Reviews and testimonials for a number of the

The Joy of Self-Pu

C000127735

I've been publishing my own books for over 2(
by more than a dozen of London's leading publi
Arrow etc. I've had books on both the *Bookseller* and *Sunday Times*
During the last two decades I've self-published scores of books and sold millions of
copies around the world. I wish I'd had Mike Buchanan's book *The Joy of Self-
Publishing* when I started. It's the best damned book on publishing in existence. It's
brilliant. I'm learning stuff from it every time I open it. Writers who try self-
publishing without reading it first – and without keeping it on their desks as they go
on – are giving themselves an extra handicap. And in the business of self-publishing
we all start with enough handicaps.
Dr Vernon Coleman bestselling English author

Reviews from buyers on Amazon.co.uk

5.0 out of 5 stars
Helpful, easy to understand, and amusing
5 Aug 2011
By Richard W Hardwick
As a published writer setting myself up as a self-publishing writer I've bought at least
eight books on self-publishing and book design. And now I've designed my book
I'm finding this one is the one I'm turning to more than any other. I didn't even plan
to buy it. Mike answered a question of mine in a Yahoo group on self-publishing and
then he gave me his phone number so I could go over some issues in more detail. I
only bought his book because I felt I ought to. But here's why it worked so well. It
really is the easiest one to understand. And self-publishing (if you're new to it) is so
complicated you wonder why you ever decided to bother half the time. It made me
smile a number of times too, and I'm pretty miserable so that's no mean feat. If
you're new to self-publishing buy this book and then scout around the rest of them
and buy one more too, one that's specifically designed for what you want. You'll get
there (I almost am) and a book like this will help you.

5.0 out of 5 stars
Great reading for all budding writers
9 Sep 2010
By A Heslop
Technology has opened up a whole new world for writers and self-publishers – until
I read this book I didn't realise by just how much. So, if there's a book in you – write
it. Begin to write it now, whilst the creative urge is flowing. But before you get too
far, read Mike Buchanan's book *The Joy of Self-Publishing*. You'll learn more about
writing and publishing by investing just a few hours, than you normally would in ten
years of self-discovery: Buchanan has been there, done it, and learnt how to make it
work. This book provides inspiration (should you need it) but above all is
commercial and honest about successful book publishing – it will both motivate you
and help you avoid costly and annoying mistakes. And I've been there. I wrote a
book that was published by a mainstream publishing house. They did a good job and

the book sold okay, but their overheads were so high that by the time I received my royalties I'd worked for less than the minimum wage. Mainstream publishing makes no sense when the tools exist to do it profitably yourself – and I sense that Buchanan gets as much pleasure from the publishing process as he does from writing. My next book will be self published and the process set out in *The Joy of Self-Publishing* is exactly how I'll do it.

5.0 out of 5 stars
At long last, a comprehensive and practical guide to self-publishing
19 Feb 2011
By KateS
Unlike other books I've bought on the subject of self-publishing, this book provides practical solutions to all the problems self-publishers face, and is right up-to-date on the options available. Its coverage of Print-on-Demand ('POD') is authoritative and its comparison of the economics of different book specification options (e.g. paperbacks, hardbacks, plate sections) is very helpful. The writer delivers his knowledge of the subject with a good deal of humour and I laughed out loud on a number of occasions. The lengthy appendix of quotations on publishing, book writing etc. could be a boon for self-publishers: many are funny, many insightful.

4.0 out of 5 stars
A must read for a wannabee author
31 Mar 2011
By Mrs H Owens
I received Mike Buchanan's book *The Joy of Self-Publishing* a couple of months ago and such a valuable pack of information shouldn't be wasted on the shelf! I've been considering writing a book of my own for many months, but with the vast information available didn't know where or how to start. I especially wanted a guide to tell me about specific resources but with the internet searches I got all lost and confused and came to the edge of giving up before even starting. *The Joy of Self-Publishing* reached me just in time and I can't recommend it more highly to anyone who is wondering where to start. It's obvious that Mike has worked hard to give practical advice and detailed information on process, formatting, other resources including even the costs! Like everything in life, writing and publishing a book requires effort but with the aid of Mike Buchanan's book it seems not just possible but achievable. The invaluable resource *The Joy of Self-Publishing* gave me the hope that I (and anyone) can now make a book visible and available to book buyers around the world at minimal cost. *The Joy of Self-Publishing* takes you through the options and explain their relative advantages and disadvantages realistically. This book also provides guidance on selecting book topics with strong sales potential; writing distinctively as well as writing content-rich non-fiction. It even offers help choosing between hardback and paperback and other formats. With the aid of *The Joy of Self-Publishing* I am hoping to say, it's all much easier then it sounds! Thank you, Mike Buchanan.

5.0 out of 5 stars
Fabulous, encouraging, and hysterical (yes – this book is helpful AND very funny)
February 27, 2011
By Kelly McCarthy Barner (Shrewsbury, MA United States)

I read Mike Buchanan's first book *Profitable Buying Strategies* about a year ago, and when I was thinking of writing my own book on procurement I found he'd written another book that would help me out. I received my copy of this book not quite a week ago and I've already finished it. More than once I actually laughed out loud while reading it, which caused my husband to think I was hiding another book inside this one's cover, which I wasn't. Really.

If you're even considering writing a book of your own, I can't recommend this one more highly. Mike's practical advice and detailed information on process, formatting, other resources, and costs make the effort required to get a book into print sound just challenging enough to risk trying. The book is made available using the same POD process he outlines in the book so you're holding the last piece of encouragement you need right in your hands.

I've now proofed my review (because who would take me seriously as a potential writer if I made obvious mistakes in a simple review?) and plan to go right back to Mike's book – next to which is the pile of notes I will turn into a book of my own thanks to Mike's help.

Two Men in a Car
(A Businessman, a Chauffeur, and Their Holidays in France)

A splendid romp. *Vive la France!*
Peter Mayle 1939- British author famous for his series of books detailing life in Provence, including the international bestseller *A Year in Provence* (1989)

Mike Buchanan is the best kind of opinionated, middle-aged, middle-class Englishman abroad: the funny kind.
Andrew Heslop

If you have a sense of humour this book will put a big smile on your face. I laughed out loud many times. A refreshing absence of political correctness.
The lovely Maureen Padley

Reviews from buyers on Amazon.co.uk

5.0 stars out of 5
Seriously funny and fabulous France
7 May 2010
By Karon Grieve
This is definitely a holiday read of the first order. If you're stuck at home it will make you wish for sunshine and holidays, if you're reading it on holiday you won't get off your deck chair. Two men: different views, different outlooks, but together they create the funniest mix. This is a tour of the French countryside with a difference. It's real, it's funny, and so politically incorrect you won't stop laughing. Add to that lots of local colour and tempting details on food and wine, it will have you booking a flight or a ferry to *la belle France* right away.

5.0 stars out of 5
Brilliantly funny
23 Jan 2010
By Mrs. Rosemary Kind 'Kind of Rosie'
I read this book in 3 days – I couldn't put it down. It was just so funny. My husband kept wondering what I was laughing at as I read the book in bed, so I had to keep reading excerpts to him. It's a well written book, interesting for those people who enjoy food & fine wines, and very amusing. Well worth buying.

5.0 stars out of 5
A gem of a book
25 June 2009
By Rosanne Lyden-Brown
Mike Buchanan's little gem of a book is a definite 'can't put it downer!' I read it during a recent spell of incarceration in hospital and it made me laugh my surgical socks off. An epicure and a man of discernment if ever there was one, Buchanan's tale of his holiday in France, accompanied by his driver and fellow traveller Paul (whose preferred fodder would appear to be steak and chips and a cup of strong English breakfast tea… in the absence of a good British corner caff cheese sandwich!) is a witty, amusing, and highly informative account of how two quite different people can, in their own quite different ways, enjoy *la belle France*. Those of

us who love our Gallic neighbours and their splendid country (and even those who do not!) will find something in this book that will make them smile, laugh, and long to be back there again.

5.0 stars out of 5
Happy holiday reading
25 Aug 2009
By jan wright
The book is written with a sense of humour guaranteed to bring a smile to your face. The good rapport and the differences of character between Paul and Mike underlie the entertaining reading. Mike gives the reader a sense of the 'real' France as they tour the regions chosen for their holidays. There's a spin-off too, with a good deal of informative information on each of the areas visited. An honest account describing the many restaurants and good quality wines they tasted along the way. The book is a must for anyone who loves France and thinking of holidaying there. Certainly a book to be packed in the case.

5.0 stars out of 5
Two Men in a Car – Priceless!
10 Aug 2009
By Mr H 'ribble valley rover' (Lancashire)
Thanks Mr Buchanan! A cracking read. What could be better than lying back in a sunlounger by the pool, in the beautiful Dordogne valley, and having fellow holidaymakers look at you with puzzlement every two minutes or so because you are laughing out loud? They were so jealous! That is what *Two Men in a Car* does to you. But beware – alongside the quirky stories and lovely descriptions of the *belles* of France (of whom there are many) Mike Buchanan gives an insight into the history of the fabulous country and takes you to places off the beaten track as well as the more 'touristy' bits. My wife and I particularly liked 'The French Helpfulness Index' to which we referred many times during our own *Tour de France* this summer – very witty but true. It was so refreshing to be part of a boys' road trip across a wonderful country. Bryson-esque!

5.0 stars out of 5
Two Men in a Car (and bar)
26 Mar 2009
By Mr Christopher David 'Celticman' (Wales)
A great read especially, but not exclusively, for those of you who like to travel in France. It's confirmation that I haven't joined the realms of the politically correct as I find the anecdotes are marvellously honest and funny. Like the author, I am now in my third age (yes, that's the one after you've been sensible for years, and are now reverting back to the first age of your life) and could identify with the romps of our two men. It's educational as well. Thoroughly recommended.

5.0 stars out of 5
Two Men in a Car... it's a Classic... or should that be a Vintage!!!
12 May 2009
By Leo – the Black Labrador's lead holder! 'Alan' (Lancaster)
What a joy to read, especially given that I can say... we were there, and have pointed out to everyone who has visited in the last week that our dog is the unwitting star of

the book (for us, at least) – Leo, the Black Labrador, it may only be on one page, but that's good enough for us! Beyond that, what an easy read… full of fun, and I can imagine Mike and Paul sat by the pool recalling their many adventures, it's just like they were here… but without the guitars. Thanks Mike for adding a further reminder to a memorable holiday, I can't wait for the next instalment.

5.0 stars out of 5
A cracking read
21 April 2009
By G.R. Morris 'Molepole' (Kent)
A wonderful meander through the backwaters of France. Two more unlikely companions you couldn't imagine. One a Francophile connoisseur of food and wine who likes to indulge in both, the other an egg, chips, and cup of tea man! The only thing they seem to have in common is being politically incorrect (and thank god or whatever deity you are into for that!) A very amusing book, enough to make me want to get *Guitar Gods in Beds*. Hope there will be some more travelogues from Mr Buchanan soon. What about Italy? Plenty of good food & wine there and probably some very attractive *senoritas* as well!

5.0 stars out of 5
Two Men in a Car
4 Mar 2009
By C. Rees 'Christine Rees'
My partner and I have laughed constantly throughout this book. I didn't think that a book about two men travelling through France could be so funny. It's the way the author has written it – his style and sense of humour is second to none and I will never, ever forget the comment made by the chauffeur about Brie tasting similar to Dairylea. An absolute classic. I highly recommend this book to anyone who wants to have a good laugh while relaxing. It really lifts your spirits.

Review from a lady buyer on Amazon.com

5.0 stars out of 5
A pleasant holiday for the reader
January 25, 2010
By Laurie A. Helgoe
Mike Buchanan's road memoir allowed me a chance to get away and explore France without the packing and expense. Traveling with Buchanan and his friend/chauffeur Paul Carrington made my trip especially entertaining. The author describes himself as 'highly unfit and averse to physical effort' and as a lover of food, wine and France; Carrington enjoys a variety of sports but is indifferent to food and wine. They do have in common their single status and accumulation of ex-wives – five between the two. The author cleverly uses charts to contrast the attributes of the two travelers and their packing lists, and includes a French Helpfulness Index. Buchanan's penchant for detail helps bring the reader along, not just through the beautiful landscapes but also into the frustrating, funny, and interesting situations that make up travel. If you need to get away and have a laugh, buy *Two Men in a Car*.

The Marriage Delusion: The Fraud of the Rings?

Testimonials from bestselling authors/psychologists

A highly original and stimulating critique of the modern marriage crisis, supported by important yet sometimes uncomfortable truths.

Oliver James, clinical psychologist, broadcaster, and author of *Affluenza*, *Britain on the Couch*, *They F*** You Up*, *How Not to F*** Them Up*

Mike Buchanan's analysis of marriage in western industrialised society is courageous and thoughtful. His perspectives on the challenges associated with marriage, and solutions to them, draw on important scientific evidence and arguments from some of our leading psychologists and wisest philosophers. This is a 'must-read' for all concerned with modern marriage.

Alan Carr, Professor of Clinical Psychology, University College, Dublin, and author of *The Handbook of Adult Clinical Psychology*, *Family Therapy* and *Positive Psychology*

Reviews from buyers on Amazon.com

5.0 stars out of 5
An honest assessment of modern marriage – at last!!!!
January 10, 2010
By Mary B 'Book Chaser'(North Carolina)

This is a brilliant and honest look at the realities of modern marriage. Mr Buchanan bravely exposes the painful truths of why marriage isn't working for most of us. He paints with very broad strokes to depict the sometimes subtle inconsistencies between our assumptions about marriage and the realities. For example, why some unhappily married people continue to extol the virtues of marriage. Particularly relevant for me was the description of introversion versus extroversion and the impact the different personality traits can have on marriage. As a happily divorced introvert, I feel vindicated. I now accept and appreciate that my singleness is a valid lifestyle choice for me as an introvert, and that my yen for solitude doesn't make me a bad person. The book is filled with excellent excerpts from other writers that corroborate Mr Buchanan's observations. The writing defies political correctness, and it is well balanced. Buchanan's candor is delightfully naughty. This is truly the most uniquely written book I've read in years.

5.0 stars out of 5
A Brilliant Exploration and Realistic Assessment of Marriage
October 30, 2009
By dancing bees – See all my reviews

As one who has made almost a vocation of studying marriage and reading books on every aspect of it, I found Mr. Buchanan's book to be a welcome breath of fresh air on a subject that is too often occluded by starry-eyed optimism and unrealistic expectations. Herein the reader will find a bracingly honest discussion of the principal factors that can undermine a given individual's chances of creating a rewarding marriage, including the inherent personality characteristic of introversion. This is a topic that has been neglected in the current climate of happy talk which leads us all to believe that, given enough work, almost any marriage can become fulfilling. In view of all the negative fallout resulting from an incomplete understanding of how personality impacts on marriage, the author has made a significant contribution to future human happiness by emphasizing this underrated aspect of what can contribute to – or detract from – what most people consider their most important relationship.

This important book includes an overview of facets that are seldom sufficiently touched upon in the many superficial works on marriage. One of these is the different natures of men and women. I found this chapter especially relevant and fascinating due to the unique slant the author has taken. The chapter covering the role of political correctness in the present day and its disastrous effects on male/female interactions is in itself a courageous *tour de force*. The conclusion, dealing with the future of marriage, outlines practical and intelligent suggestions for overhauling this nearly anachronistic institution. Interestingly, the author quotes Bertrand Russell's views on marriage at some length in this chapter. It's striking how compelling and pertinent his observations still are today, even nearly 80 years after he penned them!

While the subject matter is sobering, the author's elegant writing style and sometimes laugh-out-loud witticisms make for a read that is both edifying and enjoyable. My hope is that this book will soon find its way onto bookshelves everywhere in the U.S. because marriage, if it is to survive much longer, is in dire need of a reality check. Mr. Buchanan's book is an outstanding first step in that direction.

5.0 stars out of 5
A Challenging 'Must Read'
October 4, 2009
By Brandi Love (NC USA)
I found this book to be intense and thought-provoking. Mr Buchanan brings to light many of the issues that lead to failed marriages, in a bold and sometimes unexpected manner. It's always effective (perhaps not liked) to be honest and to communicate about all topics. So many couples go into marriage with a desired 'concept', this book is an awesome read to ensure ones understanding of what marriage IS and / or CAN be. Agree with the author's philosophies or not, you can count on many meaningful and potentially life changing conversations between you and your mate. Discussions that most likely will lead to a deeper love, understanding and appreciation for one another. It's about time someone wrote a book with Mr. Buchanan's sharp, sometimes cutting facts. Open his book, open your mind and change the relationships in your life for the better. I definitely recommend.

Reviews from buyers on Amazon.co.uk

4.0 stars out of 5
The Marriage Delusion
30 Jun 2010
By Snowboot Girl
I would seriously recommend readers of both genders to read this book. Firstly it is always interesting reading about relationships from a man's point of view, because as the author rightly points out, there is little out there by men that give an honest account. Mr Buchanan has clearly spent a great deal of time reading up on his subject and the book contains extracts from other books / newspaper articles /

studies. As my husband reluctantly discusses anything to do with relationships, particularly ours, it's encouraging that there are plenty of men who are interested in the subject. Many of the book's contributors are men.

I chose this book, interested by the fact that it was about marriage and didn't have the title, 'Why men... and women don't...'! Also because it was challenging the fact that marriage should exist at all in the modern world. [Author's note: with apologies to Snowboot girl, the last sentence is incorrect. I simply assert that most people in the developed world in the modern era are unsuited to the institution of marriage.]

Having finished the book today I am left with the feeling that the author chose his extracts largely to support his theory about the reasons marriage is increasingly failing and divorce rates increasing. Many of the reasons are valid but I am not left feeling entirely convinced. For example he talks about marriages that fail and those that succeed and the reasons for both often being compared. However he doesn't really touch on the fact that within many marriages there are good times and bad times.

Marriages are either set for failure or not seems to be the general consensus. Divorce rates have been rising since the 60s yes, but that's a comparatively short time in the history of marriage. Personally I feel that in the short time divorce has become easier we haven't yet seen the effects of / or much research into people who have divorced only to regret it later. He also does not touch very much on children and how many people's lives are made worse by divorce because of the effect it has on them.

This book was written because the author wanted to explore why his own two marriages failed and why divorce is increasing. His argument that introverted men are unhappier in marriage is interesting and yet he claims that extraverted people are more likely to be adulterous – surely a situation that increases (or results from) unhappiness in a marriage?

The book is sceptical (obviously from the title) about lifetime marriage commitment. I'm divorced and have remarried with children from both marriages (statistically I'm therefore more likely than first time marrieds to divorce again). This book has made me really appreciate what my husband and I do have rather than highlight what we don't have and I feel rather sad that so many people lose physical passion and are not able to maintain willpower to save their marriages. Selfishness – something that is not really mentioned in the book but seems to come through from between the pages – is one reason I personally would suggest.

On a massive positive – a very thought-provoking book which I could not put down and has really helped me understand how men including my husband think and feel. He deserves more slack from me, more freedom and more gratitude. I have put loads of pencil marks in the margin so I can pick it up any time I want to look at those issues that are particularly relevant to us.

4.0 stars out of 5
The case for a long and happy 'relationship'
27 Oct 2009
By 'Single Man'
A couple of days before a dinner during which I was planning to propose to my girlfriend, I was in Waterstone's in Piccadilly, looking in the 'self help' section for books about relationships and marriage. In the middle of a multitude of books in the *Ten Sure Steps To An Awesome Marriage* genre was this book. The cover intrigued me

and I was soon flicking through the book. I sat down with it and an hour passed by in a flash, before one of the sales assistants starting looking askance at me, so I bought it.

After I read it I realised that I (in common with most people contemplating marriage in the modern era) was suffering from 'the marriage delusion' - the expectation that we would enjoy a long and happy marriage. I came to understand why (like most people) I'm unsuited to the institution of marriage, and why the prospects of long-term happiness with my partner were poor. My girlfriend spotted the book in my bookshelf after I'd read it, then asked if she could read it herself.

A week later – having read the book herself – she brought round a bottle of chilled champagne, and said, 'Can I make a proposal, darling?' I gulped and before I could reply, she continued, 'Can I propose that we never get married?' We both laughed, I accepted her proposal, and we've never been happier. Mr Buchanan, thank you for saving me from a lot of unhappiness, and probably financial ruin too!

5.0 stars out of 5
The Marriage Delusion
27 Oct 2009
By 'Mr. M'
I've been reading this book with interest. It deals with many aspects of relationships and the institution of marriage. The book has been well researched and has many quotes and extracts from other relevant authors on the subject. It challenges many conformist and social historic approaches to the subject and contrasts the differences between male and female views and outlooks. As I am in a happy second-time relationship it is possible to be more understanding and use one's own experience and be philosophical in looking at these issues. It seems the author highlights the difference between reality and expectation as causing a great number of problems for both individuals and consequently couples. A book to stir up opinions and discussion on what's sometimes a thorny area full of so-called experts. A very valuable read and helpful background to getting married and co-habiting.

5.0 stars out of 5
The Marriage Delusion
15 Oct 2009
Mr R Corfe
The Marriage Delusion by Mike Buchanan is a brilliantly written book and a 'no-put-down-read' with quotations and longer passages on every aspect of marriage and personal relationships between the sexes. He's not only put his own mind to the problems of marriage, but in the cause of objectivity has engaged in extensive research. This is a must read for anyone who is already married or who contemplates marriage in the near future.

5.0 stars out of 5
Thought provoking
27 Sep 2009
By A. Heslop
The title of this book should provide an indication of the writer's perspective, but overall this is a challenging and interesting review of a difficult subject. Mike Buchanan has clearly completed a deep review of literature on the subject, from academic tomes to 'how to improve your marriage' books from the 'self help'

section of bookstores. His approach is not to offer recipes to improve a marriage or even focus on the morality of whether marriage is a good thing ethically speaking – he simply asserts that most marriages are unhappy, about half fail completely, and he goes on to explore why this situation occurs. His perspective on understanding the problem focuses on personality types, gender-related factors and religious beliefs. Oh, and he rants quite a bit about the Rt. Hon. Harriet Harman MP.

I didn't expect to identify with the book's key themes as I've been happily married for 20 years and my parents have been for 50 years, but many of my contemporaries have been divorced, and the subject is worthy of consideration by everyone, happily married or otherwise. Overall the book is well written, interesting, thought provoking and at times amusing. Depending on your perspective, it may help you better understand why you've been unhappy in your own marriage, or send you into apoplexy. You will probably find his final recommendations either extremely sensible or totally outrageous: views will be polarised.

5.0 stars out of 5
1 Oct 2009
By Mr H 'ribble valley rover' (Lancashire)
I have to agree with all the comments made by A. Heslop; I too am happily married and I thoroughly enjoyed the way the author challenged my views and perception of marriage. Through extensive research (and obviously years of experience) Mr Buchanan gives an interesting thesis on the institution of marriage which created many lively discussions between my wife and I. At times I had to agree with the author, however, I often found myself 'hoping' to disagree with his argument!

Reading *The Marriage Delusion* is a thought-provoking and often enlightening experience. Mr Buchanan's wit gives the book a light touch besides the more serious topics discussed. I would recommend this book to anybody thinking of getting married, is happily (or not so happily) married, and to anybody who likes to challenge institutionalism in today's society. A great read.

5.0 stars out of 5
At last – some realism about marriage
1 Oct 2009
By Mr Gary P Lewis
Mike Buchanan pulls no punches in this book. His central assertion – that most people are unsuited to marriage – at first seems astonishing, even if the high divorce rate across the developed world suggests he might be on to something important. The book goes a long way to explaining the misery of married couples I've known (a number of whom have divorced). I learnt a lot about marriage in this book. It had – to take just one example – never occurred to me that marriage originated in an era when people couldn't expect to live many years after their offspring were independent. And yet today people are told it's natural to have a rewarding (and even sexually exciting) relationship for 30-40 years after the kids have left home. It's about as natural as flying.

I was particularly interested in the lengthy exploration of introversion and extraversion. It seems obvious that these personality types will impact on marital happiness, but I'd never come across the point before. The book explains how both personality types can be a problem in marriage.

The book contains some welcome humour to balance the serious messages. This includes a lengthy appendix of quotations about Love, Sex and Marriage. My personal favourite, from Shelley Winters: 'In Hollywood, all the marriages are happy. It's trying to live together afterwards that causes all the problems.'

5.0 stars of 5

A fresh view on an old institution

24 September 2009

By D Lomax

Mike Buchanan's take on married life is undoubtedly coloured by his two divorces (so far), so he certainly speaks from experience, but by combining his own views with existing material and interviews with other interested parties, he has put together a fascinating insight into why he feels a large number of modern marriages are destined for failure.

Maybe failure is the wrong word because Mr Buchanan attempts to show us that actually we shouldn't expect so much from the institution of marriage in the first place, while exploding a number of myths along the way. The book is well researched and it is sprinkled liberally with quotes and references to other works.

This would be great subject matter for a book club as the issues raised almost demand to be discussed further and every page has the ability to divide opinion. Mr Buchanan stokes all kinds of fires within the reader – religious, political, idealist – then stands back and lets the sparks fly. Depending on your status – male, female, married, single or divorced – this book will either have you nodding and smiling in agreement, or tearing the pages out, but you won't put it down.

The Marriage Delusion is unashamedly written from a male perspective which is surprising as blokes aren't good at buying, much less reading books on relationships, but maybe that's part of the problem Mr Buchanan is trying to explore, and if you have an interest in how men and women ever manage to get along, you should certainly buy this to provide a bit of balance to your bookshelf.

It's not for men only though. The style of the book is more akin to a technical thesis, and anyone studying relationships would be well advised to get hold of a copy. This book should also be compulsory reading for any couple contemplating that all too short walk down the aisle, although you'll wonder why church aisles don't have an escape lane after reading this. I can also recommend it as a great resource for a best man's speech, particularly if you don't like the bride.

The Marriage Delusion lacks the laugh-out-loud humour of some of Mr Buchanan's other books, but that's because he approaches this complex subject with detail and accuracy, making it easy to connect with his way of thinking, even if it is not in line with your own. It's not without humour though and I couldn't help noticing that Mr Buchanan seems to have an unhealthy fascination with Harriet Harman MP, delivering a number of very funny jibes and comments that pull Harman's speeches and policy apart. (She was given the right to reply, but never bothered.) A picture comes to mind of Buchanan as a schoolboy, teasing Harman in the playground because secretly he quite likes her. Hang on, that's the answer – Mike should ask Ms Harman to be the next Mrs Buchanan. Now there's a book...

5.0 stars of 5
Compulsory reading
19 Sept 2009
By G. Williams
Informative, amusing, and invaluable. This book offers great insight into the long-term pitfalls of an age-old tradition that so many people seem to naively drift into. Its objectivity provides a real wake-up call for those struggling with an unhappy relationship and a warning to those who've not yet taken their vows. This should be a compulsory read for anyone considering marriage – it could save you thousands in divorce lawyers' fees!

David and Goliatha:
David Cameron – heir to Harman?

At long last Mike Buchanan has courageously taken on the radical feminists. For too long this group has dominated the public policy agenda. Pay equality, gender balance in the boardroom, all-women shortlists have been given far too much prominence in public life. We needed the other side to be put and in his book Mike Buchanan does just this. His description of the Prime Minister having a female-pattern brain is an interesting aspect of David Cameron. Without being insulting it explains some of the current direction of Conservative policy.

The book calls for a fight back against the radical feminists. It deserves to succeed. Women had a long hard justifiable fight to obtain the vote in our democracy (see my book *Our Fight for Democracy*) but now they have it, the radical feminists want special treatment. This isn't acceptable, each person's vote should have an equal value regardless of gender. Manipulating prospective parliamentary candidate shortlists to give preference to women is a distortion of democracy and anyone who believes in democracy should oppose it.

John Strafford Chairman of the Campaign for Conservative Democracy

The Glass Ceiling Delusion:
the real reasons more women don't reach senior positions

The Glass Ceiling Delusion is an important and brave book, the best book on social economics and society in general published for decades. It's irresistibly compelling, cogently argued and superbly put together. It should be in all school and college libraries. It should be compulsory reading for social science, economics and politics students. It should be force-fed to male and female politicians. This is definitely a five-star book. Brilliant. Brilliant. Brilliant. Brilliant. Brilliant.
Dr Vernon Coleman bestselling English author

The Joy of Self-Publishing

By Mike Buchanan

for LPS publishing

Feminism
(scheduled for publication November 2011)
The Glass Ceiling Delusion:
the real reasons more women don't reach senior positions
David and Goliatha:
David Cameron – heir to Harman?
The Joy of Self-Publishing
Buchanan's Dictionary of Quotations for right-minded people
Buchanan's Dictionary of Quotations for right-minded Americans
The Marriage Delusion: the fraud of the rings?
The Fraud of the Rings
Two Men in a Car
(A Businessman, a Chauffeur, and Their Holidays in France)
Guitar Gods in Beds.
(Bedfordshire: a heavenly county)

for Kogan Page

Profitable Buying Strategies
(How to Cut Procurement Costs and Buy Your Way to Higher Profits)

The Joy of Self-Publishing

mike buchanan

lps publishing

publisher's note
every possible effort has been made to ensure that the information contained in this book is accurate, and the self-publisher and the author cannot accept responsibility for any errors or omissions, however caused. no responsibility for loss or damage occasioned to any person acting, or refraining from action, as a result of the material in this publication, can be accepted by the author. nope. first published in great britain in 2010 by lps publishing. this slightly revised edition printed after 1 september 2011

lpspublishing.co.uk

lps publishing
8 putnoe heights
bedford mk41 8eb
united kingdom

isbn 9780955878466

british library cataloguing-in-publication data

this paperback edition was printed and distributed worldwide by the clever chaps at lightning source inc

this book is dedicated with thanks to vernon coleman

an inspiration to self-publishers for over 20 years

CONTENTS

ACKNOWLEDGEMENTS

My first thanks must go to my readers, especially those who've taken the trouble to post reviews on Amazon's websites. I'm sure I speak for many writers when I say that positive reviews – on Amazon and elsewhere – lift the spirits in a way that little else can.

My thanks to my beloved and beautiful daughters Sarah Mercedes and Kerry Portia for their tolerance of the time I devote to writing and self-publishing, and for telling me, 'Your books are brilliant, Dad, can we change the subject now?' Their unbiased appreciation is always welcome.

My thanks to Dr Vernon Coleman, an English gentleman and a highly successful self-publisher, for his extensive and important body of work; for the effort and time he's devoted to a number of important campaigns and causes; for inspiring self-publishers for over 20 years; and on a personal note, for penning testimonials for a number of my books which have given me great encouragement, particularly the one he wrote for *The Glass Ceiling Delusion*. Self-publishers who are disappointed at not being contracted to a commercial publisher should read the Mission Statement of The Publishing House, Vernon Coleman's self-publishing concern, which I reproduce in the second half of chapter 1. They might then be heartened and *proud* to be self-publishers; they should be.

My thanks to friend, businessman and Yorkshire-based author Andrew Heslop for his feedback on a number of chapters, most notably the chapter on the financial aspects of the commercial self-publishing model. If he weren't a highly successful business consultant he'd possibly write more books so we must hope – for our sakes, if not for his – that he runs out of work. I expect to publish his book *Music For Grown-Ups* soon, and I hope to publish a book of his short stories one day. His story about football-playing nuns is a favourite.

My thanks to the talented freelance professionals without whom this book wouldn't be what it is: Charlie Wilson, my proofreader/copy editress; Roger Day, my photographer; and John Rose of John Chandler Design Associates. Particular thanks to John Chandler and Doug Morris of Wordzworth for their appendices. What's that? No. I *don't* mean they gave me body organs. Give me strength. The appendices in this book.

My thanks to the editors and publishers of the dictionaries of quotations I draw upon in this book, as well as those who run quotation websites. Thanks also to Wikipedia for most of the biographical details I've associated with the quotations.

My thanks to you, dear reader, for buying this book. I hope it at least meets your expectations. If you enjoy reading it, would you be so kind as to post a review on Amazon? Thank you.

Please feel free to email me with comments or queries you might have about self-publishing, or indeed about any of the topics covered by my other books: Mikebuchanan@hotmail.co.uk.

INTRODUCTION

What's money? A man is a success if he gets up in the morning and goes to bed at night and in between does what he wants to do.
Bob Dylan 1941– American singer-songwriter and musician

Making a living by writing is a great way to live, and self-publishing only adds to the pleasure. You keep full control and make more money with every copy sold. You even have the opportunity to live somewhere you'll enjoy living, possibly in contrast to where you're living now.

This book will tell you all you need to know about self-publishing without resorting to vanity publishers. All that's required from you is the ability to write well on topics that the book buying public will find interesting. How difficult can that be?

If you already self-publish, or plan to do so, you're in good historical company. At one time or another so did Stephen King, Percy Bysshe Shelley, Horace Walpole, Honoré de Balzac, Walt Whitman, Virginia Woolf, Gertrude Stein, John Galsworthy, Rudyard Kipling, Beatrix Potter, Lord Byron, Thomas Paine, Mark Twain, Ezra Pound, DH Lawrence, Alexander Pope, Robbie Burns, James Joyce, Anaïs Nin, Lawrence Stern and William Blake. Blake even mixed his own inks. I'm not going to suggest you go that far.

I must include the writer who started off his book writing career by self-publishing and who doubtless deems himself fortunate in having his travelogues in some book stores next to my *Two Men in a Car*, which no doubt helps increase the sales of his books: Bill Bryson.

If you're going to succeed as a writer, I recommend you do so on your own terms. By all means read books about writing, but only use the advice that is consistent with how your mind works – not how you might like it to work, perhaps like Stephen King's – and reject the advice that isn't consistent. Become a distinctive writer. That's surely the way to maximise your chances of becoming a successful writer. At the very least it's the way to enjoy writing, which is important too.

In his bestseller *On Writing* Stephen King advises against using adverbs in association with dialogue: 'she added, dreamily' and the like. Well, I *love* adverbs in association with dialogue. Used well, they add a whole new dimension to dialogue. George Orwell used adverbs all the time.

As a writer I'm an optimist, but when I was an optimist as a publisher in my early days self-publishing I ordered sizeable print runs to lower the price per copy, and ended up with unsold copies – all at a low price per copy. So I developed the model for self-publishing which I've outlined in this book. It's a low-risk and low-cost model which I term 'commercial self-publishing'. If your books sell well – and I hope they will – you can very speedily move from one form of the model to another. If you only take one piece of advice from this book, let it be this: be an optimistic writer but a pessimistic publisher. Then, if your books don't sell as well as you hope, at least you won't have half a room or a garage filled with boxes of books to remind you daily that your books didn't sell in the numbers you'd anticipated.

When reading books on self-publishing I was struck by the paucity of information on the business aspects of self-publishing. My business career had been in procurement, buying goods and services for major organisations. Over my 25 years in that field I'd dealt with a large number of printers and I realised I could bring this experience to bear on my own venture into self-publishing. It seemed obvious to me that the most economical approach to self-publishing books – which looked as though they had been published by commercial publishers – was to deal directly with the same printers and freelance professionals that the commercial publishers dealt with. So that's what I did. Yes siree.

It has to be said that most self-published books are all too obviously self-published, including those published by most of the vanity publishers. Although vanity publishers seldom call themselves by that term, that's what they are. They often present themselves as the catalyst required to deliver your undoubted genius to an otherwise inaccessible book-buying public. In reality there need be no such catalyst as that public is highly accessible at minimal cost.

A tip for you: go onto your Amazon website and key in a few of the book titles from the vanity publishers' websites and check out where the books lie in Amazon's sales rankings. As I'll explain later, I did this with a number of book titles showing on a major vanity publisher's website, where the writers were enthusiastic about the service they had received from the publisher. The books had all been published in recent years, and their sales rankings on Amazon were all between two and seven *million*. I recommend you don't buy into the vanity publishers' hype. Or if you do, don't come moaning to me about the outcome.

The vanity publishers' websites often intimate that they employ expert cover designers. Why, then, do most of the book covers on display on their websites – and you have to assume they pick the best designs for their websites – look so unimpressive? Because they use design templates, as we'll see. Some of the vanity publishers' business models and pricing structures are difficult to understand, and when services are offered they generally cost more than you'd pay for a top-flight freelance professional. And when they cost less, my hunch is that's because they won't do a professional job of, for example, proofreading. But you'll never know that; you'll only know they've improved your manuscript *to an extent*.

On the afternoon of 12 January 2010 I was busy working on my fifth book, a book of quotations, when my search led me to the Bob Dylan quotation which kicks off this introduction. Like all good quotations, it sparked off some thoughts. To be more precise, it made me think about my whole life.

At the age of 52, after 30 years working in business, I could claim to have had some success as a businessman. A good income had financed a good standard of living for many years, but I just wasn't getting fulfilment from my work any more. I was much happier in the gaps between my assignments, when I could write and self-publish books.

At the age of 50, in 2008, my first book, *Profitable Buying Strategies*, was published internationally by Kogan Page, a leading publisher. It's a book on corporate cost management, the field I'd worked in for 25 years. It's been translated into Chinese, one of the odder-looking books in my library. Writing that book gave me the writing 'bug' and I wrote and self-published four more books in the ensuing two years, before this one (and I've written another two since, as at September 2011):

Guitar Gods in Beds. (Bedfordshire: a heavenly county) – the colourful biographies of eight guitarists living in or near my adopted home town of Bedford.

Two Men in a Car (A Businessman, a Chauffeur, and Their Holidays in France) – a travelogue about two holidays in France with my friend and socialist chauffeur, Paul Carrington, whose autobiography is contained in *Guitar Gods in Beds* . The paperback edition of *Two Men in a Car* isn't currently available to order outside the United Kingdom, for reasons I shall be outlining; if you'd like a copy please email me on Mikebuchanan@hotmail.co.uk. I've just made the book available at a recession-busting price as an ebook for the Kindle, iPad and other major e-readers.

The Marriage Delusion: The Fraud of the Rings? – a book inspired by the breakdown of my second marriage. It argues that most people in the developed world in the modern era are unsuited to marriage. The title is available in both paperback and ebook editions as *The Fraud of the Rings.*

Buchanan's Dictionary of Quotations for right-minded people – a collection of quotations for people with right-of-centre political persuasions. It was inspired by the then forthcoming 2010 general election in the United Kingdom, an election that the execrable left-wing administration which had been in power since 1997 was expected to lose – and duly did, I'm pleased to say. The American edition, which has virtually identical content, is imaginatively titled *Buchanan's Dictionary of Quotations for right-minded Americans.*

I can honestly say I prefer self-publishing to being published, for a host of reasons. Higher income per copy sold, full creative control, no deadlines to distort the project, and more besides. Self-publishing can be very fulfilling if you go about it the right way, and it's lucrative for a small number of writers. Dr Vernon Coleman, about whom I shall be saying more, has been a self-publisher for over 20 years – he now has over 100 books to his name – and he owns homes in Devon, London and Paris.

On occasion, when I was particularly fed up with my normal working life, I fantasised about taking early retirement and focusing full-time on writing and self-publishing. It would require some 'downsizing' and a willingness to live more modestly, but that was an ever more appealing prospect with every month that passed. I just needed a gentle push or two in the right direction.

The Bob Dylan quotation at the start of this Introduction was the first push. The second push arrived ten minutes later. I was visiting Amazon.com to see if I had any new reviews from American readers. *The Marriage Delusion* had already received a couple of 5-star reviews from American lady readers, and a new review had been posted the previous day:

5.0 out of 5 stars
An honest assessment of modern marriage – at last!!!!
January 10, 2010
Mary B 'Book Chaser' (North Carolina)
This is a brilliant and honest look at the realities of modern marriage. Mr. Buchanan bravely exposes the painful truths of why marriage isn't working for most of us. He paints with very broad strokes to depict the sometimes subtle inconsistencies between our assumptions about marriage and the realities. For example, why some unhappily married people continue to extol the virtues of marriage. Particularly relevant for me was the description of introversion versus extroversion and the impact the different personality traits can have on marriage. As a happily divorced introvert, I feel vindicated. I now accept and appreciate that my singleness is a valid lifestyle choice for me as an introvert, and that my yen for solitude doesn't make me a bad person. The book is filled with excellent excerpts from other writers that corroborate Mr. Buchanan's observations. The writing defies political correctness, and it is well balanced. Buchanan's candor is delightfully naughty. This is truly the most uniquely written book I've read in years.

I stood taller that day, I can tell you. And I've stood taller ever since. My thanks to Bob Dylan and Mary B for helping me realise that I should take the plunge and focus full-time on writing and self-publishing.

So at the ripe old age of 52 I took early retirement, cashed in my pension plans, and I am now enjoying spending my days writing and self-publishing. It's been about eighteen months so far and I haven't once regretted the decision to retire. I sometimes have to stop myself writing seven days a week – it doesn't seem like work. I've rarely been happier.

Books about self-publishing rarely cover the topic of quality adequately, if they cover it at all. I wanted to see if I could write and publish books which didn't *appear* self-published, and after a lot of hard work I'd like to think I've succeeded. My readers tell me I have. And I'm doing what I want to do with my days so Bob Dylan thinks I'm a success, although he hasn't had the good grace to tell me so. Typical.

In my professional career I bought countless different goods and services, but I never bought dreams. When writers – and especially new writers – spend money on vanity publishers' packages they're buying dreams. Whatever a publisher may say, if you're spending your own money to have the company publish your work, the company is a vanity publisher. Full stop. The only question is what type of vanity publisher they are, and how good or bad they are.

I shudder when I visit some of the vanity publishers' websites offering publishing packages. One is currently selling packages for almost £11,000. Another publisher states that your books can be printed in any one of a variety of fonts. Wow, like, amazing, man. They often have a range of templates for your material to be put into, which helps them keep their costs down and your costs too, to be fair. But I don't like *any* restrictions when it comes to my writing and publishing. I want to retain full creative and business control at all times.

The only restrictions I will accept – because I must – are those imposed by technology. And even then I'm not happy if I want to do something with a book that isn't technically possible, or only possible at an uneconomic cost. Researching for this book led me to a vendor, CPI Antony Rowe, prepared to manufacture a single copy of a book with a colour plate section at a low cost, something I'd been seeking for some time.

At the time of writing this – September 2011 – if you order any of my books for delivery outside the UK, the chances are that it will have been printed by Lightning Source's print-on-demand (POD) model. The copyright page early in the book will tell you who the printer was. Lightning Source is the largest POD book printer in the world, and Chapter 7 gives an account of its business model, a boon to publishers and self-publishers alike.

If you adopt my self-publishing model you'll probably only need to deal with three parties: the printer, a copy-editor/proofreader, and a cover designer. Maybe a photographer too, if your cover requires a bespoke photograph. You may be surprised to learn that most book printers, even the largest, will be delighted to deal with you directly. Margins in the printing sector are perennially low, and printers can make a better margin from individual customers than they can from large corporate customers with buying power.

Self-publishing by dealing directly with third parties has a number of benefits other than cost. If you're dealing directly with a printer which prints digitally – and indeed by offset lithography too, if you're selling enough books to merit ordering in quantities of 300 copies or more – you will have a huge array of options when it comes to your book's specification. There are fewer specification options with POD, where the book is only manufactured after a buyer has ordered the book. But the POD model has a number of benefits, financial and other, and I'll be taking you through them.

At a number of points in the book I refer to a 'standard' book specification, especially when I'm trying to make points about costs. The specification should be taken to mean a 272-page paperback with a colour cover and black content text. The specification of this book, as it happens. What are the chances?

I've adopted the increasingly popular convention of leaving the 'www.' prefix off website addresses, and I've put them in a smaller font than the surrounding text.

It took a lot of time and effort to track down the quotations I put into this book. If you're a fan of quotations you might like to read through Appendix 1 before you start on Chapter 1. If you're not, then don't. Take my advice: reject my advice whenever you feel inclined to do so.

A few words about the cover images showing myself and my *œuvre* shortly before the publication of this book. The more fashion-conscious reader of the male persuasion interested in adopting the English gentleman look – and how could he *not* be? – will wish to learn the provenance of the elements of the look. He may be surprised that I'd be willing to divulge this information, but that's the kind of chap I am.

The bespoke pure new wool suit was tailored by Austin Reed of Regent Street, London – tailors to the stars – and the shirt was bought from Charles Tyrwhitt of Jermyn Street, London. The silk tie came from Christian Dior's legendary 1992 spring/summer collection, while the very comfortable brogues were manufactured by Cheaney in Desborough, Northamptonshire. The latter were recently repaired by Morgan, a family-run business in Cardiff, cobblers to the Welsh. I am informed by an acquaintance of the American persuasion that brogues are termed 'wingtips' in America. Extraordinary.

The umbrella was made by Fox Umbrellas in England, 'Makers of the world's finest umbrellas'. Their motto is, 'Keeping you dry since 1868'. If you're at least 143, then possibly. Out of sight but contributing to my evident joy are my navy blue pure cotton boxer shorts (Marks & Spencer's 2009 autumn/winter collection) and red silk blend socks (Moorland Hosiery).

Spectacles from Specsavers – opticians to fashionable and well-heeled Englishmen and Englishwomen for generations – and hair by the lovely Samantha at Bedford's Toni and Guy completes the look.

I wish you well in your self-publishing venture and I hope this book helps you. If it does, and you feel sufficiently generous to send me a complimentary signed copy of your book, I should be most appreciative. My address is provided on the copyright page.

A word on my use of the word 'he' throughout the book when I refer to writers and readers generically. The term should be understood to imply both genders. Political correctness raises my blood pressure – don't get me started on militant feminist politician Harriet Harman – and this is all I have to say on the subject.

A final thought on the terms 'writer' and 'author'. Which should you call yourself? I'm inclined to call myself a writer on the grounds that until and unless a writer become very successful the term 'author' can sound a little pretentious. A bestselling writer once said he always called himself a writer, on the grounds that, 'I write, I don't auth.'

Until the next time.

mike buchanan
bedford, old england
1 september 2011

1

MOTIVATION, PERSISTENCE, ADVICE, WRITING AND SELF-PUBLISHING

Well, I try my best
To be just like I am,
But everybody wants you
To be just like them.
Bob Dylan 1941– *Maggie's Farm* (song, 1965)

This chapter covers:

- motivations for writing books
- the importance of persistence
- taking advice
- developing distinctiveness as a writer
- plotting and characterisation: Stephen King v. Iain Banks
- adverbs: Stephen King v. George Orwell
- rules of grammar
- introverts' and extraverts' leanings towards reading and writing different types of books
- *Write Great Fiction*
- arguments for preferring self-publishing over being published
- Vernon Coleman: a role model for self-publishers
- marketable writers
- Tom McNab and *Flanagan's Run*

I'm a Bob Dylan fan, but if you're not one yourself you may be relieved to learn that there are only two Bob Dylan quotations in this book, and you've now read both of them. Let's consider the motivations that lay behind writing.

> There are three reasons for becoming a writer. The first is that you need the money; the second, that you have something to say that you think the world should know; and the third is that you can't think what to do with the long winter evenings.
> **Quentin Crisp** 1908–99 English writer: *The Naked Civil Servant* (1968)

Learn as much by writing as by reading.
Lord Acton 1834–1902 British historian

These two quotations capture my prime motivations for writing. But I have two more. Firstly, I find writing very fulfilling and I increasingly resent anything that takes me away from reading and writing. As a happily divorced man who has taken early retirement and whose children have left home, I have plenty of free time in which to read, write, and self-publish. Joy.

I suspect that writers who claim to hate the writing process – and there are many of them, some of the finest writers included – are extraverts. The solitude that is such an important part of the writing process must be hell for them. But that solitude can be heaven for introverts, especially in the modern era with the availability through the internet of so much information at no cost.

The second motivation occurred to me after a friend, the author Andrew Heslop, made an insightful comment about my travelogue *Two Men in a Car*. He said that in 100 years' time someone would read it and laugh at the exploits and attitudes of two wildly different men on holiday in France. This, he pointed out, was more than could be said for the innovative fork lift truck buying strategy I'd devised for Exel Logistics in the 1990s, which was no doubt superseded years ago. He'd hit upon a motivation which hadn't occurred to me previously, but I think it had been in me all the same. I was writing with an eye on posterity.

Andrew is a published author himself – Kogan Page published his bestseller *How to Value and Sell Your Business* – and I am hoping to publish a book of his short stories one day. He could be the next Somerset Maugham. His story about nuns playing football is possibly my favourite. Or maybe the reminiscences of the wartime fighter pilot with whom he had worked as a young man. The book will surely become another international bestseller for LPS publishing.

I recommend you spend time honestly working out your motivation(s) in writing books. Dogged persistence is one of the factors behind the success stories of many successful writers: read Joanna Trollope's article (Appendix 7) if you have any doubts on the matter. What if she'd given up writing books after her tenth commercially unsuccessful book in 20 years? We should never have heard of her. Are *you* prepared to be that persistent? Can you afford to be? What are you prepared to sacrifice?

If your prime motivation is to write commercially successful books you might like to read Chapter 3. If you're like me, you might prefer instead to focus on writing about what you're interested in – even if you're not very knowledgeable about the topic of the proposed book at the outset – and hope for commercial success too. If you're intellectually curious the journey of discovery will in itself prove rewarding, regardless of whether or not the book sells well.

Of course you can combine the motivation of selling lots of books with the motivation of writing about something you're interested in. I did exactly that when selecting the topic for this book. I knew more and more writers were self-publishing, but many books on the topic were hopelessly out-of-date, particularly with respect to book production options, and some of the books were downright poor. I also suspected that many writers were using vanity publishers because they simply weren't aware that true self-publishing had become a highly viable option.

I also wanted to better understand a number of aspects of self-publishing that I hadn't explored before, such as ebooks. I thought I could present some perspectives on writing with the objective of informing and inspiring the reader, not of terrifying him – all served up with a dash of humour that you'd struggle to find in the existing books on the subject of self-publishing.

The Marriage Delusion was the result of my lengthy exploration to better understand my unhappiness in my two marriages. As a twice divorced third generation divorcee I knew a thing or two about marriage and unhappiness. I read numerous books in the 'how to improve your marriage' genre but none explained my own unhappy experiences of marriage.

After reading many books on relationships, psychology, religion and more besides I finally understood the factors that were making me unhappy. But what I hadn't anticipated was the realisation that they were factors I shared with *most* married and divorced people. This led me to write the book which has received strong positive reviews from readers – both male and female – and testimonials from psychologists and bestselling writers Oliver James and Professor Alan Carr.

After his well-publicised marital difficulties I mailed a complimentary copy of *The Marriage Delusion* to Tiger Woods, who was then playing in the British Open golf tournament at St Andrews. The poor man looked like he could do with a copy.

We move on to the tricky area of taking advice as a writer and as a self-publisher. As a writer every piece of advice you take on board – including advice on grammar – will inevitably make you less distinctive, especially if you're taking heed of the same advice as other writers, such as that in Stephen King's *On Writing*. How on earth can you develop distinctiveness as a writer if your brain is full of rules dictating to you all the time?

Among my favourite quotations on advice are the following:

> I owe my success to having listened respectfully to the very best advice, and then going away and doing the exact opposite.
> **GK Chesterton** 1874–1936 English essayist, novelist, and poet

> I once complained to my father that I didn't seem to be able to do things the same way other people did. Dad's advice? 'Margo, don't be a sheep. People hate sheep. They eat sheep.'
> **Margo Kaufman** American writer

My advice is to read books giving advice on the *craft* of writing, with a view to you supplying the *art* when you settle down to the task of writing your books. I have yet to embark on my first work of fiction, possibly because I'm not a big reader of fiction and I always have plans to write more non-fiction books. I read the four books in the *Write Great Fiction* series which gave me plenty of insights into the craft of writing fiction, but few about the art. And that is surely how it should be if you're going to bring your own creative spark to writing fiction – or non-fiction, come to that.

If I ever write fiction I want my first or second books to be as good as my favourite work of fiction, *Nineteen Eighty-Four*, thereby winning the Man Booker Prize for Fiction. I do like to set the bar high when it comes to intellectual challenges. I read *Nineteen Eighty-Four* as a teenager, I read it in my thirties, and I read it two years ago at the age of 51. That was in 2009, in the 13th year of a dire left-wing administration then led by Gordon Brown and the dismal 'Mad Hattie' Harman. The book explained to me why so many people in the United Kingdom were so unhappy with the administration. The parallels between the book and the administration were uncanny.

We sometimes forget that 'rules' on writing, including grammar, are man-made and not handed down from on high. I tend to fully agree (rather than agree fully) with Raymond Chandler's perspective on one matter in particular, which he related in a letter to his publisher:

> Would you convey my compliments to the purist who reads your proofs and tell him or her that I write in a sort of broken-down patois which is something like the way a Swiss waiter talks, and that when I split an infinitive, God damn it, I split it so it will stay split.
> letter to Edward Weeks, 18 January 1947

I greatly admire Raymond Chandler's books. He wrote one of my favourite sentences in modern (post Twain) American literature:

> It was a blonde, a blonde to make a bishop kick a hole in a stained glass window.
> *Farewell, My Lovely* (1940)

I wish I'd written that. Along with many of the Mark Twain lines in Appendix 1.

Aspiring writers are often given the advice to 'write about what you know'. I think the advice is *terrible*, especially when it comes from writers. The sentiment reflects the idea that people don't have the necessary authority to write about subjects they're not familiar with. I shudder to think how many authors have abandoned promising book projects in the light of such advice.

Most fiction – most good fiction, at least – wouldn't pass the test. A number of genres wouldn't exist, including science fiction and much of the fantasy genre. Did JK Rowling write about 'what she knew'? No. 16 years after bashing out the first *Harry Potter* book on an old manual typewriter, she's now worth over £600 million.

Much non-fiction, for that matter, isn't written by writers about 'what they know'. It's created by writers seeking to understand complex subjects in the absence of satisfactory books; writers seeking to shed light on topics about which they – and hopefully their target readers – wish to learn more.

Because you've bought this book it's likely that you've read books giving advice on writing. I've read a number of them myself, and I am often surprised at how prescriptive they are. The underlying premises of most of these books seem to be:

1. I'm a successful writer.
2. I'm presenting the principles behind my writing.
3. If you adopt these principles, you'll be a successful writer too.

On the basis that nobody ever became a millionaire after reading books with titles such as *How to Become a Millionaire*, let's challenge this model. Let's start with Stephen King, possibly the world's best-selling fiction writer, and his book *On Writing*, published in 2000. In June 1999 King was hit by a van while he was walking along the shoulder of a country road in Maine. Six operations were required to save his life and return him to a semblance of physical normality. When he returned to writing it was to write *On Writing*. 11 years after publication the book remains a bestseller in its genre, and with good reason. But you won't be able to write like Stephen King after reading the book. The best you'll be able to do is *imitate* him by obeying some or all of his guidance, which is a different thing altogether. And you won't enjoy writing that way.

Iain Banks is one of my favourite British authors, and his approach to writing couldn't be more different that Stephen King's. Let's start with plotting. Stephen King claims not to know the ending of his books before embarking on the writing, and he has an interesting rationale for adopting this approach. If he doesn't know how the book is going to end – while he's writing it – then nor can his readers. I suspect it also makes the writing process far more interesting for him. Iain Banks takes a completely different approach and spends a great deal of time on detailed plotting through to the end, before the bulk writing commences. Neither approach is right or wrong. They're simply approaches which suit these individual writers. They also differ on the matter of characterisation. Stephen King's success is often attributed to his skilled characterisation, while Iain Banks goes in for relatively little characterisation.

There's a good reason for being selective about taking advice on writing. Let's say that you slavishly follow Stephen King's advice. You'll then be in the company of all the writers who are doing likewise. How many? 1,000? 10,000? 100,000? Who knows? But I can see from the sales ranking of *On Writing* on Amazon that it's still selling well, ten years after publication. Why would you want to compete head on with even 1,000 writers writing under the same guidance? What satisfaction could there possibly be in that?

I imagine many of those writers have written numerous books in the style of Stephen King and are puzzled by their lack of success. You could probably spot them by their haunted expressions. I'd rather be *distinctive* and enjoy the writing process. That way, even if my books don't sell, I'd at least have enjoyed writing them.

Amid much advice King tells us that 'the adverb is not your friend', and continues:

> Adverbs . . . are words that modify verbs, adjectives, or other adverbs. They're the ones that usually end in –ly. Adverbs, like the passive voice, seem to have been created with the timid writer in mind. [Author's note: ironically, and rather sadly, the timid writer – after reading King's advice – will thereafter cease to use adverbs.] With the passive voice, the writer usually expresses fear of not being taken seriously; it is the voice of little boys wearing shoepolish moustaches and little girls clumping around in Mommy's high heels. With adverbs, the writer usually tells us he or she is afraid he / she isn't expressing himself / herself clearly, that he or she is not getting the point or the picture across.

King proceeds to back his thesis with examples of dialogue where the adverbs add little or nothing. But could it be that King is simply not adept at using adverbs, and is therefore disinclined to use them? He advocates having the spoken words explain the emotion or emotions that the speaker is feeling. Well, at least in the country I live in – England – people often *don't* put their emotions into the words they employ. Life can be altogether more pleasant as a result. An English writer will naturally use adverbs to convey the emotions associated with the spoken word.

It's time to bring in one of my favourite authors of his generation, George Orwell. Let's look at a few unrelated lines picked off random pages of his 1949 masterpiece *Nineteen Eighty-Four*.

'The past is more important,' agreed O'Brien gravely.
Winston looked up at him. 'In the place where there is no darkness?'
he said hesitantly.

'These things happen,' he began vaguely.

'Smith?' said the woman. 'Thass funny. My name's Smith too. Why,'
she added sentimentally, 'I might be your mother!'

It's a good thing Orwell didn't take heed of anyone's views on adverbs associated with dialogue. In a bookstore the other day I chanced upon *How to Write a Blockbuster*, a book written by Helen Corner and Lee Weatherly. My wild hunch is that Lee Weatherly is of the female persuasion, given the books published under the name. Anyway, they give the same advice as Stephen King on adverbs. Marvellous. I plan to use *plenty* of adverbs in my first work of fiction.

Flick quickly through any Stephen King and George Orwell books and one major difference will strike you at once: the former have a great deal more dialogue. You read 12 pages of *Nineteen Eighty-Four* before you come to the first line of dialogue.

Let's move on to the formal rules of grammar and punctuation. It's inexcusable to have more than a very few unintended mistakes in your books with respect to grammar and punctuation, and a good copy-editor / proofreader will help you avoid them (and spelling mistakes, too). But consider the following section of a book first published in 2006. The book is surely a proofreader's worst nightmare.

The falling snow curtained them about. There was no way to see anything at either side of the road. He was coughing again and the boy was shivering, the two of them side by side under the sheet of plastic, pushing the grocery cart through the snow. Finally he stopped. The boy was shaking uncontrollably.
We have to stop, he said.
It's really cold.
I know.
Where are we?
Where are we?
Yes.
I dont know.
If we were going to die would you tell me?
I dont know. We're not going to die.

If a child wrote that he'd be told off. But it's an extract from Cormac McCathy's Pulitzer Prize winning *The Road.* McCarthy is considered one of the greatest fiction writers of his generation, and his ten previous books include the remarkable *No Country for Old Men.* If you're writing fiction take your lead from McCarthy and choose the extent to which you follow the 'rules'. Never forget the immortal advice about lesser people: *Illegitimi non carborundum.*

Writers of guides to writing fiction frequently distinguish between 'literary' novels and 'commercial' novels, the latter being what they generally seek to help you with. In his excellent *Plot and Structure* (2004) James Scott Bell differentiates between two types of novel:

> The difference between a literary and a commercial plot is a matter of feel and emphasis. A literary plot often is more leisurely in its pace. Literary fiction is usually more about the inner life of a character than it is about the fast-paced action. A commercial plot, on the other hand, is mostly about action, things happening to the characters from the outside.
>
> Of course these are simplifications. There can be both literary and commercial elements in a book. Scott Smith's *A Simple Plan* reads like a literary novel – what happens inside the first-person narrator is primary – while moving ahead like a commercial crime novel.
>
> The strength of Stephen King's commercial plots is his characterisations. He always seems to be writing about real people, and not merely players for his high-concept concoctions.
>
> Literary fiction is much more comfortable with ambiguities. The endings may be downers or leave the reader wondering. We don't know what's going to happen to Holden at the end of *The Catcher in the Rye,* and that's part of the power of the book.

While researching for *The Marriage Delusion* I read many books on psychology in general, and the personality trait of extraversion in particular, as manifested in introversion and extraversion. While the proportions of introverts and extraverts in the population are consistent in societies around the world – a little over 50% of men are predominantly introvert, a little over 50% of women predominantly extravert – most societies have cultural preferences for either introversion or extraversion. An American psychology professor told me he considered Australia to be the country with the strongest cultural preference for extraversion, closely followed by the United States. Britain has a mild cultural preference for extraversion, while Scandinavian countries and Japan have strong cultural preferences for introversion.

I've read most of George Orwell's literary novels and none of Stephen King's commercial ones. It seems obvious to me that introverts will more naturally be drawn to reading literary novels while extraverts will be drawn to reading commercial novels. If this thesis is correct, I think it follows that introverts will more naturally be inclined to *write* literary novels and extraverts commercial novels. I suppose a case may be made that a writer is more likely to enjoy good sales – and as a self-publisher enjoy a good income as a result – by writing commercial rather than literary novels. But I, for one, would rather spend my time writing literary novels, assuming of course that I turn out to have any aptitude for doing so.

James Scott Bell's book is one in a series of books titled *Write Great Fiction*, the others being Ron Rozelle's *Description and Setting*, Nancy Kress's *Characters, Emotion and Viewpoint*, and Gloria Kempton's *Dialogue*. I've read all four books and plan to do so again before starting on my novel, being careful to reject any advice that doesn't accord with how my mind works.

Why might you consider self-publishing rather than going down the traditional route of seeking an agent to represent you to major publishers? The most obvious reasons are:

Time

By all means spend some time exploring whether your proposed book might be of interest to literary agents and thereby possibly to publishers. Buy a copy of the latest *Writers' and Artists' Yearbook* in which you'll find contact details for literary agents, some of the writers they represent, and a large number of informative articles as well. Appendix 4 details the contents of this excellent book.

But – and it pains me to say this – unless you have an idea for a book with obvious and substantial sales potential, and you're clearly a very gifted writer, you're more likely to have a major win on the National Lottery than find a good agent prepared to represent your work to publishers. There are simply too many good writers seeking too few good agents, and it's getting more difficult with each year that passes.

So self-publish and save yourself a lot of time. If you do send copies of part or all of your manuscript to literary agents, expect either rejection or to not hear back from them at all. Get on with writing.

Creative control

This is a big one for me, and I suspect for most self-publishers. It was a pleasure working with a major publisher on my first book, a book about cost management in major organisations. But they insisted on a minor change to what I had submitted – the details don't matter – which I felt might impact negatively on sales, and I believe it has. However they have kindly agreed to return the publishing rights to me when the current stock has sold out, and they have been highly professional at all times.

The lesson I learned? Self-publish and retain full creative control.

Specification control

One of the ways in which you can make your books distinctive is to explore the specification options including:

- format (hardback, paperback, coil bound...)
- cover finish (matt, gloss, foil blocking, raised sections...)
- paper specification and 'feel'
- page sizes
- colour graphics, photographs
- place-marking ribbons

A reputable printer will take you through the options, which will be more numerous than if you publish through the print-on-demand (POD) route. But POD may still have its place: my own books would currently not be available to order outside the UK without the POD model.

So self-publish and retain full specification control.

Cost control

There are numerous book manufacturing and distribution options available to the self-publisher. While I was working on my first self-published book, *Guitar Gods in Beds.*, I had a meeting with a local publisher that was selling a book I much admired, a book of local interest with high production values. With hindsight the company was what is often termed (with justification) a 'vanity publisher'. As my book was of local interest too – the biographies of eight guitarists well-known in the local music scene – I met with the company and went through the practical issues and costs.

I was *stunned* by the high costs the company quoted. I couldn't possibly make any margin on the book unless it sold at a price which seemed wildly optimistic. I had to abandon the idea of using the company and instead explored the option of dealing directly with companies and freelance professionals to get my book published. The outcome of this exploration forms much of the content of this book.

So self-publish and save yourself a lot of money.

I was considering writing a book about British politics in 2009, but thinking and writing about left-wing politicians including Gordon Brown and Harriet Harman became too depressing and I eventually abandoned the project. A shame because I had some good material, a good title and cover design, and the project had taken up a good deal of my time. Some of the material was later included in my book *David and Goliatha: David Cameron – heir to Harman?* which was later extended to form the content of *The Glass Ceiling Delusion (the real reasons more women don't reach senior positions)*.

The abandoned book's title was *Harriet Harman Drove Me to France*, the idea being that if Labour won the then forthcoming general election, expected in May 2010, I would emigrate to France by way of protest, and pay my taxes to the French government rather than the British one.

France is frequently rated the country with the highest quality of life in the world, and it's seldom outside the top three. It's always placed well ahead of the UK. Many English people emigrate to France, some of them to retire. The only reason French people move to the UK is to earn more than they could in France. I've never heard of a French person retiring to the UK.

I'm a lifelong Francophile. But a paradox had always puzzled me until recently. The incidence of depression among French people has long been markedly higher than among British people. What might account for this? The answer dawned on me one day as I was compiling *Buchanan's Dictionary of Quotations for right-minded people*. It all goes back to

Liberté, egalité, fraternité – Freedom, equality, brotherhood – the motto of the French Revolution. I blame the plonker from Geneva, Jean-Jacques Rousseau, myself. With his books he arguably sowed the seeds of socialism and communism which were to ultimately lead to the deaths of more than 80 million people (mainly in China and the Soviet Union) in the 20th century.

My thesis is that a constant search for *egalité* is bound to induce envy and therefore misery in people, as is the relentless pursuit of its ugly sister 'fairness'. Because the French are on the whole more left-wing than the British – hell, they're more left-wing than the Chinese – they are accordingly more prone to being miserable and even depressed. The Welsh tend to be a miserable lot for exactly the same reason – that, and their perennial gnawing hatred of their more successful neighbours, the English. Envy is one of the seven deadly sins, and having been educated in Christian boarding schools I never commit any of them. I'm very proud of that.

I made the mistake of buying (for £120) the rights to a photograph for use on the cover of *Harriet Harman Drove Me to France*, thereby illustrating a point I shall be developing later: that if you don't follow a logical process for moving from a book concept to the final book, you're likely to waste time and possibly money too. I've changed the titles of all my books numerous times while engaged in the process of writing them.

The cover image for the book was taken with a camera positioned just above the shoulder of a lady looking out of her open doorway during an election campaign. A smiling Harriet Harman was looking up to, and speaking to, the woman from just outside the house. Behind Harriet Harman was Gordon Brown, wearing the smile which could make small children cry. My idea was to have a speech bubble directed at Harriet Harman and a thought bubble directed at Gordon Brown:

Harman: 'Good morning, Ms Johnson! I hope we can count on your vote again for the anti-men, anti-family, anti-business, anti-taxpayer, and anti-democracy party?'

Brown: 'Dear God. On the campaign trail with Mad Hattie. Livin' the dream, eh? Roll on the 2010 election and *freedom*.'

But one very good thing came from this project. I had at one time considered titling the book *Gordon Is a Moron*, the title of a popular music hit in 1978 for English comedy actor and musician Graham Fellows, under the name of his alter ego 'Jilted John'. Fairly confident that nobody would have used the title for a book, I looked on Amazon anyway, and was surprised to find that the title *had* already been used, by English writer Dr Vernon Coleman. Coleman is a highly successful self-publisher, publishing through his own creation, The Publishing House. From Vernoncoleman.co.uk:

> Vernon Coleman is the author of 114 books which have sold over 2 million copies in the UK, been translated into 25 languages and now sell in over 50 countries. His non-fiction books include *Bodypower* (voted one of the nation's 100 most popular books by British readers) and *How To Stop Your Doctor Killing You* and his novels include *Mrs Caldicot's Cabbage War* (which has been turned into a major movie starring Pauline Collins) and the Bilbury series of books.
>
> Vernon Coleman has a medical degree and has worked as a General Practitioner and a hospital doctor. Often described as an 'iconoclast' he has organised numerous campaigns for people and for animals. Although he now concentrates on writing books he has in the past presented numerous programmes on television (he was breakfast television's first doctor) and radio and has written over 5,000 columns and articles for over 100 of the world's leading newspapers and magazines.

The Publishing House, it transpires, sells only books written by Vernon Coleman and his wife. His biography on the website ends with the following gem:

> Vernon Coleman, born in Walsall, Staffordshire, England, is balding and widely disliked by members of the Establishment. He doesn't give a toss about either of these facts. He is married to Donna Antoinette, the totally adorable Welsh Princess and is very pleased about this.

Jerome K Jerome, author of the Victorian classic *Three Men in a Boat*, was born in Walsall. There's obviously something in the local water. I used a quotation from *Gordon Is a Moron* in my *Dictionary of Quotations* and sent Vernon Coleman a complimentary copy by way of appreciation. He replied and was very complimentary about the book, which quite made my day. We have since had further correspondence from which I learned that he was working on several titles simultaneously – from his prodigious output, this is clearly his custom – and he employed four members of staff.

The Mission Statement of The Publishing House is as insightful, punchy, and lengthy as we might expect from the good doctor:

The Publishing House Mission Statement
(Why We Believe Small Publishers Are The Only Real Publishers Left)

Compared to the big international conglomerates Publishing House is very definitely a 'small publisher'. We don't have a massive sales force (actually, we don't have a sales force at all). We don't have a board of eminent directors (since we're not a limited company we don't have any directors). We don't have offices in a skyscraper (we do have offices but we just have an upstairs and a downstairs). And we don't have a PR department full of bright young things called Hyacinth and Jacoranda. (We don't have a PR department at all). But we have one enormous advantage over the conglomerates. We care passionately about books.

They have marketing departments which decide which books will sell. They then commission books that the sales force think they will be able to flog. They won't even consider a book until they've done a marketing feasibility study.

We publish books we believe in. We then try to sell them. Naturally, we try to make a profit. If we didn't we wouldn't last long. We have to pay the printing bills, the electricity bills, the phone bills, the rates, the insurance and so on.

But we've been publishing for 15 years. In that time, we've sold over two million books. Our books have been translated into 22 languages and are sold by other publishers (including some big ones) in over 50 countries.

The conglomerates insist that every book should make a profit. We don't. Some of our books make more money than others. But that's fine with us. We don't mind if the better sellers sometimes subsidise the other books. We don't mind if a book is a little slow to sell. Like good parents we love all our children equally – however successful, or unsuccessful, they might be.

Despite all the talk about the need for each book to stand on its own two feet many big publishers make an overall loss. They are kept alive – effectively as vanity publishers – by other parts of the conglomerate. So, for example, the TV division or the magazine division may help to subsidise the book publishing division. We believe that book publishing can, and should, be allowed to stand alone. We believe that small publishers are now the only REAL publishers alive.

The big publishers often accept sponsorship from outside companies. We never do. We rely on the sale of books to earn our living and pay our bills. None of our books are sponsored or carry any advertising. We believe this helps us to remain truly independent. We publish books which international conglomerates wouldn't dare touch.

Big publishers have lost touch with people's needs. They are slow and unwieldy. It can take them two years to turn a typescript into a finished book! (We can, if pushed, get a book out within a month – while the material is still topical.)

They are too market orientated and derivative. They produce more of what other publishers did well with last year. We look forwards not backwards.

They pay huge amounts as advances to film stars, politicians and young hot shot authors. Much of the time they don't earn back those advances. They don't care because the books are just seen as 'tools' to help other parts of the empire. For example, a conglomerate will publish a politician's dull biography as a way of putting money into the politician's pocket.

Despite their huge marketing departments they are often out of touch with people's needs. If we published as many 'turkeys' as they do we'd be out of business.

They worry enormously about upsetting powerful politicians and other corporations. The big conglomerates need to co-operate with the establishment because they are part of the establishment. We stand outside the establishment. They don't like us much at all. They often do their best to shut us down.

But we don't give a fig for what politicians or corporate bosses might (or might not) think of us. We're only interested in publishing books that inform and entertain. When they try to shut us down we fight back.

At big publishers there are loads of men and women in suits who slow things down and interfere with the artistic process. Literary originality and integrity have been replaced by marketing convenience.

We have no men or women in suits to tell us what to do. We do what we believe is right. We publish books the old fashioned way. We're a small, independent publishing house. We publish books we believe in; books we want to publish and which we hope that our readers will want to read.

That's what we think publishing is all about.

Visit the website if you're looking for inspiration. I would only do one thing differently from Dr Coleman, if and when I become as successful. I *would* employ bright young things with names like Hyacinth and Jacoranda. I'm sure I could find them *something* to do.

Everyone in the literary world appears to agree these days that publishers will only consider book proposals put forward to them by literary agents. For male writers, especially those writing books with a male perspective, that can pose a problem. DH Lawrence wouldn't have had a hope of attracting an agent in the modern era. Why? The vast majority of literary agents are female. It should come as no surprise that major publishers take on few new authors writing books sympathetic to male perspectives.

But I believe – all right, I hope – that the pendulum will swing back again. How much more thin 'chick lit' can the book-buying public consume? I think there will be an increasing appetite for sometimes challenging books which have reasoned arguments at their core. I hope so, anyway – before we all drown in a tidal wave of books on astrology, the healing power of crystals, and dead children who reappear to friends, parents, and grandparents as angels. My blood *boils* at the cynicism of authors who dupe their readers for personal gain.

Literary agents and publishers are looking for 'marketable' authors, we are told. Often this appears to mean authors who are young, female, attractive, and able to speak fluently about their work, dropping terms such as *zeitgeist*, *schadenfreude*, hubris, and post-modern into their conversation. For those of us who fall into few or (in my case) none of the categories deemed desirable for new authors, self-publishing is the way forward. We end the chapter with an interesting story – my thanks to AuthorHouse:

> In 1982 Olympic Coach Tom McNab topped the *Times* Bestseller list with his first novel, *Flanagan's Run*. Translated into 16 languages, the book occupied the top spot in both the UK and Europe, selling hundreds of thousands of copies worldwide. But when Tom approached his publisher to release a new edition in 2009 he was refused. Despite the new generation of readers yet to be introduced to the novel, and the imminent release of a Miramax film adaptation, the publishing house was not interested.
>
> Undeterred, Tom approached AuthorHouse to enable him to re-publish the best-selling novel himself. During an interview on BBC Radio 4's *Open Book* programme in May 2010, he explained the rationale behind his decision:
>
>> 'My attitude was that if *Flanagan's Run* was good enough to be read by hundreds of thousands of people all over the world in 1982, then there must be another group of people equally capable of enjoying it… I read about self-publishing in a newspaper, it told me AuthorHouse was one of the best companies, so I simply found them on the web and wrote to them – that was it.'

Published to widespread critical acclaim, *Flanagan's Run* tells the epic story of a 3,000 mile marathon across the United States. Set in the depression-era, the book follows 2,000 hopefuls as they begin the gruelling race from New York to Los Angeles; a race ultimately beset by danger as the American sports establishment try to scupper the event.

Praised for both its well drawn cast, which includes such disparate characters as an ex-miner from Scotland, a Mexican trying to save his famine-struck village, a feisty showgirl from New York, a bare-knuckle boxer and a team of Young Nazis, and its vivid descriptions of the race, *Flanagan's Run* captures the pain, motivation, commitment, and satisfaction of running, while offering an enduring look at human experience and ambition.

About the author: Royal Air Force officer, triple jump champion, physical education teacher, Olympic coach, author, athletics historian and motivational speaker, Tom McNab has enjoyed a hugely varied and successful career. Born in Glasgow in 1933, he became national athletics coach for Southern England in 1963, and published his first non-fiction book, *Modern Schools Athletics*, in 1966. Over the next forty years he established a reputation not only as one of the world's leading sports coaches, but a talented author and historian. Two-time British Coach of the Year, he worked with a number of international athletes, the British Olympic Bobsleigh team and England's silver medal-winning Rugby squad in the 1992 World Cup, while also winning the Scottish Novelist of the Year award in 1982, bringing TV-AM into being in 1983 and working as technical advisor for the film *Chariots of Fire*, which won four Oscars. Now a commentator for ITV and Channel 4, a freelance journalist for the *Observer*, *Sunday Telegraph*, *Times* and *Independent*, two time novelist and prolific playwright, Tom's talents have no bars [author's note: *bars?*]. In the past twenty years he has become a much sought-after lecturer and is recognised as one of the world's top business speakers.

2

THE WRITER'S DELUSION AND ITS EXPLOITATION BY SOME PUBLISHERS

delusion *n* the state of being deluded; a false belief *(esp psychol)*; error.
exploitation *n* the act of using for selfish purposes.

This chapter covers:

- vanity publishers
- the writer's delusion
- publishing packages
- sales rankings
- 0 per cent cholesterol margarine
- retaining copyright

Let's start with a definition of the term 'vanity publisher'. Many of the publishers seeking your custom will go to great lengths to distance themselves from the term'. So ask yourself one simple question, 'Will I have to pay this company to have my book produced and distributed?' If the answer is 'Yes' the company is a vanity publisher. It's not rocket science.

The publisher's input can be small or large. The publishing elements – whether or not bundled up in 'publishing packages' – may be priced modestly or extravagantly. I have no objection to vanity publishers in principle. What I *do* object to is the marketing hype which leads aspiring authors to believe their books will have a significant chance of being commercially successful. The reality is that the prospect of commercial success for a new writer's books, regardless of how good a writer he is, and regardless of how expensive a publishing package he is willing to buy, is small. If the author believes otherwise, he is almost certainly deluded. Vanity publishers survive by exploiting that delusion.

Some of the vanity publishers' websites are as interesting for what they don't tell aspiring writers as for what they do. You could be forgiven for thinking that as a self-publisher you won't be able to obtain ISBNs for your books, or retain copyright. Vanity publishers don't *say* these things, of course. They subtly lead you to draw such false conclusions.

In July 2010 I was conducting a survey of the vanity publishers' websites. I planned to compare the various offerings as far as it was possible to do so, with a view to presenting you with some comparative information.

Some of the companies appeared professional; some didn't. Some had clear contract terms; some didn't. Some had clear pricing structures; some didn't. One major publisher had a pricing structure for books which would have baffled an accountant. I was used to understanding complex pricing structures – I'd been doing so for the previous 25 years in my working life – but after an hour I had to give up the challenge of determining what my book would cost if published by them. Anyway, the service seemed squarely aimed at attractive authors in their early 20s, as far as I could tell. They presumably spent hours in the publisher's online forums telling one another how *amazing* each other's books are.

I reviewed the website of a large vanity publisher which offered publishing packages, some of them for eye-watering sums: up to £11,000. As you'll find with many companies offering such services, their website had testimonials from satisfied writers. I thought I'd investigate how well the books in question were selling by looking at their sales rankings on Amazon.com. The books were all published in America between 2004 and 2009. The highest-selling title ranked at 2,278,217. The lowest-selling title ranked at a jaw-dropping 7,883,223.

And so it was that that I decided to discard all the comparative information I'd drawn up on vanity publishers. It seemed to me that compared with the self-publishing model I shall be presenting to you, these companies were offering models which delivered books more expensively, with a poorer range of specifications, and with less creative control for you, the writer. All too often vanity publishers offer packages which exploit writers' – and especially *new* writers' – lack of knowledge of the options available to them. They are trying to sell you a dream.

If you look at these companies' websites through a businessperson's eyes – as I have – you see marketing hype running through so much of what they assert. I was reminded at one point of the British food manufacturer which was selling margarine and making a great play on the claim of '0 per cent cholesterol' in the product. Well, no margarine has *ever* contained cholesterol, but '0 per cent cholesterol' might lead you to think otherwise.

What reminded me of the margarine case was a point made on a number of the publishers' websites: that you would retain copyright of your work if you published through them. The inference was that if you went to other publishers you would lose it – and to be fair, with some of them, you would. But – in the UK at least – copyright is automatic, and if you contract directly with a printer, as I shall be recommending in Chapter 4, you will certainly retain copyright.

3

SELECTING BOOK TOPICS WITH
STRONG SALES POTENTIAL

It's embarrassing, you try to overthrow the government and you wind up on a Best Sellers List.
Abbie Hoffman 1936-89 American social and political activist, in response to the success of *Steal This Book* (1971)

This chapter covers:

- writing books with an eye on future sales potential
- writing books related to future major events
- anticipating centenaries, bicentenaries etc. of births, deaths, events
- writing biographies of increasingly prominent figures
- determining topics of growing interest through research
- Nielsen's BookData service
- Nielsen's BookScan service
- chickens – who'd have believed it?

A seminar for publishers and self-publishers at Nielsen Book gave me the idea for this chapter, and specifically the presentation on their BookScan service, which enables publishers to review the book market. More on this later.

Many successful businesses have been founded on a vision of the future. They are established to make a product or service available that does not have current demand but will have in the future. There was no demand for mobile phones until companies made them along with the networks that enabled them to work. And in the early days the buyers – the 'early adopters', to coin a marketing phrase – were prepared to pay huge sums for huge phones with minimal functionality, the sight of which would today render a child helpless with laughter.

If your primary goal as a writer is to write books which sell well – maybe even bestsellers – it may help to write books on topics which are currently of no interest or minimal interest to the book-buying public, but which for a variety of reason will, or at the very least *might*, be of considerable interest to that public one day.

By the time a topic is covered by the major publishers, and their books are selling well, it's already too late. If you're an unknown author you'll have to come up with a radical new slant on a topic to have even a chance of commercial success. I'm hoping that when more people start to challenge the suitability of marriage for most people in the modern era, *The Marriage Delusion* will be well positioned as the only book which covers the topic in the way it does. I remain optimistic of it becoming a bestseller and I have my eye on a villa in Monaco with a large outdoor heated swimming pool; a villa with Keira Knightley as a neighbour on one side, and Cameron Diaz on the other.

Back to the real world. The challenge with this model is to predict the topic(s) that will interest the book-buying public of the future. A few ideas on how you might do this:

Writing books related to future major events

The idea here is to have your book available at a time when the public becomes particularly interested in a topic, or people related to it. An idea off the top of my head: a series of official biographies of prominent British athletes, to be published before the 2012 London Olympics. The Olympics have not been held in London since 1948, in an age of post-war austerity, and Britain will be determined to show a confident and modern face to the world. There will be enormous interest in British athletes with a serious prospect of winning a gold medal in sports requiring more athletic prowess than tiddlywinks.

You'd probably get plenty of support from the individual(s) in question, and their families. They'd surely be delighted to lend you photographs of themselves as children, as adults graduating from college, their wedding photographs, their sporting triumphs etc. Record material with a digital recorder as outlined in the chapter 'Writing other peoples' autobiographies', have the interview transcribed online, scan the photographs, employ the digital short print run or ebook option, and you could have your book on the market in a few weeks.

Anticipating centenaries, bicentenaries etc. of births, deaths, events…

The idea here is to have your book published before – and possibly even years before – the centenary or bicentenary of the event in question. There are numerous internet sites which can help you with the search. In a few seconds my search turned up an American site, Timelines.com. Let's say you want to publish a book in 2012 or 2013, in anticipation of it catching a wave of public interest in 2014. The website has around 200 references for 1914. In addition to the references to World War I there are many others, the following being a very small selection:

> 1914: *Tarzan of the Apes* is published.

> 22 January: Gordon Zobrod is born. An American oncologist who played a prominent role in the introduction of chemotherapy for cancer.

> 13 February: American Society of Composers, Authors and Publishers (ASCAP) is founded in New York City.

> 14 February: Babe Ruth signs first contract with minor-league Baltimore Orioles.

> 11 March: Toronto Blueshirts win Stanley Cup.

> 31 March: Octavia Paz is born. A Mexican writer who won the 1990 Nobel Prize for Literature.

> 9 May: President Woodrow Wilson proclaimed the first Mother's Day. [Author's note: And we've all had to buy Mothers' Day cards ever since. Thanks, Woodrow. Only joking, Mother.]

> 15 June: James Joyce's *Dubliners* is published.

The website expands on each topic. So it was that I learnt that the first print run of *Dubliners* was for 1,250 copies, the publisher having made the preconditions that Joyce personally had to buy 120 copies and would receive no royalties until 500 copies had been sold. Joyce started off his career by self-publishing. A little trickier then than now, one imagines.

Biographies of increasingly prominent figures

The figures may come from any walk of life. Let's consider up-and-coming politicians, especially those about whom opinion is strongly divided. Sarah Palin is very much in the 'love her or loathe her' camp. I'll bet the person who published the first biography of her made a fortune.

Determine topics of growing interest through research
The idea here is to either anticipate topics which will be of growing public interest, or spot a 'hot topic' in its early days before numerous books are written about it. Unlike major publishers, self-publishers can often write and publish a book within a couple of months, sometime less. Major publishers – or at least those not using the POD model – can take six months from receiving a writer's final manuscript to having stock available in stores. They often have books printed in developing countries and ship them to their final markets by sea to save money.

Nielsen's BookData Online service (global data from major English-speaking countries) is a good way to review in many ways books available in the market. They offer a 14-day free trial to publishers and special subscription rates for publishers subscribing to their Publisher Enhanced Service. To find out more email Sales.bookdata@nielsen.com. From this service I learned that they had records of some 69 books with 'self-publishing' or 'self publishing' in their titles or subtitles, many of which were no longer available. The table on the next page shows information about the nine top-selling titles.

With this information a few months ago I may have modified this book in line with what book buyers were buying. However, this might have compromised my desire for distinctiveness, so I probably wouldn't have. But if your prime objective is commercial success you might look at the matter quite differently.

BookData Online sorts search results in sales rank order without giving the actual sales data itself. For sales data you need to use Nielsen's BookScan service, and you can then analyse data by country and in numerous ways. Both could be useful services for writers seeking topics of growing interest.

The nine top-selling titles on self-publishing in the UK, available to order (12 July 2010, via BookData Online)

Title	Author / contributor	Imprint	Date	Format	Price (£)
Aiming at Amazon	Shepard, Aaron	Shepard Publications	1 Jan 2007	P/back	10.00
POD for Profit	Shepard, Aaron	Shepard Publications	1 Mar 2010	P/back	12.00
Perfect Pages	Shepard, Aaron	Shepard Publications	1 Feb 2006	P/back	7.50
Book Publishing DIY: The Do It Yourself Guide to Self-Publishing Using Lulu and CreateSpace	Loton, Tony	LOTONtech Limited	5 Dec 2008	P/back	10.50
Self-Publishing for Dummies	Rich, Jason R	John Wiley & Sons	12 Sep 2006	P/back	13.99
Adventures in Publishing	Sampson, Brent	Outskirts Press	5 Nov 2008	P/back	6.95
The African American Writer's Guide to Successful Self-Publishing	Powell, Takesha	Amber Books	1 Jun 2000	P/back	12.50
Ask Ron – The Plain Truth About Self-Publishing	Pramschufer, Ronald	Quilling Publishing	6 Aug 2007	P/back	8.00
A Cheap and Easy Guide to Self-Publishing E-Books	Perkins, Wayne F	AuthorHouse	20 Oct 2000	P/back	9.16

The speaker from BookScan at Nielsen Book's publisher seminar asked if any of the publishers present could name their firm's current top-selling title. A young lady next to me said her firm's top-selling title was on breeding and raising chickens. I regret to say that I laughed along with some of the other publishers. The speaker tapped the book title into his computer and declared it was the highest-selling book that any publisher at the annual seminars had ever put forward. The laughter stopped. Expect more books on chickens to be published soon.

You may wish to look at gaps in the market or pick up early signs of new trends. BookScan has been measuring sales in the UK, Ireland, and many other key English-speaking territories since 1998. This data allows you to see what is selling, the format, and the price. It gives commercial publishers the opportunity to research new books prior to commissioning. BookScan can provide simple title/ISBN or author reports for relatively low costs, or you can have more in-depth analysis using their subscription service.

Once you have published your title you can set realistic targets, compare your performance with your competitors, and make more informed print decisions. See Chapter 8 for more details or go to their website: Nielsenbookscan.co.uk.

4

THE COMMERCIAL SELF-PUBLISHING MODEL, WRITING AND SELLING DISTINCTIVE CONTENT-RICH NON-FICTION

Writing a book is an adventure. To begin with it is a toy, then an amusement. Then it becomes a mistress, and then it becomes a master, and then it becomes a tyrant and, in the last stage, just as you are about to be reconciled to your servitude, you kill the monster and fling him to the public.
Sir Winston Churchill 1874–1965 British politician, prime minister of the United Kingdom during World War II and again 1951–5, soldier, historian, writer, artist, first person to be recognised as an honorary citizen of the United States

This chapter covers:

- distinctive writing
- the commercial self-publishing model
- time saving tips

Let's say, for the sake of argument, that you're planning to write a book about marriage. It includes the idea that improved communications are central to making marriages work well, which means you'd probably be of the female persuasion. More than 90 per cent of the countless books on marriage and relationships – mostly written by women – already say that. What's the point in saying the same thing yet again? Let's turn to a *distinctive* take on the subject, an excellent book co-written by Patricia Love and Steven Stosny, *How to Improve Your Marriage Without Talking About It.* The publisher's product description on Amazon:

> Men are right. The 'relationship talk' does *not* help. Dr. Patricia Love's and Dr. Steven Stosny's *How to Improve Your Marriage Without Talking About It* reveals the stunning truth about marital happiness: Love is *not* about better communication. It's about connection.
>
> You'll never get a closer relationship with your man by talking to him like you talk to one of your girlfriends. Male emotions are like women's sexuality: you can't be too direct too quickly. There are four ways to connect with a man: touch, activity, sex, routines. Men want closer

marriages just as much as women do, but not if they have to act like a woman.

Talking makes women move closer; it makes men move away. The secret of the silent male is this: his wife supplies the meaning in his life. The stunning truth about love is that talking doesn't help. Have you ever had this conversation with your spouse? Wife: 'Honey, we need to talk about us.' Husband: 'Do we have to?'

Drs. Patricia Love and Steven Stosny have studied this all-too-familiar dynamic between men and women and have reached a truly shocking conclusion. Even with the best of intentions, talking about your relationship doesn't bring you together, and it will eventually drive you apart. The reason for this is that underneath most couples' fights, there is a biological difference at work.

A woman's vulnerability to fear and anxiety makes her draw closer, while a man's subtle sensitivity to shame makes him pull away in response. This is why so many married couples fall into the archetypal roles of nagging wife / stonewalling husband, and why improving a marriage can't happen through words.

How to Improve Your Marriage Without Talking About It teaches couples how to get closer in ways that don't require 'trying to turn a man into a woman'. Rich in stories of couples who have turned their marriages around, and full of practical advice about the behaviours that make and break marriages, this essential guide will help couples find love beyond words.

Amazon.co.uk has a five-star review from a lady reader who calls the book, 'the best marriage guidance book I've ever read in over 20 years of marriage education work'. She continues:

Stosny and Love have put together a very balanced explanation for both men and women, which explains the psychological and emotional realities, and in addition put forward a really practical exercise which can be repeated over and over to bring hope and reassurance to any couple who are sincere about making improvements in their relationship. It can also be practised unilaterally with good results too.

What lesson can we draw from this example, beyond the insight itself? There's merit in adding a new perspective on a subject, and this might translate into strong sales of your books. Correspondingly there is little merit in broadly repeating what other people have already written, and book sales will probably be low.

This book is my sixth and I've slowly developed a model which reliably enables me to write distinctive content-rich non-fiction. This book took me three months to write and 120 hours of that was spent on the quotations element. I've yet to write my first fiction but it seems obvious that much of the model could also be used by writers of fiction. I hope that at least some of the model will help you. If nothing else it should help you minimise the amount of time and money you spend on individual books.

When I reflect on my early books and how I wasted both time and money, I recognise that my problems largely resulted from not following a logical sequence of events. I didn't have a sound process, or model. In short, I wasn't applying the sound business principles which had served me well in my career. But producing books is like any other complex activity, you'll find. The more you do it, the better you will become. Having a sound model really helps. *Ce n'est pas rocket science.*

My commercial self-publishing model – excluding the marketing of books, which I cover in Chapter 10 – consists of the following stages:

1. Decide the book's topic(s).
2. Identify and analyse competing books (if there are any).
3. Understand the characteristics and cost implications of the various sales channels for books; set a prospective price for the book.
4. Collect quotations for chapter headings and for an appendix of quotations (if required).
5. Provisionally decide the book's format(s), order fulfilment method(s), and price(s).
6. Carry out background research (if required).
7. Obtain a critique of your book project and a sample of your writing (optional).
8. Write and 'sculpt' the book.
9. Allocate quotations to the starts of individual chapters.
10. Tidy up formatting; insert headers and page numbers (if the book is not going to be professionally typeset).
11. Finalise the book's format (hardback, paperback etc.) and pricing.
12. Finalise the title (and sub-title if there is one).
13. Prepare the first draft of the index of cited publications, references and further reading, and the subject index (as appropriate).
14. Have the book professionally proofread and copy-edited (optional, but recommended).
15. Have the book professionally typeset (optional).

16. Adjust the number of pages in the book to suit the printer's multiple page requirement (not required for ebook or POD models).
17. Add the page numbers and headers
18. Revise the cross-references, index of cited publications, references and further reading, and the subject index (if required).
19. Design the cover.
20. Do a final check of both content and cover; convert to PDFs and/or JPGs.
21. Email PDFs to appropriate parties; order and approve proofs.
22. Register book details, cover design etc. with Nielsen or Bowker.
23. Place order for stock (if required).
24. Fulfil orders for the book (if required).
25. Send a copy of the book to the British Library.

Although I'm recommending a formal sequence of stages it's my belief that – at least if your mind works anything like mine – your non-fiction book should *evolve* over the course of its development as new ideas and insights come to you, new information is gleaned, and so on. It helps keep your mind alert, for one thing, and that freshness will hopefully come out in your writing.

In this book, as in some of my previous ones, I've been well into stage 8 – the actual writing of the book – when it occurs to me that the chapter titles, contents, and even their sequence could and should be changed to produce a stronger book. It must have happened at least five times during the writing of this book. But I look on the time spent on making the changes as an investment in the quality of the book so I'm never resentful when it happens. Well, almost never...

One of the joys of writing in the era of the computer is that making such changes need not take up a lot of time or effort – you can 'cut and paste' to your heart's content. If the result is a better book of more value to your readers, why not do it? Only you will know. I imagine that in the era of the manual typewriter an author would have kicked his cat – or, preferably, his neighbour's cat – when he realised the chapter sequences and contents should be changed.

Please, no letters about cruelty to animals. I'm a cat lover, and I happen to own a terrific cat, Albert, whose sister Victoria died many years ago. I'm prepared to make an exception to my 'not kicking cats' policy in the case of the evil-looking black male cat which somehow manages to foil every cat flap security technology known to man and sprays inside my house in the early hours of the morning once or twice a month. The smell in the house is unbelievable. Oh, and he does this after eating Albert's food. Talk about an attitude problem.

1. *Decide the book's topic(s)*

This may seem a rather obvious stage, barely worth including, but it will be a critical stage if your prime motivation is to write a book with the hope of commercial success, making you a reasonable amount – or even a lot – of money. You might then decide to write a book on a topic which will be of interest to book buyers at some future time, in an effort to be 'ahead of the wave' at the point of publication. I made some suggestions on how you might do this in the last chapter.

You might have the ambition to become a recognised authority on a subject, thereby driving your book's sales and possibly preparing the ground for future editions, especially if the book's topic is one which develops over time. With my commercial self-publishing model you can readily and inexpensively change the book's content over time. Just don't publish the book as a new edition if there's little content change compared with the previous edition, because you'll only alienate readers who buy both editions. And you can't expect an alienated reader to even consider buying your future titles.

2. *Identify and analyse competing books (if there are any)*

Even if you're not planning on writing a bestseller you should never lose sight of the fact that you want to write a book with a market, however small. If you adopt the advice in this book, in the worst case scenario you will have lost little money, even if not a single copy of the book is sold.

Too many self-published books are not distinctive, or they have small page counts, or thin content which is exposed by the use of Amazon's 'Look Inside' tool. When I write books I like them to be distinctive, content-rich, and ideally with no competition. My *Profitable Buying Strategies* remains, to the best of my knowledge, the only book written *in plain English* showing organisations how to reduce the costs of the goods and services they buy.

How many books on marriage and relationships have been written? At least a gerzillion, surely. But *The Marriage Delusion* is the only one putting forward the thesis that it does, and the thesis remains unchallenged two years after the book's publication. Whatever you write, try to make your book distinctive. Make it stand out from the crowd. That way you won't be competing heavily on price against publishers with deep pockets.

Before I start on a new book project I spend some time on Amazon to see what other books on the topic in question are already available, or are due to become available in the coming months. They're my forthcoming book's competition. I order books which appear to be putting forward a similar thesis to the one I plan to put forward. I search for titles using keywords, in the case of this book 'self-publishing' and 'self publishing' because both terms are in common usage.

I find that sorting the books on Amazon by 'Relevance' rather than 'Bestselling' gives superior results for the purpose of this exercise, because in the latter case Amazon searches both the book's title and inside the book for references to the keywords. What else could explain Daniel Goleman's *Emotional Intelligence*, published in 1996, topping the bestseller list for 'self-publishing'? I emailed Amazon to ask what 'relevance' meant in the context of keyword searches. They responded with the following:

> Relevance as asked in your inquiry, is the criteria in which the search results are based on the keyword match from the bestsellers pool of items.

That's clear, then.

I like to write distinctive, content-rich books – they're more satisfying to write and suffer less price competition than indistinctive, content-poor books – so I analyse a number of the existing offerings on the topic in question. The table on the next page illustrates the nature of the analysis I carried out before I started writing this book.

Analysis of leading titles on self-publishing on Amazon, May 2010

Title, author(s); date of publication; price direct from Amazon inc p&p; sales ranking; number of customer reviews and average review (out of five stars)	Number of pages; book dimensions (cm); content viewable with 'Look Inside'?	Index?	Content summary (1)	Content strengths and weakness, overall assessment of the book (2)
Dan Poynter's Self-Publishing Manual: How to Write, Print, and Sell Your Own Book Dan Poynter March 2007 £9.55 #22,067 12 reviews, avge 4.5 stars	463 pages 21.3 x 14 x 2.5 Yes	Yes		<confidential>
Aiming at Amazon: the NEW Business of Self Publishing, or How to Publish Books with Print on Demand and Online Book Marketing on Amazon.com. Aaron Shepard January 2007 £10.00 #60,856 21 reviews, avge 4.5 stars	208 pages 22.6 x 15 x 1.8 No	?		<confidential>
Self-Publishing For Dummies Jason Rich September 2006 £7.89 #188,416 No reviews	384 pages 23.1 x 18.8 x 2.3 Yes	Yes		<confidential>

(1) Include table of contents if available through 'Look Inside' or from Amazon's description.
(2) Look at what the book's reviewers on Amazon have to say about the book – what do they like, what don't they like? Compare the book with what I could write, possibly after some research.

I came to the conclusion after conducting this analysis that I *could* write and publish a distinctive content-rich book on the subject – you may beg to disagree, to be fair – and I wrote down what I wanted it to deliver to prospective buyers:

- *up-to-date* information on self-publishing options available, including ebooks
- material on writing, encouraging self-publishers to write in a way that is more in tune with their strengths rather than aping bestselling authors
- give readers the benefit of my 30 years' experience in the business world to show them how to maximise profits – or at least how to minimise losses
- give readers the benefit of my 25 years' experience of buying printed materials
- show the readers how to deal directly with the various parties involved with getting a book to production
- inject some humour from time to time, to improve the reading experience
- include a lengthy section of quotations relating to books, writing, reading etc. to give readers continuing value long after they've finished the book

From previous books I knew that preparing each page of quotations in a book this size, using the methodology I use – which I shall outline shortly – would take about three hours. In the event there were more high quality insightful or amusing quotations relating to books and related subjects than I'd anticipated, and I collected 40 pages of them, so the exercise took about 120 hours to complete. But the result is, to the best of my knowledge, the only collection dedicated to the topics available.

You may well think that a writer would have to be barking mad to spend 120 hours selecting quotations for a self-published book. I couldn't possibly comment. Woof.

3. Understand the characteristics and cost implications of the various sales channels for books; set a prospective price for the book

This is an important stage if you wish to maximise your earnings from writing books, or at the very least minimise your losses. The current viable approaches to self-publishing are the following:

- ebooks
- print-on-demand (books printed digitally and manufactured in response to an order from yourself or a buyer or a bookseller, a single copy if required)
- short-run digital print (1–300 copies)
- offset lithography (300+ books)

Digital printing is the only viable and cost-effective printing option for print runs of 1–300 copies. With Lightning Source you have the option of making your physical (Print on Demand) books printed in the US, UK, Europe and Australia for buyers living in or near those territories. For runs over 300 copies (approximately) offset lithography printing will be cheaper, and the 'per copy' cost will then reduce as the run length increases.

Each of the self-publishing options has advantages and disadvantages. Appendix 6 covers the topic of formatting files so as to create ebooks to suit the different e-readers available, and later in this chapter I explain how you can have your books formatted for all major e-readers for a one-off payment of US$149.00 (about £95.00). Or go for a cheaper option. I've now made four titles available as PDF ebooks – viewable on free-to-download Adobe Digital Edition software available from such websites as bookdonboard.com – through Lightning Source at no cost, and specified that readers will be able to neither print nor copy material from the titles. The PDF files were created directly from Word 2007.

Give some consideration to having your books available in a number of editions, getting the best out of each model. If you have a colour plate section in your book you'll be able to include it in your ebook edition at no cost, and in your short-run edition at low cost (about £0.07 per page with MPG Biddles and CPI Antony Rowe). To the best of my knowledge POD editions can't currently have colour plate sections in an otherwise mono book – let me know if you know differently – other than apparently through CPI Antony Rowe, although I haven't yet explored this option myself.

A comparison between POD and short-run digital print is provided in Chapter 5. Lightning Source's POD model is impressive – it's at the heart of many vanity publishers' business models – and I cover it in Chapter 7.

In the days shortly after publication your books will probably not appear in 'bricks and mortar' bookstores, other than your local ones if you can persuade them to hold them. You'll be making your books visible and available to users of online bookstores and to 'bricks and mortar' bookstore staff who will order on their customers' behalf. You need not allow their wholesalers/distributors (principally Bertrams and Gardners in the UK) the discount they would require if they were to physically hold a stock of your books in their warehouses: usually 50–60 per cent. Allow them just 20 per cent, as I do. They don't respond to my letters seeking formal agreement for a 20 per cent discount, but they always settle my invoices in full, and that's what matters.

Assuming you're publishing a book and you're uncertain about sales – and won't that always be the case? – don't launch with an offset litho print run. Decide provisionally which of the three other formats (ebook, POD, short digital print run) you wish to use. You can offer one, two, or all three of them, and have different offerings in different geographical markets.

If the book is on a serious topic you might wish to launch it in a hardback edition. The cost premium over a paperback could well be less than you'd expect, and you'll then be delivering additional perceived value to the buyer. Hardback editions are available through both the POD and short print run models, but not through the ebook model, my extensive researches has revealed. Now that's something that other writers of books about self-publishing won't have pointed out to you.

From the analysis of competing books you should have some sense of a viable price point for your book. Hopefully you'll be writing a better book than those already available on the topic(s) in question, so you'll be able to command a higher price. If you've written a distinctive book, with distinctiveness of a type that the book buyer can be expected to value, again you'll be able to command a premium price.

Now decide what your sales channels are going to be. Whether you use Nielsen's basic service (free) or their enhanced service (a charge is made per title) bookstore staff around the world will have online visibility of your book, as will buyers ordering from online bookstores.

If you're going to make profits as a self-publisher you'll obviously have to cover your costs, so you need to set your book's price with some care.

So, what are the costs in self-publishing? Some are fixed – payable even if you don't sell a single book – while others are variable and rise (in overall cost terms, not per copy) in proportion to the number of books sold.

Fixed costs include:

- preliminary costs including proofs
- cost of book manufacturing (if any) or ebook formatting
- costs associated with making the book available to buyers: the copy editor, proofreader, typesetter (if used), cover designer, Nielsen Enhanced Service (if used)…
- cost of book storage if you use an order fulfilment company
- overheads required for the book to be produced, which should be at least partly tax-deductible: use of a room as an office, computer, utilities etc.
- ISBNs and possibly also a charge for the graphic designer to source individual ones – although if you use Lightning Source they ISBNs you provide will be present on the design templates they email

Variable costs include:

- order fulfilment (including postage and packaging) whether or not you use an order fulfilment company
- sums paid to intermediaries (e.g. online bookstore fees – read Chapter 9 on dealing with Amazon to understand Amazon's selling models and associated costs)

In a conventional business, when setting the price of a product or service you might start with a sales forecast and divide your fixed costs by that number. You'd then add the variable costs to arrive at a cost per item, and this figure can be used as a figure to help you set the selling price and therefore the margin.

But as self-publishers we have a problem. We don't know in advance how many books we're going to sell, and our forecast may well be wildly wrong. We won't be able to forecast more accurately until the sales of our titles have become at least reasonably predictable, and that's only likely to happen if we keep writing books in the same genre which I, for one, do not wish to do.

I set my forthcoming books' prices by guessing what the market will bear, not forgetting that the more distinctive it is, the higher the price I can charge. If the book doesn't sell as well as I'd hoped I might reduce the price, making sure that the book's costs are covered.

4. Collect quotations for chapter headings and for an appendix of quotations (if required)
It's time for me to reveal a dark secret. I'm a quotation junkie.

You might be surprised that I suggest collecting quotations at this early stage, but if you're writing only or mainly non-fiction books as I do, you may be glad you did so. A quotation can work on any level but the best ones provide insight(s) which can trigger intriguing lines of enquiry. If they're humorous as well then they're more easily digested and remembered.

When I wrote *The Marriage Delusion* I wanted apt quotations at the start of each chapter, reflecting the chapter's topic: a common feature in non-fiction books. I looked in my dictionaries of quotations – *The Oxford Dictionary of Quotations* provided some – and visited Quotationspage.com for more quotations on love, marriage, men, women, sex, relationships, and more. In the end I had far more than I could use at the start of chapters, and it occurred to me that I might add an appendix to the end of the book, containing those quotations not used as chapter starters. The appendix ran to 18 pages, maybe 220-plus quotations in total.

I was intrigued to receive feedback from readers saying they'd much enjoyed the section of quotations, coming as it did after a book with so much serious content. A number said that the quotations section brought some light relief and was an unexpected 'freebie', something they could enjoy time and again long after they'd read the main book content.

But I had benefited from the exercise too. The quotations sparked off a number of ideas and questions which considerably changed the proposed content of the book. I adopted the same process for this book, looking for quotations on books, reading, writing, publishing, and so on. And again they proved very useful in stimulating my thinking.

Well-selected quotations can be a real asset in a book, especially books with serious content, where they bring some light relief to the reader. The more serious and thought-provoking the book's content, the greater the need for light relief, in my view. It can take a surprisingly long time to select and transcribe a substantial number of high-quality apt quotations. Think of it as sorting the wheat from the chaff: a little wheat amidst a lot of chaff. I want every quotations I employ to earn its keep: it must provide insight or humour, ideally both.

In my books which contain an appendix of quotations as well as quotations at the start of chapters, such as this book, I can take two weeks or more locating and transcribing quotations. I've developed a process which works well, although it's time consuming. But it's thorough and I seldom experience the frustration of coming across a quotation which would have been perfect for an earlier book.

The process I'm about to outline provides me with about one page of quotations every three hours, using the font and page sizes I've used in this book. The section of quotations – Appendix 1 – along with the quotations at the start of each chapter took me about 120 hours to track down and transcribe. If you want to gather a substantial number of high quality quotations I recommend you start with the best available source, *Oxford Dictionary of Quotations* ('ODQ'). This and other dictionaries of quotations I've bought and draw upon are critiqued below, the prices being the lowest prices advertised (including postage and packaging) for copies of the latest edition in 'new' and 'used' conditions on Amazon.co.uk in June 2010:

Oxford Dictionary of Quotations ('ODQ')
(2009, £18.69/£12.64) – 20,000+ quotations.
This dictionary is famously accurate. If your budget is tight you might opt for an older copy: on Amazon you can currently buy used copies of the 1999 edition for £0.44. If you're of Scottish extraction – as I am – you could always of course not buy a copy, and instead spend several days perusing a copy in your local library and write the quotations down. I predict, however, that after a few days of doing this, you'll go howling-at-the-moon crazy.

The *ODQ* is arranged principally in alphabetical order of the writers or speakers of quotations, and it also has sections dedicated to individual topics or publications – for example, 2 pages of advertising slogans, 48 pages of selections from the Bible (authorised version, 1611), and catchphrases (3 pages).

Keywords are the principal method used by the *ODQ* to help the reader track down suitable quotations. Knowing the topic of your book will guide you to the most relevant keywords. For this book I chose a selection of keywords including 'book', 'books', 'publish', 'published', 'publisher', 'publishers', 'publishing', 'read', 'reads', 'reader', 'reading'…

The index consists of the keyword followed by an extract of the line it's drawn from, then an indication of the author, then the page number, and finally the quotation number on that page. The section devoted to the keyword 'publish' starts with:

publish P. and be damned   WELL 827:15
   p., right or wrong   BYRO 182:8

The quotations are from the Duke of Wellington and Lord Byron respectively. You might find sources cropping up which are *never* usable. I've given up any hope that Chaucer ('CHAU') will ever yield a usable quotation, and this is my first book to include quotations from Shakespeare. The key thing to remember is that the more discriminating you are in your choice of quotations, the richer the contribution they will make to your book and by extension to your reader's appreciation of your book.

The *ODQ* has a few words about the speaker or writer, their years of birth and (where appropriate) death, and the source material and its year of publication. You might want to offer the reader more biographical detail on the quotation contributors, as I did in this book, in which case I can recommend Wikipedia (Wikipedia.org).

Oxford Dictionary of Quotations by Subject
(2010, £7.14/£7.13) – 7,000+ quotations.
An excellent work. The quotations are provided under 600 themes. No keyword search but there's an author index indicating the subject matter of quotations attributable to them in the book.

Bartlett's Familiar Quotations
(2002, £16.02/£15.80) – 25,000+ quotations.

The first edition of this book was edited and self-published in 1855 by John Bartlett, a bookseller from Cambridge, Massachusetts. I guess that must be where Cambridge, Cambridgeshire, took its name from. The book was itself to be the subject of comment by Winston Churchill in his *Roving Commission: My Early Life*, published in 1930:

> It is a good thing for an uneducated man to read books of quotations. *Bartlett's Familiar Quotations* is an admirable work, and I studied it intently. The quotations when engraved upon the memory give you good thoughts. They also make you anxious to read the authors and look for more.

The *ODQ* cites only the first sentence of the above extract. *Bartlett's Familiar Quotations* has an unusual organisation, in that the primary system used to order the quotations is the originators' birth dates. That said, contributors' quotation locations in the book are readily found in the 'Index of Authors'. A keyword section enables the reader to search in much the same manner as he would in the *ODQ*.

Due to the sometimes differing content of the *ODQ* and *Bartlett's*, if writers can only afford one major dictionary of quotations, the *ODQ* is possibly more suitable to writers in the United Kingdom, and *Bartlett's* most suitable for writers in North America. Buy both if you can afford them.

Oxford Dictionary of Humorous Quotations
(2009, £7.75/£6.75) – 5,000+ quotations.

The fourth edition still bears the name on the cover of the late lamented Ned Sherrin, although he died in 2007. His preface to the third edition (2005) is included as are his prefaces dating back as far as the first edition (1994). This book is ordered in alphabetical order of themes, the index of themes taking up three pages. The book is therefore a very helpful source of quotations for writers who know the themes they are exploring in their books. A quick glance down the index of themes may well lead you to add quotations on themes that are relevant to your book, but which you might not have thought of yourself. There's also a keyword index.

Oxford Dictionary of Modern Quotations

(2008, £6.99/£4.55) – 5,000+ quotations.

The book provides quotations from 'key voices and events of the 20th and 21st centuries, from literature, politics, film, television, journalism and popular song' and is arranged in the alphabetical order of the contributors' surnames. The book has a keyword index.

Cassell's Humorous Quotations

(2003, £7.41, £3.62) – 5,000+ quotations.

This book was edited by the British writer and radio presenter Nigel Rees. It covers an astonishing 1,200 themes and is laid out in alphabetical order by theme. Particularly welcome are the short biographies of the authors, their years of birth and death, the source of the quotation, and sometimes some background to the quotations to shed some light on the context in which they were created. A keyword index completes an excellent dictionary.

Funny You Should Say That

(2006, £2.76/£2.76) – 5,000+ quotations.

This is an absolute gem of a collection and clearly the result of an enormous amount of work. It has the theme/sub-theme structure of *The Funniest Thing You Never Said* (below) but so much more besides:

- the source of the quotation, and its date of publication
- a 35-page section of author biographies along with the authors' years of birth and death
- an author index including the themes to which the quotation is question is related
- a keyword index

The Funniest Thing You Never Said (The Ultimate Collection of Humorous Quotations)

(2004, £5.73/£2.76) – 6,000+ quotations.

The organisation of this book is unusual. It doesn't have a keyword index; it has an index of contributors. The material is sorted into 13 themes/sub-themes, not in alphabetical order, under which appear individual themes, again not in alphabetical order. To illustrate the point, the first super theme – 'Humanity' – contains the following themes:

People	Cheating
Men	Divorce
Women	Friendship
Battle of the Sexes	Character
Gender	Voice
Attraction	Upper Class
Sex	Snobbery
Kiss	Ego
Dating	Manners and Etiquette
Love	Advice
Marriage	Profession
Family Planning	Work
Children and Family	Success and Failure
Home	Awards

No biographical details are provided on the individual contributors, not even the years of their births and deaths.

The Mammoth Book of Comic Quotes
(2004, £2.80/£4.10) – 10,000+ quotations.
This book has twice the number of quotations as *The Funniest Thing You Never Said* but suffers from the same shortcomings, notably the absence of biographical information on the authors and a keyword index.

A mention must be made here of a masterpiece written by the American journalist and satirist Ambrose Bierce. It's his satirical classic *The Devil's Dictionary* (1911), a dictionary rather than a dictionary of quotations, but you may well find useful definitions to pep up your book. A selection of words starting with the first two letters of the alphabet should tell you whether you're likely to find the book a useful resource:

Abroad, adj. At war with savages and idiots. To be a Frenchman abroad is to be miserable; to be an American abroad is to make others miserable.

Accord, n. Harmony.

Accordion, n. An instrument in harmony with the sentiments of an assassin.

Alcohol, n. (Arabic al kohl, a paint for the eyes.) The essential principle of all such liquids as give a man a black eye.

Altar, n. The place whereon the priest formerly ravelled out the small intestine of the sacrificial victim for purposes of divination and cooked its flesh for the gods. The word is now seldom used, except with reference to the sacrifice of their liberty and peace by a male and female fool.

Bacon, n. The mummy of a pig embalmed in brine. To 'save one's bacon' is to narrowly escape some particular woman, or other peril.

Bang, n. The cry of a gun. That arrangement of woman's hair which suggests the thought of shooting her; hence the name.

Barometer, n. An ingenious instrument which indicates what kind of weather we are having.

Barrister, n. One of the ten thousand varieties of the genus Lawyer. In England the functions of a barrister are distinct from those of a solicitor. The one advises, the other executes; but the thing advised and the thing executed is the client.

Belladonna, n. In Italian a beautiful lady; in English a deadly poison. A striking example of the essential identity of the two tongues.

Betrothed, p.p. The condition of a man and woman who, pleasing to one another and objectionable to their friends, are anxious to propitiate society by becoming unendurable to each other.

Brandy, n. A cordial composed of one part thunder-and-lightning, one part remorse, two parts bloody murder, one part death-hell-and-the-grave, two parts clarified Satan and four parts holy Moses! Dose, a headful all the time. Brandy is said by Emerson, I think, to be the drink of heroes. I certainly should not advise others to tackle it. By the way, it is rather good.

Once I've worked through the dictionaries of quotations I start to search for quotations online. I always carry out this stage *after* reviewing books of quotations because online sources tend to be less reliable and seldom include the level of biographical or source material I'm looking for. They also often duplicate the quotations I already have. But sometimes they offer some terrific ones – often quirky - although you can rarely be sure of their provenance. Wikipedia will again furnish the biographical details you want, and sometimes even the source material details. On occasion a name is not recognised even by Wikipedia.

After experimenting with a number of websites I now use only Quotationspage.com. As well as offering the customary keyword search facility, the site offers a useful subject index. At the time of writing – June 2010 – it covers 247 subjects.

Finally, there's a strong *practical* case for including an appendix of quotations – and, for the same reason, excerpts from any previous books you've written – in your books, at least if you're opting for a digital short print run with a page multiple requirement. If you're opting for a non-POD digital print run or offset litho run, the printer will probably specify a page multiple, usually 8 or 16 pages. When I finish a book it's never exactly in line with the required multiple so I see what I can do rather than leave unsightly blank pages. I find that adjusting the quotation appendix or the size of extracts from my other books speedily leads me to the magic multiple.

The POD model printers ask for a multiple of two pages: if you supply them with a PDF with an odd number of pages they'll simply add a blank page side behind the last page, and Lightning Source add another page at the end, on which they print some details including the location of the plant which printed the book.

5. Provisionally decide the book's format(s), order fulfilment method(s), and price(s)
Next comes the matter of format, particularly whether you'll be publishing your book in hardback or paperback format (or possibly both, at different price points). Many commercially successful books are first launched only in hardback format, at a premium price, and you'd reasonably assume that the price reflects the high cost of manufacturing hardbacks. But it doesn't.

The chances are that the latest blockbuster from a leading writer, retailing for £15.00, cost the publisher under £2.00 to have printed, especially if it was printed in a developing country such as India. The price of £15.00 reflects *what the market will bear.*

Don't rule out initially publishing your book as a hardback at this stage, even if you're publishing under the print-on-demand (POD) model. The marketplace for books can bring surprises. My titles available to order outside the United Kingdom are all printed by Lightning Source's POD model, and I am initially making this book available worldwide through the model. In September 2009 I published my hardback *The Marriage Delusion* with a cover price of US$30.00 in the United States. It sold steadily, and in an effort to attract more sales I published it as a paperback – *The Fraud of the Rings* – in February 2010, with a retail price of US$18.00.

If you look at either of the books on Amazon you'll very quickly see that the other edition is available. If you key in the first title you'll be directed at first to the second; presumably Amazon have a policy of directing buyers to the best value-for-money edition in the first instance. And yet, five months after the launch of the paperback, the hardback continued to markedly outsell the paperback, to my surprise.

Give some consideration to pricing your different book editions differently, maybe to some extent reflecting their costs of production. But always have an eye on the buyer's perspective, and ultimately do what the big publishers do: price your books to maximise profit, not revenue.

I recently learned from Lightning Source that 20 per cent of my North American POD sales originate with Amazon, the other 80 per cent originating from other sources which they wouldn't divulge. I do wonder whether the latter mainly originate from 'bricks and mortar' booksellers, where eagle-eyed sales assistants inform customers of the hardback rather than the paperback edition of my book, so they can make a larger margin.

So, the big question: how should you provisionally set your book's recommended retail price? Your research into the competition should give you some indication, but even major publishers admit that setting selling prices is as much an art as a science.

Don't be intimidated by the often low prices of competing titles which are selling well, as evidenced by their sales ranking on Amazon. These are likely to be by well-established writers whose sales volumes justify books being printed by offset lithography rather than by the digital process. Books are only printed by offset lithography when production runs of 300+ copies are undertaken, and the cost *per copy* is then lower than for books printed digitally. The longer the production run, the lower the price per copy, whereas for digital print runs the cost per copy remains largely unaffected by production run length, although a minimum order quantity (often 100 copies) is commonplace.

The greater the extent to which your book is distinctive from the competition – and is visibly so to potential buyers – the less will your book's sales be price-sensitive.

You can adjust the price of your books over time by informing Nielsen. So why not start off with a relatively high price, then reduce the price if and when you think your profits will improve as a result? If income is more important to you than sales volumes, you should seek to arrive at a price which provides the maximum profit as opposed to the maximum margin per copy. It's surely better to sell 50 copies with a margin of £2.00 per copy than 10 copies with a margin of £5.00 per copy.

If you adjust the price of your book by informing Nielsen (and Lightning Source if they print the book), with the POD model you'll have the cost of changing the cover PDF as well as the cost of the designer processing a new cover PDF. Lightning Source currently charge £25.20 to process a new PDF. Alternatively, if all your sales are to be online, consider not having a price printed on your book in the first place.

Matters are more complicated if you have your books printed under the short digital print run model, for the obvious reason that you have printed stock bearing the price you now wish to change. Your printer will be a good source of self-adhesive bar code labels bearing the new price – the ISBN itself will remain unchanged – but of course you still have the problem of the stock in bookstores (if any) being incorrect. This probably won't matter too much, because while the buyer will be expecting to pay the price printed on the book, he will be pleasantly surprised to be charged less at the till. The bookseller may not be happy that he's getting a lower margin than he'd anticipated, but I've found in practice that they're very philosophical about it. Until and unless they're selling large numbers of your books, booksellers won't be too bothered by such discrepancies.

6. Carry out background research (if required)

It could be that you don't need to carry out any research at all. But if you're writing non-fiction and wish the book to be authoritative, you might decide that there are some areas where research could strengthen your book, especially if topicality would improve the book's perceived value.

On the other hand you might decide a substantial amount of research is required, especially if you're trying to put forward an original or possibly even controversial thesis. In *The Marriage Delusion* I recognised that the central thesis of the book – that most people in the developed world in the modern era are unsuited to marriage – was sufficiently controversial that I had to back it up with material from authoritative sources.

And so it was that I read or partially read some 50 books related to the subject in some way – covering psychology, the different natures of men and women, the law relating to marriage and divorce, religion, love, sex and much more besides – and included material from 30 of the books in my own. It hardly needs saying, I hope, that this approach was highly time-consuming.

7. *Obtain a critique of your book project and a sample of your writing (optional)*
This is a sensitive issue but it merits some consideration. I've been offered a number of manuscripts by other writers with a view to publishing them, which have been poor in the extreme: sometimes on a number of levels. I often find that the writers of such manuscripts are not frequent book readers, so they may be excused for failing to understand how far short of commercially acceptable their manuscript is. Some have even become abusive at my failure to recognise them as the literary heir to Ernest Hemingway and I'm disinclined to spend time on publishing other people's books when I can spend time on publishing my own.

It could be that you're not as good a writer as you'd like to believe. If this is the case, it could be that workshops and courses might help you improve your material markedly, but it's possible they might not. There's a risk that you could put in a superhuman effort for years with not even the remotest prospect of success.

Unless you're very confident about the quality of your writing, or you're allergic to criticism like I am, it might be worth investing in an editorial critique of your proposed project and material. Don't rely on the opinions of family or friends, and be wary of feedback from vanity publishers. I imagine that if you present them with a real stinker of a manuscript, the publication of which might open them to ridicule, they might provide strongly negative feedback. But otherwise you can reasonably expect them to comment favourably on your material whilst making some minor recommendations with which you could readily comply.

Most of the money vanity publishers make from most of their customers comes from the sale of publishing packages and allied services rather than the sales of customers' books. There may be exceptions but you shouldn't count on being one of them.

My confidence as a writer has been sustained by positive reviews on Amazon in particular, and I fear that my confidence and optimism as a writer might be dented if I had my work critiqued. On the only occasion I have had a proposed book critiqued – *Two Men in a Car* – the (female) reviewer said I needed to make major changes to the book, lest the potential female readership be offended. In the event I rejected her advice – I felt she was simply being politically correct – and I published the book as it was. In time I was pleased that I had rejected her advice: the book has attracted positive reviews from women as well as men.

If you're less averse to potentially negative feedback than myself you might want to have your book – or at least part of it – professionally critiqued. After some research I came across The Writers' Workshop whose website (Writersworkshop.co.uk) is well worth visiting. There's a section on editorial critiques which has some interesting case studies relating to both fiction and non-fiction.

At the time of writing (July 2010) for fiction, non-fiction, short stories, children's books, opening chapters, and manuscripts they're charging £160.00 plus £3.50 per thousand words, which seems reasonable to me. The fees are to be increased from 1 August. I asked The Writer's Workshop for some details on themselves and they sent me the following:

> When The Writers' Workshop was set up a couple of years ago it was a small operation with just two editors. Now, with around 80 editors, a vast amount of editorial activity, a multitude of courses, and a thriving online community at Thewordcloud.org we are the biggest writers' services company in the UK. The Writers' Workshop is run entirely by writers

for writers. We passionately believe that only successful authors are fully capable of helping amateur authors come to grips with writing publishable work. This is reflected at every level of the organisation: the phone will be answered by a writer; decisions about passing material on to agents or publishers will be made by a writer; your manuscript will be assessed by a writer. We understand the issues you're facing as a fellow writer.

We've helped dozens of clients go on to secure representation with top agents. We've even sold clients' work direct to publishers – helping one lucky client to a £21,000 advance. Our goal is to help you develop and market your work, and we've got stunning contacts with agents, publishers, and production companies. We also offer workshops, where you can spend an entire day being taught by a professional writer. In addition to this, we offer free advice by phone & email. Feel free to just give us a ring on 0845 459 9560 or email to info@writersworkshop.co.uk and we'll be happy to have a chat about anything writing-related. For more information, visit our website at Writersworkshop.co.uk or join our free online community at Thewordcloud.org.

If you use The Writers' Workshop I should very much like to hear of your experience of it so I can reflect it in any future editions of this book. Please email me on Mikebuchanan@hotmail.co.uk. Thank you.

I understand there has been something of a boom in writing courses but I've never been attracted to them myself. I suspect that writers who are extraverted will get more from them than writers who are introverted. I'm perfectly happy working on my notebook computer for hours at a stretch. I'm content to wait for feedback from people who will (hopefully) buy the books.

8. *Write and 'sculpt' the book*

Chapters give books structure. Before you start the business of writing your book, I recommend that you break down the book's overall subject matter into chapters, each covering one topic or a small number of related topics. When I've started on my more serious non-fiction books, such as this one, I've usually found that the subject matter fell naturally into something between 10 and 14 chapters.

Take some time to decide the topics you want to cover and – critically – sequence them logically. When you've done this to your satisfaction decide on the sub-topics (if any) in each chapter. I've started the chapters of most of my books with a section headed, 'This chapter covers:' and I then work out the sub-topics. This forces me to order my material before starting on the lengthy business of writing the book, and greatly enhances my productivity. I think of this as the book's 'road map'. If you're struggling to structure your books effectively, you may hire a book editor to help you.

I recommend you develop a model for writing books which is in harmony with your basic nature. I could no more adopt the model for writing non-fiction employed by Simon Winchester (Appendix 8) than jump over my house. That level of routine would probably lead me swiftly to a mental breakdown. But it might be perfect for you.

So I decided to develop my own model and through trial and error arrived at one which suits me well. Sir Terence Pratchett once said he couldn't have written his books before the era of the computer. I couldn't either, he'd be pleased to learn. It's easy to assume that writers in the 21st century must all be writing with computers, but it's not the case. One of the most remarkable books I've read in recent years is Ian Clayton's *Bringing It All Back Home* (2007). Used copies of the paperback edition (2008) are available on Amazon.co.uk for £0.01 plus postage and packaging. Throw caution to the winds and order a copy. If you don't love the book I'll refund your £0.01. The book was hand-written, and the acknowledgements start with, 'Pat on the back and ruffle of the hair to Pam Oxley for typing.' Isn't that nice? The book's initial pages consist of reviews of his books, an idea I pinched for this book.

If you're anything like me you must be prepared to accept, as you write your book, that you'll probably revise the chapter contents, the order of the chapters, and more besides. While this can lead to some frustration, especially if the changes have implications that necessitate some rewriting, you must remind yourself of the eternal truth that the more effort you put into writing the book, the less effort the reader will have in reading it, and the more he will enjoy the book.

You'll probably be changing some chapter numbers and referring to material which has been moved. For this reason I always highlight text which is likely to alter, or have it in a red font. This includes chapter numbers up to the point that the book is finalised. And I don't finalise those detail until step 16 of the model, when everything else has been done. The whole manuscript can then be allocated a black font. The easiest way to do this – while highlighting any remaining text which needs to be turned into a black font – is to employ Word's 'Zoom' function. Have maybe eight to ten pages visible on your monitor and scroll down whilst highlighting. When this is completed you can make all the text black.

I abandoned the writing of *The Marriage Delusion* several times. I gave up in despair that I could convincingly support the central thesis of the book. The topics I was covering in the book – love, sex, religion, psychology, gender roles – appeared in my mind's eye like enormous boulders which couldn't be made to fit together. And that's when I stumbled upon the craft of 'sculpting' books.

I started to spot intriguing linkages between seemingly disparate topics. Each question I answered – mainly through research – led me on to other questions. And slowly but surely the pieces started to fit together. In the end it wasn't until I had read or partially read over 50 books, extracting material from about 30 of them, that I was finally satisfied that I had a strong thesis to present to the world. A great deal of chapter changing and rewriting was required. But I'm pleased I made the effort, as have been the readers who have given the book feedback on Amazon and elsewhere. The central thesis of the book flies in the face of all the countless books in the *Ten Secrets of Happy Marriages* genre. And yet, two years after publication of my book, I have yet to receive a single challenge to the book's central arguments.

Onto the subject of drawing upon material from books written by other authors. The purpose of this book is not to give detailed advice on copyright matters; for one thing, copyright law is different in different countries, and this book is aimed at a worldwide readership. But I do advise this: *always* obtain permission(s) in advance from the publisher(s) of the material(s) in question, *in advance of* the publication of your own book(s). You may be pleasantly surprised to discover some publishers permit you to use material at no charge, particularly if the material has been around for years and the book in question is not well known. Some publishers will ask for a small sum and some for larger sums, possibly beyond your means. You may also find that the rights to the material are owned by different publishers in different geographical territories, and have been sold on from one publisher to another. You may have to pay separate fees for your physical and electronic editions. If you're publishing with the POD model you can in all honesty state that the print run is 1 copy: explain that it's a POD edition.

It may be worth looking into obtaining permissions *before* you embed other writers' material in your book, in case you can't ultimately afford the permission rights.

9. *Allocate quotations to the starts of individual chapters*

Try to resist the temptation of allocating quotations before this stage. As your book evolves you might change your mind as to the most appropriate quotation to start a chapter. And you might just stumble on a terrific quotation as you're writing the book. So wait until the rest of the book has been written, relax with a cup of tea and possibly a scone and butter – add jam and clotted cream if you're in a suitable mood – then print out and read the list of contents. Work through the quotations on your computer and I guarantee you'll soon be saying to yourself, 'Ah! This would be perfect for the chapter on...' Highlight these quotations in red along with the chapter numbers they relate to, making a separate note of which chapters you've found a quotation for. You'll probably find that two or more quotations are obvious candidates for particular chapters. It's one of my favourite steps in the book creation process.

I recommend not having the same quotations at the start of chapters and in the appendix of quotations lest the reader feel 'short changed' by the repetition.

10. *Tidy up formatting (if the book isn't going to be professionally typeset)*

This is the time to make sure you have all the presentational aspects of the book correct: font sizes, line spacing, margins, page numbers etc. Formatting to the point that the file is ready for publication is known as typesetting. It can be done in Microsoft Word and presumably other word processing packages too. By the time of writing the revised edition of this book (August 2011) I'd typesetted (typeset?) all seven of my self-published books, and found Microsoft Word 2007 allied with Windows 7 a good combination for typesetting, and better than previous editions of the software.

11. *Finalise the book's format (hardback, paperback) and pricing*

Take another look on Amazon to see what's now available on your topic. New titles may have become available – or are scheduled for future publication – since you first looked into the matter. You should be able to come to a view on the format to launch the book in, and the price. Check again that you'll make a margin on the exercise. If the book is to be made available in bookstores outside of your country of residence, have the price of the book printed in several currencies on the back cover, possibly above the ISBN. I price my books in sterling, euros, and American / Canadian / Australian dollars.

12. *Finalise the title (and sub-title if there is one)*

You may have had ideas for the title (and possibly a sub-title) as well as a cover design concept from the outset of your project, and remained with them so far. No matter. The thinking behind placing the stage of *finalising* these areas late in the overall process is sound.

Many writers find, as I do, that the final book is somewhat different to the book they anticipated at the outset. This will probably be the case if you're following to any significant extent my model for writing non-fiction. So a cover design and title that made sense at the outset of the project may no longer make sense or – more likely – as time passes you'll think up stronger titles and sub-titles. By leaving these areas to this late stage you'll have avoided wasting time and money (the latter on a graphic designer, if used).

For some time I was going to title this book *Professional Self-Publishing*. But as the book developed I came to realise that the term 'professional' might not be deemed positive by some of my potential readership. For example, in the United Kingdom the term is sometimes used in a pejorative sense, as in a 'professional' foul in soccer.

Inspiration for a title can come from anywhere. The title of *Two Men in a Car* was a nod to Jerome K Jerome's Victorian classic *Three Men in a Boat*, the book which prompted the first of the two holidays in France which are described in the book. Book titles are not subject to copyright and you might even be cheeky and give your book the same title as a bestseller for increased exposure.

Legend has it that Mike Harding, the British comedian, folk music enthusiast, and broadcaster, was struggling to decide the title of a new book in 1988. His publisher apparently suggested that he should give some consideration to bestselling genres at the time. Research led him to conclude that those genres were cookery, the monarchy, and pets, which possibly explains the title of his book – whose content was utterly unconnected with any of the three genres – *Cooking One's Corgi*.

In the modern era most of us are familiar with the use of keywords in carrying out searches, and you may use them if you look on Amazon for books about particular topics. It may have been your keyword search for books on self-publishing that led you to this book. I don't know – was it?

If you subscribe to Nielsen's Publisher Enhanced Service – or Bowker's equivalent in North America – booksellers who enter keywords will effectively be looking for books with those keywords in a number of sections: short and long descriptions, table of contents, review quotes, author biography, and all the title fields including title, subtitle, series title, and part title. I asked Nielsen how Amazon used keywords, and received the following plaintive reply:

> I have checked with my colleague – we assume Amazon use descriptions for searching keywords, but we don't know for sure.

If your non-fiction book is about topic 'x', put 'x' in the title (or at the very least, the sub-title). You may recall that Aaron Shepard, an American writer, wrote the three top-selling books on self-publishing in the UK. He doesn't make use of Amazon's 'Look Inside!' facility but his book covers do reveal him to be one handsome son of a gun. Hot dang, if I were *that* good looking I'd have images of myself on my own books' covers.

Shepard uses subtitles so we can reasonably assume that they facilitate his book becoming visible with keyword searches. In March 2010 he published *POD for Profit* with the sub-title *More on the NEW Business of Self Publishing, or How to Publish Your Books With Online Book Marketing and Print on Demand by Lightning Source.*

Taking my lead from Mr Shepard, I gave this book the snappy subtitle *Self-Publishing and Publishing with the Print-on-Demand and Digital Print Models* of Lightning Source and Others, and Selling to Amazon and Other Online Booksellers and Traditional Bookstores.

13. Prepare the first draft of the index of cited publications, references and further reading, and subject index (as appropriate)

Now here's something I didn't know until today. Or maybe I knew it once, but have since forgotten it. I don't know. I was taught as a schoolboy to keep a dictionary beside me whilst writing, and for the life of me I couldn't remember if the plural of 'index' was 'indexes' or 'indices'. So I looked it up in my trusty *Chambers Dictionary*. It turns out that the plural form is 'indexes' in the case of books, but otherwise 'indices'. You truly do learn something new every day. Or possibly relearn.

One of the frustrations of doing your own formatting and typesetting in Microsoft Word – even with Word 2007, I find – is that you sometimes find that when you remove the formatting marks (¶) minor changes in the positioning of text will result. So remove the marks before carrying out the indexing.

Indexes are important in non-fiction to help the reader find exactly what he wants speedily, although the current norm for non-fiction ebooks is not to have indexes. I like to do my own indexing because sometimes I can add a little more 'colour' to my books. In the index of *Guitar Gods in Beds.* I wanted to give a flavour of the colourful life stories and the serious topics as well as the humorous topics to be found in the book. The following selections from the index illustrate the point:

I have a simple methodology for developing an index. I work through the book and write down the words and terms I want to go into the index, but I *don't* put page numbers against them. Page numbers aren't added until stage 17 for reasons which will become clear. If you add the page numbers at this stage, you may be cursing yourself later.

There is a convention in indexing that for certain terms – for example, the title of a book or show – the initial 'The' is ignored for indexing purposes. In this book I have a quotation from *The Golden Girls*. In the index this would be positioned under 'T', so I wrote in red font *Golden Girls, The*. Then when the index was finalised and had been sorted into alphabetical order I simply moved 'The' to the start of the term.

Another tip. Write the index in 10-point text, and – unless the index in question runs to only one or two columns on a single page – write the index only on the left hand column of a two column table, possibly running to many pages. You don't need to order the terms alphabetically because Microsoft Word can do that at the end for you in an instant.

You may prefer to have your book professionally indexed. Like all professional bodies the Society of Indexers has an interest in improving the lot of its members, so you may well find freelance indexers willing to work for rates lower than those deemed appropriate by the Society. Their website Indexers.org.uk offers the following guidelines for clients with respect to fees:

> In negotiating fees, whether based on hourly or page rates, indexers will consider the complexity of the text and other factors listed below.
>
> Negotiation of fees
> Before being asked to agree a fee the indexer should see the proofs, or at least a few specimen pages, in order to make a fair assessment of what is involved. If time is too short for that, at least the following details should be given:
>
> - subject, length and format of book
> - readership aimed at, to allow the indexer to assess the level of speciality required
> - pages/number of lines allowed for index
> - time available to produce the index
> - format in which the index is required (rtf, html, PDF)
> - whether the fee includes incidental expenses or whether these can be charged separately
> - any factors listed below that affect time required.

Preparing to contact an indexer
Completing this MS Word (RTF) form and emailing it to potential indexers will help them assess their availability and suitability for the job and quote a realistic fee. If you need an indexer urgently, try telephoning first to check availability.

Factors that may increase the time required for indexing
- reference and research texts requiring indexes equal in importance to the textual content
- detailed indexing of figures and tables
- foreign language text content
- need for consultation of reference sources to ascertain correct form of index entry
- requirement to consult author
- proofs of poor quality, or of an awkward size or format, which are difficult to read or handle
- proofs received out of sequential order
- late amendments to proofs
- non-standard house style or presentation
- embedding of tags or insertion of hyperlinks

Factors that may increase the rate charged
- complex text which needs a detailed understanding of the subject matter
- pressure to produce an index in a very short time
- necessity to work unsocial hours

As from 1 January 2009 (unchanged for 2010), the Society recommends that indexing rates start from £20.50 an hour or approximately £2.30 a page, £5.25 per thousand words for an index to a straightforward text.

It is recommended that these figures be used as a basis for estimating the total cost of an index. It should be noted that experienced indexers working on specialised texts will normally charge well above the minimum rates quoted above, which are applicable to non-specialist texts and less experienced indexers.

Further advice on commissioning indexes is available here.

A sample indexing contract is available to download.

You might consider using the indexing functionality of your software package, especially if you expect the book to be modified in the fullness of time, with the index having to be renumbered as a result. I haven't used the indexing functionality of Word 2007 for this book, so I don't know how good the functionality is, but my experience of the indexing functionality of an earlier version of Word (2003, I think) was a frustrating one. When I was preparing the index of *Guitar Gods in Beds.* most of the words were indexed correctly, but some weren't. The wartime bandleader Glenn Miller – who was well known for performing with his band in the throbbing metropolis of Bedford and the surrounding areas – comes to mind as an example. 'Miller, Glenn' was always placed in the wrong part of the index, and always in the *same* wrong part.

14. Have the book professionally proofread and copy-edited (optional, but recommended)

I cannot recommend too strongly that you do this. When I published one of my early books money was very tight, and I didn't use the services of a copy editor/proofreader. When I open the book and read more than a few pages I invariably spot an error or two and wince. Most of my books have been copy-edited and proofread by Charlie Wilson, who is of the female persuasion despite her first name. She has proofread and copy-edited the content of this book – other than the back cover – and it's all the better for it. I learned only this morning from one of her corrections that I'd used the word 'proscriptive' instead of what I should have used, 'prescriptive'. You can imagine my embarrassment.

15. Have the book professionally typeset (optional)

If you have the money for this, or you'd rather spend time doing almost anything else, have the book professionally typeset by a graphic designer, possibly using Adobe InDesign software. I spoke to several typesetters and most charge around £0.80 – £1.00 per page. Both Wordzworth and John Chandler offer the service; contact details are in Appendix 2. You should give the typesetter the target page multiple, if there is one.

16. Adjust the number of pages in the book to suit the printer's page multiple requirement (not required with ebook or POD models)

If your printer has a page multiple requirement – it will probably be 8 or 16 – and you're not having the book professionally typeset, you'll need to adjust the number of pages in your book. Don't just leave a number of blank pages at the end of the book.

It's quite straightforward to arrive at the exact multiple. Don't forget that you may have indexes which will reduce in page number when you fill both columns, so take that into account. Simply adding page numbers to the indexes in the next stage may add one or more pages.

I find that using one or more of the following tricks leads me close to the required page multiple fairly quickly:

- Check that the introduction is on a right-hand page, adding a blank page before it if it isn't.
- Add a blank page before every chapter.
- Find chapters that end towards the bottom of a page, and add a paragraph or two in the chapter to force an extra page – or break up lengthy paragraphs to achieve the same effect.
- Find chapters with little material on the final page and extract a little material to remove a page.
- If you have appendixes which run over two pages you might want to have them side by side if they aren't already, so add a blank page before them.
- Expand or contract the appendix of quotations if there is one, or the extracts from your other books.

Don't forget to highlight in some way (coloured font or shading) any text you add, because you will need to have this text copy-edited and proofread.

17. Add the page numbers and headers
This is the only aspect of book formatting I'm happy to leave to another person, and I turn these days to my glamorous assistant, Sharon Smith. She manages to sort out these areas in a tenth of the time that I would take.

18. Revise the cross-references, index of cited publications, references and further reading, and the subject index (if required)
Work through the book and where you have chapter numbers, cross references etc. highlighted by text colour or background shading, insert the correct text. Don't allocate page numbers in the table of contents just

yet. Print off the indexes and working slowly through the book, add the page numbers to the individual terms. Keep the indexes in the left columns of a two column table: you'll be able to calculate the impact of later putting the text into both columns. Then make whatever adjustments are required to arrive at the required page multiple. The later in the book you make your alterations, the less will be the need to adjust the page numbers in the indexes.

Now you can cut and paste the text in the indexes so as to fill both columns, one page at a time. Take care when you're doing this, and go slowly. It's all too easy to get this wrong, and you'll be very frustrated if you have to re-do it. There's probably a smarter way to do this but I don't know of one.

Finish off the book by adding page numbers to the table of contents.

Don't forget to make the borders of the table of contents, the indexes, and possibly some tables in your book invisible.

19. Design the cover

The reason for carrying out this stage after the book's content is finished is simple: you won't be sure of the number of pages, and therefore the spine width, until this stage. If you're using Lightning Source you need to use their tool to input the paper specification and number of pages, and they'll email you the design template to forward to your designer, complete with the ISBN (which can be moved from the location on the template they send).

Potential buyers of your book need not know from its cover design that the book hasn't been published by a commercial publisher. Nor should they know, either before or after they've bought it. However, the design of most of the covers of self-published books are amateurish, including many from the leading vanity publishers, and this surely impacts negatively on books' sales potential, regardless of their contents. The good news is that good cover design need not be expensive. The combined cost of a professional photographer and a professional graphic designer for this book's cover was just £125.00.

A few words on the book's design 'template'. You need to be very sure that your designer is creating the design within a template which is *exactly* the right size, and for the right book format: paperback, hardback with a printed case, hardback with a dust jacket, other? Beyond this consideration is the issue of which company is going to print the book.

Most of my titles selling in the UK have been printed by MPG Biddles. But when they sell in North America they're printed by Lightning Source's POD model, which uses thinner paper. If you've bought a copy from the first edition of this book it will have been printed by Lightning Source and the spine width will be 14.5 millimetres, while the MPG Biddles edition – should sales justify a print run with them – will have a spine width of 20 millimetres.

The cover designs obviously need to reflect these spine width differences. Lightning Source offer a cover template generator on their website which has always worked very well for me. I order the template in the InDesign software format used by my graphic designer.

I like to come up with the cover design concept; for me it's all part of the creative process of producing books. I will sometimes visit online photograph libraries for inspiration, searching with keywords, and I can recommend bigstockphoto.com. If you're struggling to come up with a concept, your designer may have some ideas.

Unless you're lucky enough to know a talented book cover designer, you should seriously consider using the services of an experienced freelancer. MPG Biddles has a close association with the book designer John Chandler – Chandlerbookdesign.co.uk – and I've used John's firm for my last four books' covers, including this one.

John and his designers are very talented, and whilst not cheap at £75 per hour, you'd be amazed by how much can be accomplished within an hour if you're disciplined. All my book covers have been completed in an hour or less. John charges by the minute and I've always been delighted with both the quality of his firm's work and the cost. And I retain copyright of the final cover designs.

Because most of John's work is connected with book titles, which is not the case for most graphic designers, he'll often come up with ideas which would never have occurred to me. For *Two Men in a Car* he had the idea of having the cover's spine printed in sections with the backgrounds to the text elements being blue, red and white, reflecting the French flag. When on a bookshelf it stands out as a book that surely *must* be about France, which can only help if it's in a bookseller's 'Travel' section amongst many competing tomes, most of them not connected with France.

For this book's cover design – using three photographs – I used one of John Chandler's new designers, John Rose. I had him whiten up my eyeballs on all three images. Vain, *moi*? I later interviewed John Chandler for the content of Appendix 5, 'Notes from a successful book cover designer'.

It happened that when the time came to produce the cover design for my latest book *The Glass Ceiling Delusion* I didn't have the use of a car to drive to John Chandler's studio, and through an internet search I tracked down a cover designer who lived only a few minutes' walk from me. He was familiar with Adobe InDesign but had never produced a book cover before. Despite this lack of book cover design experience, and using Lightning Source's design template, the cover design was completed to my full satisfaction within 90 minutes, and as he worked from home his charge rates were more competitive than John Chandler's, at £30.00 per hour.

Because you're so familiar with your book's contents and theme, cover images might suggest themselves to you. You might of course use one of your own photographs, or have a talented friend or relative take one for you. Better still, why not use a professional photographer? It may well prove less expensive than using an image from a major photo library.

I used the services of Roger Day (Rogerdayphotography.com), a well-known local professional photographer, to take the photographs used on the cover of this book. The session lasted an hour, Roger was very helpful and creative, and I paid £50.00. I asked him whether the pose I struck for the photograph for the back cover made me look gay. 'Not *too* gay,' he replied, unconvincingly.

We'd settled on the final three images but he later emailed me the image that is now on the front of the book. Roger took the picture as I was struggling unsuccessfully for the umpteenth time to balance the pile of books on my head. We both liked the quirkiness of the image, and its representation of something other than joy contrasted nicely with the book's title.

Roger had agreed beforehand that I was to retain the copyright of the photographs. You need to settle the copyright issue in writing – an email from the photographer will suffice – before you meet with him. If he won't let you have copyright of the forthcoming images, politely suggest he enter the 21st century, and then find another photographer who *will* let you have the copyright.

Even if you're not considering having a photograph on the cover of your book (and possibly on the back and spine too) you might still look at some online photo libraries. You'll be able to look at countless photographs, tracking them down by the use of keywords, and they may well lead you to some good ideas for the cover design. The cover of *The Marriage Delusion* contains two photographic images (the intertwined rings and the background galaxy) sourced from iStockphoto.com. They cost under £20.00 apiece. The image of the young lady on the cover of *The Glass Ceiling Delusion* cost £6.99 from Bigstockphoto.com. A search using the keywords 'angry woman' led to over 7,000 images being made visible.

Sometimes you may be able to track down photographs which are free or low cost. For *Buchanan's Dictionary of Quotations for right-minded Americans* I was fortunate to buy an image of a young Ronald Reagan for just $12.00 from the Ronald Reagan Library, while the image of Gordon Brown for the British edition cost me £120.00 from Gettyimages.co.uk.

If you're having books printed with the POD model you need to be aware that there might be a small variation in the horizontal attachment of the cover to the book's contents, so the spine design might go slightly into the front or back cover. Look on the manufacturer's site for guidance on this, or contact them. Lightning Source publish their tolerance but I've always found the actual drift to be very small. It's just something you should bear in mind if your spine design runs to the edge of the spine, as it does on this book.

If you're looking for a representation of one or more people on the cover of your book but you're disinclined to use a photograph, you might commission a caricature. Stan Hurr (Stanhurr.co.uk) created caricatures of Paul Carrington and myself from photographs for the cover of *Two Men in a Car*. I've never met Stan. The backdrop of the original photograph was the villa Paul Carrington and I were staying in, and Stan had the idea of replacing that backdrop with a rural landscape which suggests Provence to anyone familiar with that particularly beautiful part of

France. He also slipped Paul Carrington and my cherished Mercedes S-class saloon – my *wunderwagen* – into the image.

As an alternative to a caricature, why not consider a cartoon? For the cartoon on the cover of *David and Goliatha: David Cameron – heir to Harman?* I employed a gifted English cartoonist I'd long admired, Martin Honeysett (Martinhoneysett.com). In the early to mid 1970s, as an avid reader of *Punch* magazine, I always found Honeysett's cartoons to be among the highlights of the magazine, and I've enjoyed his output ever since. For non-British readers I should perhaps explain that the woman in the cartoon holding the battle-axe is the militant feminist Labour politician Harriet Harman while the male figure is our current prime minister, David Cameron.

If you're not using Lightning Source the designer will add the ISBN and bar code to the back of the book, and may charge a small fee for sourcing it.

If there's anything you're not quite happy about with the image you use – whether it's a photograph or a caricature – your graphic designer should be able to rectify the matter. In the case of *Two Men in a Car* I wasn't quite happy with the colour of the sky in the original caricature. The designer replaced it with the perfect colour in a matter of seconds.

When you're happy with the final cover design you should ask the designer to prepare electronic files in the file format appropriate for the organisations that will be using them – Nielsen or Bowker, and the company that will be printing your books. Two file formats should satisfy their requirements: PDF and JPG. I recommend that you ask your cover designer to provide PDFs and JPGs of three cover images, to cover all eventualities:

- full cover (for the printer if you're not opting for POD)
- front cover (for a POD edition and Nielsen or Bowker, and possibly for your own promotional purposes)
- back cover

The JPG for conventional printed editions will need to be in CMYK format, POD editions (at least from Lightning Source) will need the PDF based on their template, and JPGs of the front cover for ebooks and Nielsen or Bowker need to be in RGB format.

20. *Do a final check of both content and cover; convert to PDFs and/or JPGs*
This is the last chance to detect mistakes before the proofing stage. Given that you'll have to (at best) spend time making any corrections after the proofing stage and (at worst) spend some money too, the final check needs to be carried out carefully. If time allows, have family or friends look over the content on your computer – as well as spotting errors, they might have some useful suggestions to make. You might also print a copy onto copier paper for review. For some reason it's easier to spot errors when text is printed, rather than viewed on a computer screen.

You'll need to have your content file converted to PDF format so it can be used by the printer: use the PDF creation software package they recommend. Lightning Source currently (August 2010) specify Adobe Acrobat Distiller, which your cover designer will almost certainly have. Microsoft Word 2007 (and possibly earlier versions of Word) enables a speedy conversion from a Word file to a PDF with the 'Save as' functionality, and I've used it for my last two or three Lightning Source POD book editions without a problem. You may find that the act of converting a Word file to a PDF introduces new errors into the file, so check the PDF very carefully before sending it off to be processed.

21. *Email PDFs and/or JPGs to appropriate parties; order and approve proofs*
Send your files to the necessary parties as email attachments. Amazon will accept a PDF for their 'Look Inside!' programme, and you might consider using the facility for Amazon's websites selling to territories other than your own.

Ask the printer to email you the PDF of the book's content which he intends to use for the print run. It will suffice for content proofing purposes. He may have had to adjust your PDF slightly, and you should look through it carefully, searching for anything unacceptable.

You may be tempted to save money by not ordering a full colour proof of the cover, but I urge you to resist the temptation. I was once very busy when my cover designer – this was before I started to use John Chandler's firm for my book covers – emailed through a PDF of my new book's cover. I glanced at the file, couldn't see anything wrong, and proceeded to place my order for 100 copies, at a cost of around £500. It was only when the books arrived that I spotted an error. The cover design on the books was acceptable but it wasn't the final one agreed with the cover designer. However, in accepting the PDF I had contractually waived any redress from the designer which I might otherwise have sought. A proof copy would have brought the problem to my attention.

I strongly recommend you resist any temptation to send the entire book as a PDF to friends or family, however close. Some years ago I was surprised to receive from a friend a PDF of a shortly-to-be-launched cookery book by celebrity chef Jamie Oliver. The story goes that someone in his publishing company sent the PDF to a close friend with strict instructions that he should not forward it on to anyone else. Well, needless to say he *did* forward it on, and before long many thousands of people had the PDF without having paid a penny for it. I believe the launch was cancelled and the entire print run pulped.

Even at the start of your writing career, don't send the full book PDF to anyone other than your typesetter and printer. Should you become a successful author one day, there will be interest in your earlier books. If PDFs of them are flying around the internet you won't make any money from them.

22. Register the book's details, cover design etc. with Nielsen or Bowker

The book's front cover should be sent to Nielsen as a JPG (RGB format). Provide Nielsen with details about the book to satisfy either their minimum requirements or fuller details if you subscribe to their Publisher Enhanced Service (Chapter 8).

23. Place order for stock (if required)

Unless you're opting to launch your book solely as an ebook, or as a POD book and you don't want any physical stock, you now need to place an order for stock. If you're with Lightning Source and some other POD manufacturers you could use them only to print your books, but distribute them yourself (or through another channel). Or place an order for a short digital print run (ten copies, say) with printers such as CPI

Antony Rowe. Some digital book printers, unlike CPI Antony Rowe, have a minimum order quantity of 100 copies, or 50 copies if you're lucky. The danger then is of having unsold stock which has tied up your money unprofitably.

24. Fulfil orders for the book (if required)
As a self-publisher you have a number of options for fulfilling orders for your books, and some of the options can run concurrently. Your choice of which option(s) to take will depend on the decisions you have made about sales channels, the time you have available to carry out the task personally – if any – and financial considerations. Until and unless your individual titles are selling at a rate sufficient for the major wholesalers/distributors to consider stocking them in anticipation of future sales, the main viable options are currently as follows.

- POD
- self-fulfilment: credit card orders on a website, possibly your own
- self-fulfilment: orders will be emailed to you by Nielsen
- using one or more of Amazon's schemes (these are described in detail in Chapter 9)
- using the services of a company to stock your books and fulfil your orders

If you're using the POD model you won't need to be involved with order fulfilment. Nielsen will communicate the order to your printer, whether it's Lightning Source or another company. In North America Bowker will communicate with Lightning Source. You just sit back and (hopefully) see the orders come in. The profits will go automatically into your bank account three to four months later.

If you're fulfilling orders directed through Nielsen you'll receive them on a daily basis, by way of an email about 5.30 in the morning. You click on a URL and this takes you straight to the order, which will identify the book(s) required, the quantity, and where to send them to – in the UK, almost always Gardners or Bertrams. Try to mail your books the same day you receive the order, and send them by second class mail. Always use a padded envelope as an absolute minimum, and if you're sending more than one book in an envelope wrap the individual books in bubblewrap. If you're sending more than a few books use a corrugated box, again wrapping the individual books with bubblewrap. I always place my invoice along with my book(s) – see Appendix 3 for an example invoice layout – and have always had my invoices processed efficiently.

For orders placed with you as a reseller on Amazon, you'll get an email from Amazon telling you where to post the book(s) to. I send these by second class mail too, and I'm often surprised at the reviews left by Amazon buyers, such as, 'Astonishingly fast. Great service!' I've only ever received a couple of poor reviews of my service as a reseller, and they related to my use of padded envelopes into which the books fitted too tightly.

I like to sign copies of my books even when I don't know who the recipient is going to be. By the very nature of the POD model this isn't something I can do when Lightning Source are fulfilling my orders by sending the books direct to the buyer. Some of my book orders come through Amazon's 'Fulfilled by Amazon' scheme, which is said to increase sales by giving the book buyer more confidence. I've signed all the books they stock for me with this scheme.

If you get an order from Amazon as a 'reseller' you'll be able to email the buyer. Why not take the opportunity to email the buyer to ask if he'd like the book signed and dedicated? I find buyers often appreciate the gesture. Sometimes I'm cheeky and ask if they'd be so good as to write a review on Amazon's website if they like the book, and not to write one if they don't. They're often willing to do so, and – touch wood – I've yet to receive an Amazon review for any of my books with less than four out of five possible stars. Please don't be the first person to change that.

If you don't have the time and/or inclination to fulfil your own orders you might find someone to do it for you, ideally at little or no cost. Or you could use the services of an order fulfilment company. Contact details for an excellent one in the UK, myWarehouse, are given in Appendix 2.

25. Send a copy to the British Library

Publishers and distributors in the United Kingdom and the Republic of Ireland have a legal obligation to send one copy of each of their publications to the Legal Deposit Office of the British Library within one month of publication. The requirement remains irrespective of the number of copies in a published edition. Items originally published elsewhere but distributed in the United Kingdom and in Ireland are also liable for deposit. Books should be sent to:

Legal Deposit Office
The British Library
Boston Spa
Wetherby
West Yorkshire
LS23 7BY

Tips for saving time

Whatever time you have available for researching, writing, and self-publishing books, you should clearly aim to waste as little of it as possible. After writing six books, and through much trial and error, I've worked out a number of ways to improve my productivity and make the whole process less frustrating. My first book, a 224-page business book on a subject I knew intimately, took five months to complete. This 272-page book took me three months, including the 120 hours on the quotation element. Here are my top time-saving tips:

1. Avoid unnecessary distractions. There are many elements in the course of writing a book which won't demand your full concentration. Sourcing quotations and formatting are just two that spring to mind. But if you have the objective of writing material that breaks new ground, or is highly original, you must avoid unnecessary distractions. That's not to say you have to work in monastery-level quiet surroundings. But do whatever you have to, to enable you to focus completely on your work. I hate not receiving emails when they arrive but I've been annoyed so often by trivial emails when I'm writing that I simply have to be offline if I'm trying to think deeply about a subject. What emails have *you* ever received that couldn't have been replied to in an hour or two?

When I *really* need to focus intensively on my writing I switch off my internet connection and my mobile phone, and I disconnect the house phone. This is the only way I know of to guarantee that a pair of bright-eyed smartly-dressed young American evangelical Christians will shortly knock on my door.

2. As far as possible work on the elements to which your mood inclines you. There are few days when I don't feel inclined to writing, but there are some. On those days I might work on the document formatting, on the basis that any formatting done earlier in the process doesn't have to be done later. Or I might focus on any one of the tasks other than writing which form part of the effort to become a successful self-publisher.

3. Invest some time in improving your word processing skills, if necessary. To take just one example, if you learn enough about document formatting you'll be able to avoid the need for a typesetter. You may even, as I have, eventually come to enjoy the process of sculpting your book on your computer monitor.

4. Some elements of your book will take more research and time than others because you're in the hands of third parties – both organisations and individuals – to provide the information you're looking for. It makes sense to launch these efforts early in the book writing process. There's nothing more frustrating than finishing the book except for one or two chapters where people are slow in providing you with information.

5. Highlight text which may have to be modified, or may not merit inclusion in the final draft, in some way. Coloured fonts or coloured shading works best, I find. You'll then be able to find this material quickly when you're finishing off the book.

6. If you're going to be including a good deal of text from other sources, 'copy and paste' the material if it's in an electronic 'soft' format, or use OCR – optical character recognition – if it's in a

hard format. The latter involves scanning the material and then converting it through the word processing software into the format required.

7. Always use the most appropriate 'view' in your word processing software for the task in hand. I always use the full 'page width' when writing because experience tells me I spot typing errors much more readily. Having a large monitor helps, too. Late in the process of writing your book you may be seeking any remaining text that is in a coloured font or shaded. You'll save time if you have multiple pages visible on your monitor simultaneously.

8. If you're cutting or copying material from other works and pasting them into your book, be sure the basic formatting of the former is the same as the latter. I have a blank template formatted to my current book's formatting and I ensure the formatting is correct after I've pasted material into the template. I go to this trouble because of an experience I had with one of my first books.

   I had finished the book, created a PDF, and emailed it off to my printer. As has become my custom I was preparing to open a bottle of vintage champagne, Taittinger if memory serves me correctly, to celebrate the end of the project. This was in the late afternoon, you understand.

   Then my printer called me to tell me there were a variety of page formats in the PDF. My heart sank. I put the whole of the Word file into my preferred format, only to discover the final book was 12 pages short of my intended length. I put the champagne back into the fridge. It was to be another two or three days before I opened it.

9. If it suits your style of working, and if your book is non-fiction rather than fiction, work on files of individual chapters at a time, bringing the book together at the end. This may lead to your software package crashing less frequently. Unfortunately, I do so much 'cutting and pasting' that I have to be philosophical and

accept that Word will fail me from time to time. My cat Albert has learned to run out of the house when he hears the howl that I emit when Word crashes. I then shout things about Microsoft's Bill Gates which may possibly be slanderous.

10. You may find, as I sometimes do, that material you decide to delete from the book merits reintroduction in the context of material that you write later. It saves time if you can retrieve the material in question, so save your work at the end of each day with a file name reflecting the date. I use the date in reverse order along with something identifying the book, so today's file, for 23 June 2010, will be 100623 TJOSP. And I try to remember to back up the new file onto an external hard drive at the end of every day.

11. If you're writing books which consist partly or wholly of interviews with people and you're not a fast typist, you might consider using a transcription service. This could be a person playing back your recordings and transcribing them, or you could of course instruct your wife to do the typing and promise her some nice new shoes when she's finished. They needn't be too expensive – after all, it's the thought that counts – and she'll be thrilled to bits. Or you could use one of the many online services available. You'll need to convert the output from your electronic recording/dictation device into a suitable file format on your computer. You then simply email the file as an email attachment to the company you're using.

12. This tip has only just occurred to me, maybe because it's so blindingly obvious. Why not increase your typing speed through training? For 30 years I've been typing on keyboards with only my index fingers. They should be short stumps by now.

5

THE COMMERCIAL SELF-PUBLISHING MODEL: FINANCIAL ASPECTS

Gentlemen, I agree with you that Napoleon is a tyrant, a monster, the sworn foe of our nation, and if you will, of the whole human race. But, gentlemen, we must not forget that he once shot a publisher.
Thomas Campbell 1777–1844 Scottish poet

This chapter covers:

-   the commercial self-publishing model: maximising revenues and minimising costs to maximise profits
-   the importance of both optimism and pessimism
-   ISBNs
-   Nielsen and Bowker
-   ebooks
-   the print-on-demand (POD) model
-   the short print run model
-   comparison between the POD model and the short print run model
-   Amazon's helpful Mr Nard
-   Amazon's POD model
-   Lightning Source
-   Lightning Source: cost of paperback and hardback print runs
-   profits from POD book sales
-   placing an order with a printer

The model which I term the commercial self-publishing model draws on my business experience to a considerable extent, but it is a simple model. It takes heed of the basic commercial equation of all commercial organisations:

$$\text{Revenues} - \text{costs} = \text{profits (or losses)}$$

The commercial self-publishing model is designed to maximise revenues and minimise costs, thereby maximising profits. If your books don't sell in sufficient numbers you'll make a loss, but the model will at least help you minimise your loss. And you'll certainly have saved the cost you paid for this book many times over.

A self-publisher aiming to run a profitable enterprise – whether or not sufficiently profitable to earn a living – would do well to be an optimist as a writer and a pessimist as a publisher. I'm an optimist by nature and the book I'm currently working on is always destined to be a bestseller. Or if not that one, *certainly* the one after that.

It seems to be a near-universal law of publishing that book sales will disappoint the writer – and the publisher, come to that. This is especially true of a writer's early titles, while he is developing his craft and developing a readership. I don't want to rain on your parade if you're about to self-publish your first book, but equally I don't want you to end up with a stock of books which haven't sold. Let the commercial self-publishing model spare you that at least.

I strongly recommend that you do *not* order a print run of hundreds or even – let me shudder gently at this point – thousands of copies of your book. A senior executive in the book printing industry told me he regularly advised new self-publishers to limit their initial orders to 100 copies or less. But time and again new authors, confident of the sales potential of their masterpieces, ignore his advice. They place an order for 500 copies or more to reach a cost per copy low enough to give them a margin through traditional 'bricks and mortar' bookstore sales, which commonly (in conjunction with the wholesaler/distributor) demand a 60 per cent discount to stock, distribute, and sell books. If your title retails for £15.00 the bookstore (in conjunction with the wholesaler/distributor) will take £9.00, leaving the author with £6.00 per copy sold. The executive told me that it is common for writers to sell less than 10 per cent of their first title's print run, whatever the size of the run.

Surely a better model would be to manufacture books *after* an order had been placed and paid for, or perhaps have only a few books in stock to satisfy orders, and to increase order quantities as and when justified by sales? Self-publishers are fortunate because the technologies and business models now exist to enable them to do just that. You can now make your book visible and available to potential buyers worldwide for just £50.40, as I have with this book, and I'll explain how.

I recommend that when a book is launched you don't make it available to bookstores other than local ones. And even then only allow a combined bookstore/wholesaler discount of, say, 20 per cent.

There are three key options at this stage for making your book available to potential buyers:

- print-on-demand (POD)
- a short print run (perhaps one to ten copies at the very beginning)
- as an ebook

You'll need an ISBN to identify your book. If you have a book in both ebook and physical formats they will require different ISBNs, but the good news is that one ISBN will suffice for all ebook formats, and if your only ebook is a Kindle book it won't need an ISBN. Hardbacks and paperbacks will need different ISBNs. You can, however, have books produced by different manufacturers made available in different geographical markets with the same ISBN. The titles which I distribute myself in the UK (mostly produced by MPG Biddles) bear the same ISBNs as the editions sold through Lightning Source's POD model in overseas markets.

If you're a writer resident in the UK or Ireland, writing books in English, you'll need to contact Nielsen (see Chapter 8) to buy ten ISBNs – even if you're planning to self-publish fewer books – to make your title visible and available to book buyers and bookstores around the world. Contact Bowker for ISBNs if you're a self-publisher in North America. Nielsen don't charge for making available your book cover design and some basic information about the book to potential buyers visiting online and 'bricks and mortar' booksellers throughout the English-speaking world. But you might consider subscribing to their Publisher Enhanced Service (a fixed charge is made per title for this service) to provide a good deal more information to seduce potential buyers and bookstores.

The POD business model – or at least Lightning Source's excellent version of it – is outlined in Chapter 7. Amazon also offers a POD model in certain territories, through their CreateSpace brand. With the POD model books are only produced as and when orders are placed, whether by book buyers or yourself. Most of the model's output is for single copies.

The 'low tech' and cheapest option to create ebooks at the time of writing (August 2011) is to supply Lightning Source with PDFs for to be read with free-to-download Adobe Digital Edition: Lightning Source is currently processing content PDFs and front cover JPGs (the latter in RGB format) free of charge.

But what of formatting books for e-readers such as the Apple iPad and Amazon's Kindle device? I'll be covering this topic in chapter 6. If you're interested in this area you might also like to read Appendix 6.

Let's consider the options you have as a self-publisher to get your book into your buyer's hands. For the past two years I've used MPG Biddles to print a number of my titles which sell in the UK. The company has a minimum order policy of 100 copies. While researching for this book I came across CPI Antony Rowe, which offer both a POD model and an ultra low short print run model (runs as short as a single copy). I'm more familiar with the MPG Biddles model than with CPI Antony Rowe's model, so I've used them to make a comparison against Lightning Source's POD model in the table two pages along.

Print-on-demand (POD)

With the POD model, books – paperbacks or hardbacks, as well as other format options – are printed digitally, in the exact quantities they have been ordered (usually just a single copy). The digital print technology is the same technology that has been used in office copiers for a number of years.

My printed books which are available to buy in the United States and other non-UK markets, as well as the first edition of this book, were produced by the POD model by the largest global printer of such books, Lightning Source Inc (henceforth 'LSI'). I failed to find a book distributor in North America willing to stock my books for distribution without onerous contractual or financial terms, so I had no choice but to use the POD model for sales in that region.

POD is the model whereby books are only manufactured *after* a buyer (which may be you, as the self-publisher) has ordered the book, and the buyer's funds cleared. The process has a number of advantages over the traditional model of publishing, still in operation but in decline, where the publisher places an order with a printer and holds the books in a warehouse until (hopefully) they sell.

The table on the next two pages compares Lightning Source's POD model with the short print run model of MPG Biddles.

Comparison between the POD model and the short print run model

	POD Model (Lightning Source Inc.)	Short Print Run Model (MPG Biddles)
Print technology	Digital	Digital
Available formats	Hardback, paperback, spiral bound	Hardback, paperback, spiral bound
Book specification options	Limited range of options Not viable to have colour images (e.g. photographs) in the book unless a 'colour book' throughout, with a high per-page cost Hardbacks with dust jackets: under the jacket, cloth limited to light blue or light grey (as at July 2010)	Very extensive range of options, it's worth meeting your printer to better understand them Viable to have colour images (e.g. photographs) in the book, on coated paper stock – this adds extra value for the reader at little additional cost
Minimum order quantity	One copy – and even that needn't be ordered if you have no wish for a copy of your own	100 copies (but CPI Antony Rowe will print a single copy if requested)

Comparison between the POD model and the short print run model (cont'd)

	POD Model (Lightning Source Inc.)	Short Print Run Model (MPG Biddles)
Page number options and page multiples	Virtually unlimited and multiple of two pages required	Virtually unlimited and multiples of 8, 16 or 32 pages – depending on the page sizes selected – required for economic printing
Cost of maintaining availability	Annual charge of £7.00 per title	Cost of maintaining stock; possibility of having to write off stock in the event of poor sales. Some digital printers – not MPG Biddles – make an annual charge to maintain title availability
Order fulfilment	Order fulfilment possible globally	Various options from self-fulfilment to using wholesalers / distributors. Difficult to find overseas wholesalers / distributors willing to take on stock of titles without some guarantee of reasonable sales
Receipt of sales proceeds	Three months after the end of the month in which sale is made. Payment directly into a nominated bank account	Depends upon method of payment used by the buyer. Paypal on your own website: immediate. Amazon: up to two weeks. Gardners: cheque posted at the end of the month following the month in which the sale is made. Bertrams: payment into nominated account around the 8th of the month, two months after the month in which the sale is made

I had an interesting phone conversation with a most helpful American gentleman who works for Amazon in London. Unusual first name (Burr) I recall thinking at the time. I'd heard of it used as a surname – Raymond Burr came to mind – but never as a first name. Mr Nard later sent me an email to explain Amazon's position on POD in Europe:

> We currently only have the bandwidth in the EU to deal with publishers that have 50 or more titles. Your title count is still not high enough for us to consider putting you on POD in the EU at present unfortunately. However, please do consider activating your title on our US site via our sister company at Createspace.com as there is a fully self service functionality for self publishing authors to make the books available in physical copy on the Amazon.com site via POD and on Kindle. Hope this helps.

It was at this point that I spotted on the email that his name was not Burr Nard; his first name was simply Bernard, pronounced so as to rhyme with 'barred'. Those Americans and their crazy names and accents – don't you just love 'em?

Bernard then explained that Amazon's POD books were printed in their order fulfilment centres in the US, the UK, and Germany, and if they printed the book they would be shown as 'In Stock' on Amazon websites, while titles printed by other POD printers – such as LSI – would not be. I told him he must be mistaken as my POD books were always shown as being in stock on Amazon.com. He politely explained that this was 'not possible, sir' and was so adamant on the point – *politely* adamant, it has to be said, in the manner exhibited by American customs officials – that eventually I started to doubt my sanity and had to check the matter out. I've just copied the following from Amazon.com and plan to send a copy of this book to Bernard:

Buchanan's Dictionary of Quotations for Right-minded Americans [Paperback]

Mike Buchanan

Price: **$22.00** & eligible for **FREE Super Saver Shipping** on orders over $25.
Details

In Stock, Bernard.

Ships from and sold by **Amazon.com**. Gift-wrap available.
Only 1 left in stock-order soon (more on the way).

9 new from $20.75 **1 used** from $40.30

I may have added a word there. But it just goes to prove that just because someone is polite it doesn't mean he's necessarily right, as Clint Eastwood observed in the film *Dirty Harry*, I believe.

The POD model has some disadvantages for the self-publisher compared with short print runs of, say, 100 copies. Depending on your book project they may or may not be important to you. What other differences are there between the POD model and a digital short print run? I have found the following with respect to LSI and MPG Biddles:

-   LSI offer a narrower choice of specifications: hardback book cases (not the covers) at the time I first started with LSI in 2008 were available only in light blue or light grey. One of my books benefited from having a black cover, so POD was not an ideal option.
-   The LSI paper has a nice smooth feel, but it is markedly thinner than the papers commonly used by MPG Biddles. The result is a thinner book which may have an impact on perceived value for money, although to be fair I've had no negative feedback on my books' value for money from buyers of my POD editions.
-   Colour plate (usually photograph) sections are highly uneconomical with POD, but very economical with the short run digital print model of MPG Biddles (about £0.07 per page, £0.14 per leaf). CPI Antony Rowe charge about the same.

So, what are the costs involved with using the LSI model? The following data relates to the current offering from LSI's British operation, as evident on their dedicated website Lightniningsource.co.uk. It is LSI's stated policy to deal with publishers, not writers. Presumably this is to ensure that they do not have to deal with the queries an author is likely to raise, the answers to which they might not have, but a publisher would.

However, they took me on as a customer when I told them I was planning – as LPS publishing – to produce numerous titles in my own name as well as publish other writers' books. They were kind enough to agree to my request for a meeting in their Milton Keynes facility, where a lady took me through the book specification and other options available. A tour of the manufacturing plant followed and I recall my surprise at learning that their average manufacturing run length was 1.6 copies.

One early but pleasant surprise was that LSI manufactures hardbacks as well as paperbacks. I had not long before read a recently published book on self-publishing which was adamant that hardbacks were not available with the POD model anywhere in the world – and, for that matter, that you couldn't have colour plate sections in digitally printed books (I've already mentioned that MPG Biddles and other printers manufacture such books, and have done so for me). I threw the book in the bin when I read the second error.

It may help you better understand the LSI pricing model if I start with the costs that you as a publisher would pay them for an order to be delivered to one address. You may, for example, want a number of copies delivered to your home so that you can mail complimentary copies to book reviewers. The next two tables show the costs you would pay currently (June 2010) if you ordered your 272 page, 234 x 156 millimetre paperback (the specification of this book) or hardback from LSI in the UK. When you register with LSI as a publisher you'll have access to a very straightforward tool to calculate these costs, the tool calculates the cost of any book specification or print run length you enter.

Cost to the publisher of LSI production runs of up to 100 copies of a 234 x 156 millimetre paperback, 272 pages

Order size (copies)	1	10	50	100
Unit selling price	£3.42	£3.42	£3.42	£3.42
Total selling price	£3.42	£34.20	£162.50 (1)	£308.00 (2)
Handling fee	£1.25	£1.25	£1.25	£1.25
SUBTOTAL	£4.67	£35.45	£163.75	£309.25
Shipping (3)	£1.51	£5.25	£13.81	£27.62
TOTAL COST	£6.18	£40.70	£177.56	£336.87
Cost per copy	£6.18	£4.07	£3.55	£3.37

(1) £8.50 promotional or volume discount. LSI's discounts start at this order quantity.
(2) £34.00 promotional or volume discount.
(3) Standard shipping, non-trackable. Expedited shipping and trackability options offered at extra cost.

I'll be covering the issue of paper thickness in another chapter but the LSI edition of this book is 14.5 millimetres thick, while the MPG Biddles edition (on Vancouver BookWove White 80 grams per square metre [gsm] paper) would be 20.0 millimetres thick. It's the reason I mostly use MPG Biddles to print books to fulfil orders in the UK. MPG Biddles's quotation for an initial print run of this book was a minimum 100 copies at £3.54 per book. The following table shows the costs for the same book from LSI in hardback format with a dust jacket. Discounts again apply for orders of 50 and 100 copies, reflected in the 'Total Selling Price' line.

Cost to the publisher of LSI production runs of up to 100 copies of a 234 x 156 millimetre hardback, 272 pages

Order (copies)	1	10	50	100
Unit selling price	£7.72	£7.72	£7.72	£7.72
Total selling price	£7.72	£77.20	£366.50	£695.00
Handling fee	£1.25	£1.25	£1.25	£1.25
SUBTOTAL	£8.97	£78.45	£367.75	£696.25
Shipping	£1.82	£5.25	£19.64	£36.78
TOTAL COST	£10.79	£83.70	£387.39	£733.03
Cost per copy	£10.79	£8.37	£7.75	£7.33

The LSI website enables you to cost a variety of options for your books. The required tool – along with others, for example calculating the book's spine width and weight – are to be found in a section titled, imaginatively, 'Tools'. The costing model is found under 'Publisher Compensation', the term LSI uses to denote the income you'll receive from sales of your books.

The costing model requires you to enter a number of pieces of data to enable it to perform the required calculations:

ISBN: Leave this field blank for this exercise.

Content type: Specify 'B&W' if the book content (as opposed to the book's cover) is black, or 'Colour' if there's *any* colour content.

Paper type: Specify crème (isn't that sweet?) or white.

Book type: In this case, '234 x 156mm Perfect Bound on White'.

Page count: Don't forget this is the total number of page *sides* in the book, so enter, say, '272'. But understand that there are 136 physical pages or 'leaves'.

List price: The price the book will sell for. Four market options are offered: United Kingdom, European Union, United States and Australia. When you set up the final details for the book LSI seeks pricing in sterling, euros, American and Australian dollars.

Wholesale discount: the discount shared between LSI and the organisation selling the book, e.g. Amazon. LSI's shipping costs have to be covered and it's unclear whether they're covered through the discount, the print charge, or both. LSI point out in their guidance that the higher a wholesaler discount you set, the more orders you can expect. There's clearly a trade-off and you may have to later adjust the list price and/or discount to maximise your title's profits. I set the discount at a low level for my POD books (25 per cent, as low as 20 per cent is permissible in some territories) and the lowest permissible level for my ebooks (currently 25 per cent).

Market: Specify one or more of UK, European Union, United States and Australia.

Print charge: The costing model calculates this as soon as you click on 'Calculate'.

Publisher compensation: The money you will make from each sale, which is automatically calculated.

For our 'standard book' – the same specification as this book – the costing model provides the following numbers:

<u>Lightning Source costing example</u>

	Sterling	Euro	US Dollar
List price	£9.95	€12.95	$14.95
Wholesale discount (25%)	£2.49	€3.24	$3.74
List price – discount	£7.46	€9.71	$11.21
Print charge	£3.42	€3.79	$4.44
Publisher compensation	£4.04	€5.92	$6.77

If you've bought the LSI edition of this book you'll have given me a sum of £4.04, €5.92 or $6.77 without me having to do anything beyond writing the book. Thanks. Very good of you. Pop in for a cold beer if you're passing.

We move on to working with traditional printers rather than adopting the POD model – although you might use both options, as I do, for distribution in different geographical territories.

After discussions with a representative at the printer you should be emailed a formal quotation for your proposed book, along with a reference number and contract terms. Check through the quotation very carefully, and the terms. Ask for an explanation of anything that isn't clear, and if necessary take legal advice on the contract terms. It's possible that your requirements have been misunderstood or misinterpreted, and this is your last chance before the proofing stage to rectify any such mistakes.

You may be tempted to avoid the cost of having a proof produced on cost grounds, but I recommend you don't. I once did exactly that and ended up with £500 worth of books with the incorrect cover design. I related the story in Chapter 4.

MPG Biddles have an online order form which takes little time to complete. In the following table I've reproduced the key elements along with the options offered (where appropriate). The order form is for hardback books; the order form for paperbacks is slightly shorter due to there being fewer specification options.

MPG Biddles hardback order form

Your contact details:

Supplying files
How will you send us the files? Please choose
- Via your MailBigFile upload facility
- Please set up an FTP account for me
- I will send the files on a CD in the post
- This is a reprint, please use existing files

Delivery details
Bulk delivery address: Please choose
- Same as address above
- Other

If other, please give address:

Book details
Author/title:

Book size: ?mm (depth) x ?mm (width)
Number of pages: ? (excluding cover)

[Author's note: this is not the number of sheets of paper, but rather the number of sheets of paper – 'leaves' – multiplied by two. Don't forget to include the preliminary pages, which precede the page bearing the page number '1'.]

Number of hardback copies:
ISBN:
Delivery date: dd/mm/yy (this will be confirmed on receipt of order)

[Author's note: I generally find my books from MPG Biddles are delivered about two weeks after I place the order.]

Date files due to MPG Biddles: dd/mm/yy
If this book is for a launch, please tell us the date: dd/mm/yy

Book content details
Copy type: Please choose
-   Print ready PDFs
-   InDesign file (there will be a charge for us to convert to PDF)
-   Quark XPress file (there will be a charge for us to convert to PDF)
-   Scan previously printed book

Printing press: Please choose
-   As our estimate
-   Litho
-   Digital (Publisher's Choice)
-   iGen (Illustrated Choice)

Paper text to be printed on: Please choose
-   As our estimate
-   Vancouver Opaque 80gsm
-   Vancouver Bookwove White 80gsm
-   Vancouver Bookwove Cream 80gsm [no namby-pamby crème with Biddles]
-   Vancouver Matt Coated 100gsm / 115gsm / 130gsm /150gsm / 170gsm

Text and print colour: Please choose
-   Black text only
-   Black text and black and white drawings
-   Black text and black and white photographs as plate sections
-   Black text and integrated black and white photographs
-   Black text and colour photographs as plate sections
-   Black text and integrated colour photographs
-   4 colour throughout
-   2 colour throughout

Title verso page: have you included our imprint 'Printed and bound in the UK by the MPG Books Group, Bodmin and King's Lynn' on the title verso page? Please choose:
- Yes
- No

[Author's note: including the printer's name on the title verso page is a legal requirement, in the UK at least.]

Preliminaries (pages e.g. i – xi): (if applicable)
Text (pages e.g. 1 – 240):
Blank pages (e.g. xii, 241 – 244): (if applicable)

Binding
Book type: Please choose
- Paperback
- Hardback
- Split edition

Cover / Jacket / Papercase
Type: Please choose
- Cover
- Jacket
- Papercase

Lamination: Please choose
- Gloss
- Matt

Only complete the next section if your book has a separate (plate) section of printed photographs

Print colour of plates: Please choose
- Black and White
- 4 colour

[Author's note: the term '4 colour' is used by printers to denote not four colours on the printed page, but the four inks or toners used to reproduce colour images such as colour photographs: 'CMYK'. If your book contains both colour and black and white plates, choose '4 colour' here.]

Plates extent (e.g. 4 / 8 / 16 pages):
Where do plates fall (e.g. middle of book):
Sequence of plates:

Only complete this section if you require proofs

Text proofs required? Please choose
- No

- Yes

Text proofs are charged as follows:

E-mail: no charge.

Publisher's Choice: text proofs are not available. A laser proof for text checking purposes can be sent for £40 but this will not represent final print quality.

Illustrated Choice: £25 for black and white content proof, no charge for first colour content proof.

Type of proof required: Please choose
- Soft proof by email
- Laser text proof
- Illustrated Choice black and white text proof
- Other

If other: Please specify

Special instructions and additional comments

Any special instructions or comments that we should be aware of: Please specify

□ By ticking this box I understand that I am agreeing to MPG Biddles' Terms & Conditions and that I understand that MPG Biddles may deliver 5% over or under the quantity of books that I have ordered and that I will be charged accordingly as stated in point 8d below...

6

BOOK FORMATTING AND
SPECIFICATION OPTIONS

Quality is never an accident; it is always the result of high intention, serious effort, intelligent direction and skilful execution; it represents the wise choice of many alternatives.
William A Foster (1917–45) United States Marine

This chapter covers:

- why professional presentation is so critical
- the writing environment and equipment
- the chair that would win the Nobel Prize for Office Furniture Design
- book format and cover options (hardbacks and paperbacks)
- print technologies: digital v. offset lithography
- paper specifications and their impact on spine widths
- number of pages, page sizes, and margins
- preliminary pages
- binding
- content formatting
- Blanc pages
- font and font sizes
- line spacing and paragraph indentation
- headers and footers, including page numbering
- the problem with horologists
- copy-editing and proofreading
- formatting books for e-readers
- Data Rights Management ('DRM')
- Ebook retailers

There's no reason in the current era for self-published books to be of a markedly inferior appearance when compared with books published by commercial publishers. Self-publishers can review books published by the leading publishers in the world, see how the content is laid out, and seek to copy elements to their heart's content. It was exactly how I arrived at the formatting of my first self-published book.

If writing and self-publishing take up a lot of your time, you should invest in the best equipment you can afford. The case for this is even stronger if you intend to do all the word processing and document formatting yourself. I'm not a fast typist but recently my typing speed has increased (and my frequency of typing errors reduced) as a result of buying my first notebook computer – a Sony Vaio VPCW12S1E, since you ask. The processor isn't very powerful and I certainly wouldn't have used the computer for business use, but for writing books it's perfect and it's highly portable.

I twin the computer with a Hewlett Packard HP2009v monitor. The screen of the latter measures 20 inches diagonally (about 51 centimetres). As I'm writing this I have the page taking up almost the width of the monitor screen, and the horizontal distance between the two borders of print is about 12 inches or 30 centimetres. I find that having the text so large helps me spot typing errors far more frequently than was previously the case, as does having the formatting symbol (¶) visible right up to the point of sorting out the book's indexes (sometimes the symbols annoy me and then I temporarily disable them).

If you're going to be spending a lot of time writing books, formatting them to an adequate level, then self-publishing and promoting them, you're going to be spending a *lot* of time sitting down. I therefore recommend you consider investing in a very comfortable chair, a true design wonder. If there were a Nobel Prize for Office Furniture Design it would win hands-down. It's the Aeron, designed by the American designers Bill Stumpf and Don Chadwick for Herman Miller Inc. The Aeron has to be the most comfortable office chair in the world. It's expensive to buy in new condition from retailers but you could probably pick one up in 'as new' condition on eBay for a fraction of the retail price, as I did. I'd particularly recommend the chair if you're on the chunky side. I weigh about 200 pounds – ladies, form an orderly queue – and I can spend all day in the chair in great comfort. And often do. I can even lean back in it in perfect safety. It's the nearest sensation to floating in the air that I know of.

With the Aeron chair you rest on a fabric with lots of very small holes in it. This is especially welcome if you happen to live in a country with a hot climate, such as England. As I write this I have a large fan blowing air through the back of the chair onto my naked back. Heaven. Hell, it must be over 20 degrees centigrade in here.

This book, in common with my previous books, has been word processed with Microsoft Word software. This is my second book typed into Word 2007 coupled with Windows 7, both of which I've found excellent. Still prone to the occasional crash, needless to say, but if you save your files with a different name every day, and back up onto an external device at the end of each day, you should be fine. After a crash I find myself saving material with monotonous regularity for a time.

If your word processing skills are not strong you might invest in a course or buy one of the books available on your word processing package. Alternatively, consider working with an experienced typist and/or typesetter for your final manuscript. But those might prove to be expensive options.

There are a number of aspects of book writing and presentation which require consideration, ideally before the book is even started:

- book format and cover options (hardbacks and paperbacks)
- print technology: digital printing v. offset lithography
- paper specification
- page sizes and margins
- preliminary pages
- binding options
- content formatting
- fonts, font colours, font sizes
- line spacing and paragraph indentations
- headers and footers, including page numbers
- copy-editing and proofreading

Taking each aspect in turn:

Book format and cover options (hardbacks and paperbacks)
While the usual instinct for self-publishers is to launch a book in a paperback edition, for more serious books an initial hardback edition might be worth considering. The premium over paperbacks may be less than you'd expect, and you should be able to recover the premium with a higher selling price.

Print technology: digital v. offset lithography

A rule of thumb you'll hear from book printers is that digital print technology is most economical (in the sense of cost per copy) for print runs of up to 300–500 copies, beyond which quantity offset lithography ('offset litho' or just 'litho') becomes more economical. Beyond the economic aspects you might wish to understand how the two technologies compare in terms of the final printed article.

Digital printing uses the same technology that has been used in office copiers for some years, using toners. Offset litho printing uses printing plates and inks and requires considerably more set-up time and preparation, as well as more skilled manpower. But I would defy anyone to distinguish, with the naked eye, between samples of text printed digitally and by offset litho.

Offset litho has one advantage over digital print, which digital printers tend to downplay or even deny. With few exceptions which need not detain us, coloured images – colour photographs, for example – will be printed with dots of four colours of toner or ink: cyan, magenta, yellow, and black. Printers often refer to the colours as 'four colour process' or 'CMYK', with 'K' representing 'key' because the cyan, magenta and yellow printing plates are 'keyed' against the black plate. I hope you've been paying attention because I'll be asking questions on all this later.

In offset litho the dots of ink are finer than the dots of toner in digital printing, which results in finer definition. Some self-publishing books go so far as to recommend against reproducing colour photographs in digitally printed books. My advice is to have the printer produce colour proofs. You'll probably be pleasantly surprised, especially if the source material is of a high resolution.

Sometimes digital print can enhance the reddishness of an image, so skin tones may be a little more reddish than the original image. This can be compensated for by reducing the level of magenta in the image, something best left to the book's cover designer in most cases. It's as much an art as a science, I'm told. I had the level of magenta reduced slightly in the three images of my face on the cover of this book.

Paper specifications

This is one of a number of aspects of the self-publishing process which I have found is best discussed face-to-face with a representative at the printer. MPG Biddles employ a gentleman named Nigel Mitchell who is the very embodiment of patience. But I do find we cover ground more efficiently face-to-face than over the phone or by means of emails, partly because in his office he has ready access to the materials we're talking about and can bring in other members of staff as required to answer particular questions. The MPG Biddles plant is a drive of some 70 miles from where I live: an American acquaintance described the proximity as 'practically next door'.

Most copier paper sold in the UK is 80gsm, and 80gsm paper is the grade used in most paperbacks in the UK. People commonly assume the term 'gsm' – grams per square metre – is a measure of thickness, but it's not. It's a measure of weight for a given square area of paper, a quite different thing. My books printed by MPG Biddles always use their 'Vancouver White Bookwove' 80gsm stock.

Paper thickness is generally specified in microns – thousandths of a millimetre – and the paper stock I've just referred to is 140 microns (0.14 millimetres) thick. It's an easy task, therefore, to estimate the thickness of your book: simply multiply the number of pages by the page thickness. To make things even simpler, both LSI and MPG Biddles have online reckoners to calculate the book's spine width, which will obviously have an impact on your book's cover design template.

Your printer will be able to take you through the different paper grades available. Broadly speaking, the denser and thicker the paper, the less print will 'show through' to the other side of the page. Ask to see samples they've printed, so that you're satisfied with the level of show through. And enquire about the cost of different grades – the additional cost for a thicker grade may not be large, and it will lead to a thicker book with higher perceived value for money.

If you're having colour images reproduced – and especially if there are colour photographs – they will normally be printed on 'coated' papers. The coating is usually china clay, or kaolinite. Being less porous than paper, the coating means that the dots of ink applied to the page can be smaller than if they were applied to paper, where they would spread out into the paper fibres. Accordingly, finer detail is achievable.

Coated papers are markedly smoother, heavier, stiffer, and usually glossier than the equivalent thickness uncoated papers. My books published by MPG Biddles are printed on 80gsm uncoated paper, 140 microns (0.14 millimetres) thick. Their 115gsm *coated* paper, which they use for my plate sections, is thinner: 120 microns.

The full range of paper options for book content from MPG Biddles is as follows. Note how the coated papers are markedly thinner than the uncoated papers of a similar gsm:

<u>MPG Biddles: paper specification impact on book thickness</u>

MPG paper	Weight (gsm)	Book thickness (mm) (1)
Vancouver White Bookwove	80	20
Vancouver Cream Bookwove	80	20
Vancouver Opaque	80	15
Vancouver Matt Coated	90	12
Vancouver Matt Coated	115	15
Vancouver Matt Coated	130	16
Vancouver Matt Coated	150	19
Vancouver Matt Coated	170	21

(1) Thickness of a 272 page, 136 leaf book.

If you're having your book produced through the POD route you'll find the range of paper specifications more limited. LSI's default papers – at least in both the US and the UK – have a nice smooth feel but they are markedly thinner than MPG Biddles' default papers and so, naturally, is the final book.

This book was printed by Lightning Source on their 'white' paper grade, which is 75gsm and 100 microns thick. Their 'crème' paper stock is 85gsm and 114 microns thick.

The internal content of *The Marriage Delusion* is 20 millimetres thick when printed by MPG Biddles but only 14.5 millimetres in the POD edition printed by Lightning Source. I've worried that buyers of the POD edition – only available outside the UK – will remark on the book's value for money, but so far they haven't, and reviews on Amazon's American website have so far been favourable.

I find the print in books manufactured by Lightning Source to be markedly less pronounced than in books manufactured by MPG Biddles, so the text is finer. Normally, this isn't a concern, but it can be with very small font sizes. In *Buchanan's Dictionary of Quotations for right-minded people* there is a good deal of small text, as small as 6.5 point. It can be a challenge to read print at this size at the best of times, but in the Lightning Source version the lower ink density makes reading the problem worse than in the MPG Biddles edition. But with more 'normal' print sizes – 8 point and above, perhaps, as used for the headers and page numbers in this book – readers won't have any problems.

Number of pages, page sizes, and margins

Writers are sometimes surprised to learn, when they have their (say) 234-page book finalised, that the printer is unable to produce a book with exactly the number of pages the author wants – or at least not without introducing a number of blank pages. The printer is likely to require a multiple of a certain number of pages, usually 8 or 16 pages. Perhaps the most flexible model is the POD model, at least the model offered by Lightning Source. They offer a multiple of two pages; if you send them a PDF with an odd number of pages they'll simply add a blank page at the end of the book – or, more accurately, a blank side of a page.

Matters are not so straightforward with short digital print runs or litho runs, and the printer's required page multiples may also vary according to book size. It's all to do with the printing and finishing equipment at the printer. MPG Biddles offers the following guidance (other printers may have different equipment, in which case their guidance could differ):

Book sizes best suited to MPG Biddles presses

Book format and (trimmed) page size (height x width, mm)	Page section multiple printed by:	
	Digital press	olitho press
B Format / Large Crown (198 x 129)	16	n/a
Demy (216 x 138)	16	32
Royal (234 x 156)	16	32
American Royal (229 x 153)	16	32
A5 (210 x 148)	16	32
Pinched Crown Quarto (up to 248 x 171)	8	32
Crown Quarto (246 x 189)	8	16
A4 (297 x 210)	8	16

It clearly makes sense to bear the page multiple issue in mind when writing a book. Because I like to have lengthy sections of quotations in my books, or short extracts from my other books, it's usually a straightforward matter to 'flex' the final page number up or down to the required multiple. I gave other tips on the matter in an earlier chapter.

If you have a mono or colour plate section (usually photographs) in a book otherwise full of text, you also need to bear the multiple issue in mind, because the plate section should be printed on coated paper stock, while the remainder of the book will be printed on uncoated paper stock. Two of my books have 16-page colour plate sections. The colour plate section needs to be positioned between two adjacent 16-page sections. If you have fewer than 16 pages with colour images on, the remainder would simply have text on the remaining pages of uncoated stock, which will look a little odd, although you might be prepared to live with it.

The genre of your book may help you decide on your book's size and therefore its page sizes, although if you're looking to be distinctive you might wish to plump for an unusual size. When I am starting a new book I look at other books in the same genre and measure them. It would be advisable to tell the printer the final page sizes you propose to send, because they may require a PDF with larger size pages to be submitted to allow for trimming of pages during the manufacturing process.

If you want to use a page size that is out of the ordinary you should inform the printer of what you want and see if a slight adjustment might make the size more economical to produce, leading to cost savings for you.

It is worth spending a little time considering page margins for two reasons: one technical, the other associated with making the page appearance attractive to the reader. Ask the printer for guidance on minimum margin sizes. Lightning Source makes its guidance available in a series of PDFs – if you ask your customer representative for much in the way of such information you'll be pointed gently but politely in the direction of the PDFs.

Have a look at a range of books in your possession and come to a judgement on the margins you'd like in your book. In Microsoft Word it is possible to customise margins very easily, having different margins in different sections if you wish, having different margins on left-hand and right-hand pages etc. If your margins are fairly small it might be wise to make the margins closest to the spine larger than the margins on the other side of the page. On most of my books I've opted for 20 millimetre margins on all four edges of all pages, and this book has them.

Preliminary pages

If you go to the start of this book and ignore the buyer reviews, the subsequent pages before the introduction contain what are known in the publishing world as the 'preliminary pages' or just 'prelims'. You'll find most non-fiction follow a similar sequence. I know, because I copied the sequence after looking at many commercially published books.

One convention is that the first page you see on opening a book should either be completely blank – in which case it's termed an 'end paper' and may be of a different specification to the other pages, probably thicker – or it will bear only the book's title and not the subtitle. If you move forward a page you'll see the book's title, subtitle, author's name, and the publisher name or imprint. Some publishers publish under a variety of names or 'imprints' to cover different genres.

I used to become frustrated with the process of formatting these two pages, and getting the text positioned centrally, so for this book I forced myself to come up with a solution to the problem for you, dear reader. As a result I've sorted out the pages in a fraction of the time I normally take. Word 2007 – and possibly earlier versions of the software –

helpfully has the formatting 'Show/Hide' symbol ¶ available to use as a symbol in your writing. I've used the symbol in the example that follows to show how your pages should look with the formatting marks showing on your screen.

With the formatting symbols visible, fill the title page by tapping the 'return' key repeatedly, until you get one formatting mark per line. Ensure the line spacing is single spacing, then add your book's title to roughly the middle of the page, in the format and size you want. One tip about the title – it will probably look more attractive and distinctive if you increase the character spacing as I've done for the purpose of this exercise, increasing it by 2 points.

Now count the number of symbols above your title, and the number below. Add and remove lines as required to have the same number of formatting marks above the title as below. In the example, you'll notice 23 marks above the title, and 23 below. The title line needs to be in the same place two pages later. So copy and paste the page, leaving a blank page (or perhaps I should say a blank 'page side') in between. If confused, see how the pages look at the start of this book. Ebooks – other than those based on PDFs – have quite different requirements for preliminary pages when compared with conventional books.

Keeping the title in the same position – check the number of formatting marks above it – you're ready to add the subtitle, author's name and publisher's name, and again some character spacing increases for these elements may be worth introducing. And you may want to increase the paragraph spacing between the title and subtitle. Even a little increase can make a marked difference to 'eye appeal'.

A quick point on the publisher's name. There's no need to let the prospective book buyer know you're also the publisher, and some people might be put off by the knowledge that yours is a self-published book. Some people are very stupid, don't you find? So make up a name. I simply used the three letters of my former limited company to create LPS publishing. LPS doesn't stand for anything in this context. Maybe I should start telling people it stands for 'Let's Publish Successfully'.

With the formatting showing, the two pages appear like this on my monitor:

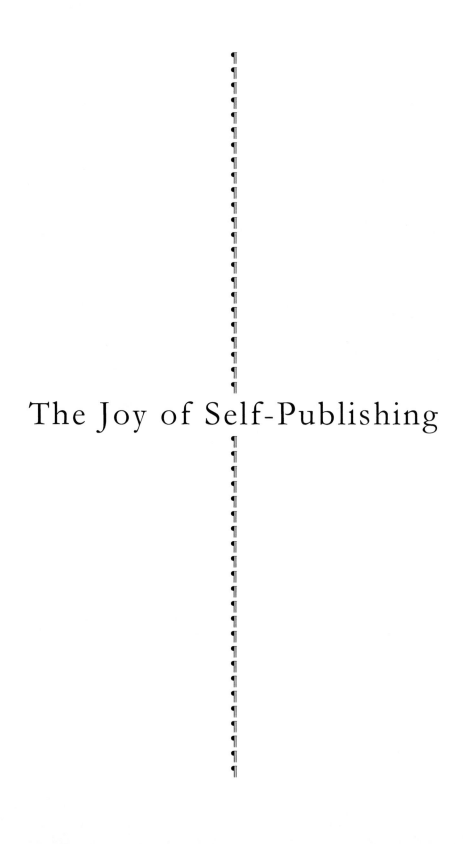

The Joy of Self-Publishing

The Joy of Self-Publishing

mike buchanan

lps publishing

Binding options

MPG Biddles wasn't the first printer I used. The first was based in the East Midlands. I was pleased with the quality of the copies of *Guitar Gods in Beds.* when they arrived and duly put them for sale on Amazon and elsewhere, including my local branch of Waterstone's. So I was horrified to hear from a friend, who had leafed through a copy of the book at Waterstone's, that the photographs were starting to fall out of the book. The printer refused to compensate me, saying this was a common problem with plate sections when individual leaves are glued together.

Gluing pages together on the spine is the most common method used to bind hardbacks and paperbacks, and it's termed 'perfect binding'. It's the commonest form of binding for POD books. One of the reasons I like to use MPG Biddles is that they bind *sections* together, rather than individual pages, so I've never had a problem with pages falling out of my books when I've used MPG Biddles. If you have plate sections in your book, ask your printer about this issue. Another British printer, CPI Antony Rowe, glues single pages together, but they assure me the pages would not fall out of the book other than after some considerable mistreatment.

Content formatting

The genre of your book may guide you in this area. Look at a range of recently-published books in the genre to get a feel for what you're competing against. Or, of course, you may wish to do something different for the sake of distinctiveness. Maybe look at books published some years ago if you're deliberately seeking an old-fashioned feel. The point is to devote some time and effort to this area, which is commonly ignored altogether by many self-publishers, judging by their output. Readers have come to expect top-quality formatting from major publishers.

In the period I was working on this book I was also involved in publishing the first book of another writer, a cookery book. Sadly the project was later abandoned by the writer. I did the text formatting myself and while it was neat I had to admit to myself – and to the writer – that I thought the book (retailing at £12.00) deserved more professional formatting. We spent some time looking through a range of cookery books for inspiration. These days they tend to be filled with a multitude of photographs. One, written by a leading British chef, contained numerous large photographs of individual vegetables, presumably for the intellectually challenged reader who has to be reminded what a potato or a carrot looks like.

We finally settled on a book written by the French celebrity chef Raymond Blanc. Published by BBC Books, it has the high design and production values you'd expect. It's his *Simple French Cookery* and I have the paperback edition, published in 2005. After the next page is my effort at copying a page of that book. The page sizes of the two books are different, but allowing for that, the final result is close to the layout in Blanc's book. The second version shows the table cell outlines which I've made invisible on the first page. I've left blank the areas where the original book has colour photographs.

So, what are the details of the formatting in this example? There are a number worth mentioning:

The Blanc page: font, font colours, font sizes
In many books you'll find the font (sometimes called 'typeface') named on an early page in the preliminaries, usually the same page showing the details of the publisher, copyright holder, and so on. In the case of Blanc's book the font is identified as Univers, which is not a standard font in Word 2007. Being 50 per cent of Scottish extraction, I'm not about to go online and buy the font for the purpose of this illustration. Happily, a number of Word 2007 fonts are similar to Univers. The easiest approach is to highlight the text in question, then simply go down the list of available fonts: I ended up using Arial Narrow.

The recipe title 'French onion soup' is in 28 point type. But there's something about the text – along with that of the text 'softening the onions' and 'caramelising the onions' – which you might not have noticed. The text isn't a solid grey colour (at least not in printed editions of this book). To be more precise, it's 'White, Background 1, Darker 25%' – one of Word 2007's many available colours. Eight shades of grey alone are provided, and that's before you even explore the 'more colours' option. If you hold the recipe title close to your eyes you'll see that the print isn't actually grey, it consists of dots of black ink which, set against the white background, give the illusion of grey text.

The text 'the humble onion... very dark brown' is 9.5 point, while the 'serves 4' box is 8 point. Text in the three lowest boxes is 8.5 point. The numbers '1' and '2' in the two lowest boxes on the right are 18 point.

Of course there's no reason why you can't use different individual fonts on the same page, but I think it takes some expertise to make the end result pleasing to the eye. You'll get some sense of how different fonts can be expertly combined on the same page from a number of the *Oxford Dictionary* series, especially the Quotations series.

The Blanc page: line spacing and other matters
Line spacing is 1.5 down to 'until very dark brown'; thereafter it is single spacing.

There's a 3 point gap above the 'serves 4' line, to better space out the text in the vertical dimension. Note, too, the absence of capital letters in this box.

French onion soup

The humble onion is very much part of the French culinary Anthology. It was probably also responsible for the second invasion of England by the French. I still remember when I first came to England, seeing men riding very drunkenly on bicycles, loaded with magnificent entwined onions.

The quality of the onions is crucial in this recipe. We want both high acidity and high sugar levels to create a fully flavoured soup. The best onions are Pink Roscoff; Spanish onions, though lacking in acidity, will also work. If you like a strong onion flavour, caramelise the onions for a further 15 minutes, until very dark brown.

serves 4

preparation time: 25 minutes

cooking time: 40–50 minutes

For the soup:

50 g (2 oz) unsalted butter, diced
4 medium Roscoff or Spanish onions, cut in half and then sliced 3 mm (1/8 in) thick
1 heaped teaspoonful plain flour
200 ml (7 fl oz) dry white wine, boiled for 30 seconds to remove the alcohol
1.5 litres (2½ pints) boiling water
1 teaspoon sugar (optional)
sea salt and freshly ground black pepper

To serve:

12 slices of baguette, cut 1 cm (½ in) thick
150 g (5 oz) Gruyère cheese, grated

1 Softening the onions.

Pre-heat the oven to 200°C / 400°F / Gas Mark 6. On a high heat, in a large non-stick saucepan, melt the butter without letting it brown. Add the onions and soften for 5 minutes, stirring frequently. Season with 10 pinches of salt and 2 pinches of pepper.

2 Caramelising the onions.

Continue cooking the onions for 20–30 minutes to achieve an even, rich brown caramel colour. Stir every 2–3 minutes to prevent burning.

French onion soup

The humble onion is very much part of the French culinary Anthology. It was probably also responsible for the second invasion of England by the French. I still remember when I first came to England, seeing men riding very drunkenly on bicycles, loaded with magnificent entwined onions.

The quality of the onions is crucial in this recipe. We want both high acidity and high sugar levels to create a fully flavoured soup. The best onions are Pink Roscoff; Spanish onions, though lacking in acidity, will also work. If you like a strong onion flavour, caramelise the onions for a further 15 minutes, until very dark brown.

serves 4

preparation time: 25 minutes

cooking time: 40–50 minutes

For the soup:
50 g (2 oz) unsalted butter, diced
4 medium Roscoff or Spanish onions, cut in half and then sliced 3 mm (1/8 in) thick
1 heaped teaspoonful plain flour
200 ml (7 fl oz) dry white wine, boiled for 30 seconds to remove the alcohol
1.5 litres (2½ pints) boiling water
1 teaspoon sugar (optional)
sea salt and freshly ground black pepper

To serve:
12 slices of baguette, cut 1 cm (½ in) thick
150 g (5 oz) Gruyère cheese, grated

1 Softening the onions.
Pre-heat the oven to 200ºC / 400ºF / Gas Mark 6. On a high heat, in a large non-stick saucepan, melt the butter without letting it brown. Add the onions and soften for 5 minutes, stirring frequently. Season with 10 pinches of salt and 2 pinches of pepper.

2 Caramelising the onions.
Continue cooking the onions for 20–30 minutes to achieve an even, rich brown caramel colour. Stir every 2–3 minutes to prevent burning.

Fonts and font sizes, italics

After spending a good deal of time analysing books from major publishers I settled on just two fonts for my books, Garamond and Goudy Old Style. Unfortunately the latter is not a standard font in Word 2007 so I now only use the former, usually in 11.5 point (the size generally employed in this book) for the main text, with materials drawn from other authors' books indented and in 10 point, along with single line spacing to distinguish their writing from my own. Here is an example of a referenced author's work from *The Marriage Delusion.* In his 1995 bestseller *Emotional Intelligence* Daniel Goleman wrote the following about divorce statistics in the United States:

> The rate *per year* of divorces has more or less levelled off. But there is another way of calculating divorce rates, one that suggests a perilous climb: looking at the odds that a given newly married couple will have their marriage *eventually* end in divorce. Although the overall rate of divorce has stopped climbing, the *risk* of divorce has been shifting to newlyweds.
>
> The shift gets clearer in comparing divorce rates for couples wed in a given year. For American marriages that began in 1890, about 10% ended in divorce. For those wed in 1920, the rate was about 18%. For couples married in 1950, 30%. Couples that were newly wed in 1970 had a 50% chance (of divorce). And for married couples starting out in 1990, the likelihood that the marriage would end in divorce was projected to be close to a staggering 67%!

Word 2007 has about 180 available fonts and you can buy countless more over the internet, should it take your fancy. Of course you might choose to only use a different font for your book's cover. The vast majority of fonts would soon test your readers' patience if used for the main content of your book.

Garamond is very unusual in having an italic version markedly smaller than the regular version. It also has a very few unusual symbols; for example '&' becomes '*&*' when italicised.

Line spacing and paragraph indentations

After some experimentation and efforts to duplicate pages from books by major publishers I've settled on a line spacing of 15.2 points, and have used it in all my books including this one.

I use a paragraph indentation of 1/4 inch, or about 6 millimetres. It's the smallest default paragraph indentation in Word 2007 and possibly earlier versions of the software too. I find the larger indentations sometimes used by other writers annoying, and I always suspect them of simply bulking out their books in this way.

Headers and footers, including page numbers

You *must* give appropriate attention to these areas. If they're done well, they'll add considerably to the perceived quality of your book's interior. If done badly, they'll annoy the reader.

Microsoft Word is very user-friendly in these areas and a little time spent with a sound guide to Word should enable you to sort out these areas competently. Different publishers have different conventions but the following guidelines will enable you to arrive at a professional-looking result:

1. On otherwise blank pages, don't have any headers or footers or page numbers.
2. Start the introduction, foreword, preface, and the first chapter on a right-hand page, even if this means having a blank page opposite.
3. The first pages of the introduction, foreword, preface, each chapter, appendices, indexes etc. should have page numbers but no header.
4. Headers start on the second page of the introduction and carry on throughout the book.
5. Left-hand page headers should be the title of the book (and possibly the subtitle too, if not very lengthy), in a markedly smaller font than the main body of the text. In the case of a book written mainly in Garamond 11.5 point, for example – such as this book – I find *italic* Garamond 8 point perfect. It's used for all the headers in this book.
6. In the book's chapters the right-hand page headers should be the title of the chapter or appendix or index in question. If not – as will often be the case in works of fiction rather than of non-fiction – simply have the book title again.
7. The book's first normally numbered page – the page bearing the number '1' – should either be the start of the introduction or the start of the first chapter. One of my books ran to 198 pages from

the start of Chapter 1 to the epilogue, so I started the pagination with the introduction and the book then ran to 206 pages. Garamond 8 point italics are perfect for the page numbers, and used in this book.

Forgive me a little ramble. We're all familiar with Roman numerals – I, II, III, IV, V, VI, and so on. But have you ever noticed that on clocks and watches – at least those of some quality, or of some age – the number '4' is presented as IIII rather than IV? I heard a story as a boy that the 'Sun King', King Louis XIV (1638–1715) – not, you will note, King Louis XIIII – designed a clock face and mistakenly wrote IIII rather than the correct IV. The court horologist pointed out the mistake and – legend has it – was guillotined as a result. The next court horologist was more flexible on the matter – *quelle surprise* – and built a clock to Louis' design, as have other horologists ever since.

The British Horological Institute begs to disagree with this version of events, however. Horologists can be so argumentative, don't you find? The Institute maintains that IIII is used because it is aesthetically pleasing, balancing out the VIII on the same level on the other side of the clock. The reader with some time on his hands, and an interest in this matter, might like to visit the following Wikipedia page to learn more:

http://en.wikipedia.org/wiki/Roman_numerals#Calendars_and_clocks

Now, what caused me to start that ramble? Oh yes. Preliminary pages – those before the introduction – should have lower case italic Roman numerals (*i, ii, iii, iv, v*) and be identified as such on the contents page and in indexes.

Copy-editing and proofreading

We come on to the critical areas of copy-editing and proofreading. If you want your books to appear professionally published to demanding book readers – and I hope you do – you'll have your work professionally copy-edited and proofread, rather than have a friend or relative do it (having said that, my 83-year-old mother could make a living from proofreading). Ideally the same person will carry out both copy-editing and proofreading at the same time.

If you're like me you'll never be perfectly happy with your book. There will always be minor changes you want to make. But you don't want to make any changes to copy-edited and proofread text if you can avoid it. If you do, highlight the text in question and have it copy-edited and proofread again.

This book, in common with a number of my self-published books, was copy-edited and proofread by Charlie Wilson, a lady who lives in the UK. I use her services whenever I can afford to do so. I email her my flawless manuscripts and she duly returns them after identifying numerous flaws and suggesting corrections to them. Any mistakes you find in this book were probably added by me after she'd been through the manuscript. I know, I know…

Among the useful resources on Charlie's Perfectly Write website (Perfectlywrite.co.uk) is a free downloadable ebook in PDF format, *101 Common Mistakes to Avoid in Your Writing*. If you ask her nicely she'll copy-edit and proofread a sample 500-word piece of your material; send it as a .doc attachment to her at Info@perfectlywrite.co.uk. Her response will give you a sense of how thorough and competent she is, and she will also then be able to give you a quotation for working on your book. The effort required can clearly differ greatly from author to author, so she does not have standard prices.

Charlie is a professional freelance writer, editor and proofreader, and published author. Her business Perfectly Write provides a wealth of book-related services including ghostwriting, book critiquing, development editing, copy-editing and proofreading. Charlie works on both sides of the publishing fence: helping authors with their manuscripts prior to submission to agents/publishers, and working on books for a range of publishers, including John Wiley & Sons (the publisher of *For Dummies* books), Folens and Routledge, Taylor & Francis, to name but a few.

Over the years Charlie has worked on hundreds of books and helped many authors find their way into print. Here she offers her advice for writers considering self-publishing:

Getting Your Writing Right: Readying Your Book for Publication

Self-publishing is on the rise
When I first started out in the industry, self-publishing authors were few and far between. Why? Several reasons spring to mind: the stigma then attached with choosing to publish by a non-traditional route; the high costs of doing so; and the fear factor – self-publishing wasn't all that common, and little information was available for the wannabe author.

Today it's a very different story. Writers have become increasingly frustrated by the cliquey nature of traditional publishing; of the miniscule odds of getting published even if your book is great. In the modern digital era, many feel traditional publishers are still stuck in the dark ages. So writers have decided to take the bull by the horns and publish their own books.

Taking control through self-publishing
Increasingly, authors I work with are choosing the self-publishing route. It's quicker, it can be more financially rewarding, and – best of all – you get to keep control of the entire process. You decide that your book is publishable. You take charge of the text. You choose the cover. You set the price. Your book remains your pride and joy, your creation, throughout.

But of course being in control also means taking responsibility for the quality of your book. You're not going to impress any reader, or make much money, marketing a book that's badly written and riddled with typing errors. That's why you need an editor.

The good news is, because you're going to hire an editor yourself, you can set high standards for your book. If you'd taken your book to one of the big one-stop-shop self-publishing companies, the book would be copy-edited as part of the fee you pay. But publishers often make this charge as low as possible, so you can't expect a great standard of editing for the price you're paying. The only way to guarantee top-notch editing is to hire a top-notch editor yourself.

Understanding copy-editing and proofreading
Copy-editing and proofreading are essential parts of the publishing process. Every publisher in the country has manuscripts copy-edited and proofread prior to publication, and the self-publishing author needs to adopt the same approach.

First things first, what do the jobs entail? It's simple really: a book proofreader ensures accuracy and style consistency; a book copy editor goes one step further and also improves the text.

A proofreader corrects mistakes in spelling, punctuation and grammar, and ensures things like numbers and capitalised words and hyphenated terms are consistent throughout. A copy editor does all this but also looks at the writing style. So, for example, the copy editor may – depending on the level of copy edit agreed with the client – ensure good flow, break down over-long sentences and revise clumsy phrasing. What a copy editor does not do, however, is work on the bigger picture of the book: things like structuring and tone and content (that falls under development editing).

The vast majority of authors who are looking to self-publish their writing need to commission a copy-edit. Very few authors are good enough writers to get away with a simple proofread.

Ideally, you should have an editor copy-edit your book, and then have another professional proofread it – this is the process that publishers follow to best ensure accuracy. However, if you pick a good enough copy editor (see the later section 'Spending your money wisely by choosing the right editor'), the copy editor can both copy-edit and proofread the book for you.

For more information on copy-editing and proofreading – what the services entail and how they differ – please see my website at perfectlywrite.co.uk.

Knowing how the editing process works

Once you've agreed the service with an editor, and paid half the fee upfront as security, the usual procedure is to email your book over to the editor, who works on it on-screen.

By far the quickest, easiest and cheapest method for editing is for your editor to work on a Microsoft Word file of the manuscript, using the 'track changes' feature to highlight the edit. The beauty of track changes is that you can see everything the editor does to the text, and you can choose for yourself to accept or reject the editor's changes, thereby keeping complete control of your book.

Once the editor has finished editing, you get an invoice for the remainder of the fee. And you will, of course, be free to go back to the editor with any queries.

An important point to note about the editing process is that you must submit your absolutely final manuscript to the editor, and restrain yourself from making further changes after the edit. Don't undo your editor's good work by fiddling with or adding to a word-perfect manuscript. Clients of mine who've done this in the past have found themselves having to pay for a second edit – a complete waste of money.

Realising that everyone needs an editor

Too many writers have a sense of arrogance in their abilities. They don't need an editor; their writing is brilliant. They don't need a proofreader; they won a prize for spelling at school, and anyway, they used the spellchecker.

The truth is, unless you're one of the elite trained and experienced professional editors and proofreaders in the country, trust me when I say you do need support.

In ten years of proofreading and editing, I have never once returned a book with no changes. Usually, authors are staggered by the level of corrections I make. And that goes for all levels of author: each day I edit and proofread text from top authors who are very intelligent, qualified, good writers, but it's unheard of that I don't find mistakes and inconsistencies in their writing, and sometimes I return files that are covered in red corrections. Yes, many famous, bestselling authors require a lot of editorial support.

The thing to remember is this: there's no shame in having an editor work on your writing. It's normal, accepted practice in every publishing house in the country.

Oh, and a quick word on spellcheckers and the accompanying grammar check. Don't fall into the trap of thinking these tools offer a DIY approach to book editing. Yes, they'll help you spot obvious problems like a double full stop, or babie instead of baby. But they'll completely miss something like 'The companies what make it programmes should big improve her gram cheques' (The companies that make IT programs should greatly improve their grammar checks). There's simply no substitute for a trained, experienced, professional editor casting their eyes over your writing.

Making the quality of your writing a priority
Imagine you're selling vases that are quite pretty at a distance, but up close are chipped, cracked and look like they've been glazed by a toddler. What customer is going to be happy with your vase?

Now imagine you're selling a book that has a nice cover and an interesting blurb, but the writing itself is weak – repetitive, inconsistent, clumsy, inaccurate. What reader is going to be happy with your book?

A mistake many authors make is not realising that their book is a product to be sold, and as such the product must be high quality to please the customer. You want your reader to see you as a professional author and be impressed by your writing. That's not going to happen if they're spotting errors in your book. And trust me, they will: readers are eagle-eyed. They're also quickly put off by mistakes. Not only will they give up on your book, but they're unlikely to buy any other titles by you, and they may even write negative reviews of your book online – disaster for sales!

An investment now in creating professional-standard text is an investment in your perceived calibre as an author, and in the potential success of your book.

Hiring a professional copy editor/proofreader
The easiest way to find a copy editor/proofreader is to search online. A simple internet search reveals plenty of freelancers. I recommend you including the word 'book' in your search terms, (for example 'book proofreader' or 'book copy editor'), so that you find editors who have solid book experience.

Take your time looking at websites and ask for some quotes. But remember, the cheapest editor is very unlikely to be the best – if you pay peanuts, you will get monkeys.

I advise steering clear of editorial agencies – websites that offer to take your money in exchange for farming out your book to one of their team of editors (often unidentified). You want to know exactly who's editing your book, and have one-to-one contact with that person.

Spending your money wisely by choosing the right editor

There are so many people offering editorial services online, it can be pretty daunting and hard to know who's good and who's mediocre (at best).

First, look at the editor's experience. You want an editor who's been working in the industry for years and who's worked on a good range of books. Make sure the editor has extensive book experience, not just proofreading reports or editing website copy.

Then look at the client list. Editing the local church newsletter doesn't cut it. Look for national organisations and established publishers on the list.

Finally, think about how the editor comes across. Will they care about your book? Will they be respectful in their editing? Do they seem to have a genuine passion for what they do?

My clients – like the author of this book, Mike – come back to me time and time again for my experience, my training, my reputation in the industry and my skills as a writer and editor. That's the kind of editor you need to get the best out of your book.

The good news is, you're in charge of publishing your book, so you can choose the best editor for the job.

[Author's note: in Appendix 2 you'll find contact details for the Society for Editors or Proofreaders, which has a directory of 440 members.]

Formatting books to be read on e-readers

The reader is referred to Appendix 6 for a detailed article on this topic.

I've already covered the 'free and easy' option for creating an ebook: at no charge (at the time of writing, anyway – August 2011) Lightning Source will process your front cover image (a JPG in RGB format) and content PDF, and make the resulting book available to a large number of ebook retailers including the one I buy my ebooks from, booksonboard.com. The PDF reading software Adobe Digital Edition is excellent and downloadable from that site among others, so you can read ebooks on your computer. One or two e-readers still handle PDFs. Given how easy it is to set up an ebook in this manner, it's difficult to think of a reason not to do so. The margin of up to 75% of selling price is attractive. Don't expect sizeable sales through this route, for the simple reason that most ebooks are read not on computers but on e-readers.

We move on to formatting your book files for e-readers such as the Amazon Kindle, Apple iPad and Sony eReader. I spent time in a vain effort to use free downloadable internet software to format one of my titles for e-readers, *Two Men in a* Car, and eventually for the sake of my sanity I gave up. Maybe a more computer-literate person would have more success than myself. Amazon offer free downloadable software to format Adobe InDesign for the Kindle, but as the content of the book in question was never converted to an InDesign file it wasn't an option I could take up.

I was keen to have a professional-looking ebook with useful functionality, such as the ability to click on chapter titles in the Table of Contents and being taken directly to the chapter in question. I sought a number of quotations but all were out of my price range. Then I saw a recommendation for a relatively new American company eBookIt.com on a Yahoo discussion forum for self-publishers – contact details for the group in Appendix 2 – and placed the work with them. The company's offering, in the form I used it for *Two Men in a Car*, was as follows:

- one-off charge of $149.00 (about £95.00) per title, payable in advance
- minor modifications made at no cost (I needed slight amendments to the text under the plate section images to change references from page numbers – which aren't used in ebooks – to chapter numbers)
- no annual charges as paid to Lightning Source for keeping titles 'live'
- no need to modify the regular book file before sending it to them, formatting of books for all major e-readers from a Word file takes 3-5 days. Resolution of queries and minor amendments another day or two
- PDF proof sent for approval before files are sent to Amazon etc.
- eBookIt.com supply the ISBN at no extra cost and are therefore named as the publisher throughout the book distribution chain; they modify the copyright page, so in *Two Men in a Car* a line now reads, 'First printed in Great Britain in 2008 by LPS publishing, this ebook edition published August 2011 by eBookIt.com.' They have, however, left a reference to 'LPS publishing' under my name on the first page of the book, the title page.
- eBookIt.com distribute the formatted book files to all the major e-reader device manufacturers, covering almost all the ebook reading market:

Amazon Kindle, Apple iPad, Sony eReader... this is paid for through a 15% commission on *net* margins. Distribution is an optional service but I thought the commission reasonable to avoid the time and effort required to deal with Amazon, Apple, Sony...

- publishers are paid on the 15th of the month following the month of sale: *much* faster than Lightning Source
- contract terms are flexible and available to view online; you're free to end your contract if you wish to do so

It's worth visiting the website and spending some time running down the FAQs as well as reading the short ebook written by the company's founder and owner, Bo Bennett. I had a number of exchanges of emails with Bo and found him to be friendly, speedy and efficient, in the American manner. Melissa, the lady who actually formatted the book, was speedy and accurate and answered a number of queries expertly. The whole experience was a very positive one, and I recommend the company to you. I plan to convert all my titles to ebooks through eBookIt.com in the coming months.

Amazon offer free downloadable 'Kindle for PC' and 'Kindle for Mac' software so Kindle books can be read by anyone with a computer. I'm considering launching my next book *only* as an ebook through eBookIt.com. One advantage ebooks have over physical books is that there is no secondary market for ebooks; no resellers on Amazon selling titles for low prices, some as low as 1p + p&p, which is a problem for commercial publishers and self-publishers alike. That said, I buy quite a few books every year from Amazon for such prices. I just don't like to see *my* books sold at low prices, and if a title exists only as an ebook it won't happen.

A few words on Data Rights Management. For PDFs you supply (to Lightning Source, for example) to be read on Adobe Digital Edition you can choose how much (if any) of your book's content may be copied or printed by the book buyer. I always specify that no such copying or printing can take place, and I do the same with my titles destined to be read on e-readers. DRM is a topic which creates a good deal of heated debate among writers and publishers. I cannot for the life of me understand why anyone would allow unregulated copying or printing of their work. Maybe DRM suits some writers and publishers but not others.

I put too much time and effort into my books to see their content given away in this manner. I'm sure if anyone asks to use a not unreasonable amount of material from one of my books, and it was to be properly attributed, I should be happy to grant permission at low cost, or possibly at no cost if I happened to be in a good mood at the time.

Ebook retailers

There are a number of ebook retailers supplied by companies such as eBookIt.com and as well as Amazon they include Borders Borders.com, Barnes & Noble BN.com, Sony eBookstore Ebookstore.sony.com, Google eBookstore Ebooks.google.com and Ingram Digital Diesel-ebooks.com. You could, of course, supply these and other retailers directly.

The following retailers placed orders with Lightning Source for (Adobe Digital Edition PDF) ebooks and eaudiobooks in July 2010:

Retailer	Country	Website(s)
1st Books (AuthorHouse)	United States	Authorhouse.com
All Romance eBooks	United States	Allromanceebooks.com, Omnilit.com
Artech House	United States	Artechhouse.com
AudioBooks.com	United States	Audiobooks.com, Edigitalmediastore.com
BOL	Netherlands	Bol.com
Book Masters	United States	Atlasbooks.com
Books on Board	United States	Booksonboard.com
Booksense/IndieBound (ABA)	United States	Indiebound.com
Campus eBooks A/S	Denmark	Slbooks.dk
Center for Creative Leadership	United States	Ccl.org
Centraal Boekhuis	Netherlands	Eboekhuis.nl
Cokesbury	United States	Cokesbury.com
Computer Manuals Ltd	United States	Ereadable.com
Cyber Read	United States	Cyberread.com
Diesel eBooks	United States	Diesel-ebooks.com
Digital Pulp Publishing	United States	Dppstore.com
Direct eBooks	Ireland	Directebooks.com
DittoBook	United States	Dittostore.com
DK	United States	Us.dk.com, Dorlingkindersley-uk.co.uk
eBook Mall	United States	Ebookmall.com
eBook Pie Inc	United States	Ebookpie.com
eBookshop	South Africa	Ebookshop.co.za
eCampus.com	United States	Biggerbooks.com, Ecampus.com

eChapter One	United States	Echapterone.com
Entourage Systems Inc	United States	Entouragesys.com
Fictionwise	United States	Fictionwise.com, ereader.com
Hachette	United States	Hachettebookgroupusa.com
Highbridge Audio	United States	Highbridgeaudio.com
Interead Ltd	US & UK	Coolerbooks.com, Coolerbooks.eu, Coolerbooks.co.uk
iUniverse	United States	Iuniverse.com/bookstore
Lulu Press Inc	United States	Lulu.com
Lybrary.com	United States	Lybrary.com
MacMillan	United States	Macmillan.com, tor.com
MBS	United States	Textbooks.com, Digitaltextbooks.com
McGraw Hill Professional	United States	Mhprofessional.com
Payloadz Inc	United States	Payloadz.com
Pearson Technology	United States	Informit.com
Penguin	United States	Us.penguin.com, Penguin.ca, Penguin.co.uk
Powell's	United States	Powells.com
Publisher Services Inc	United States	Onebookshelf.com
Sentient 6/MedUsa LLC	United States	Keebra.com
The Book Depository	United Kingdom	Bookdepository.com
Walk the Talk	United States	Walkthetalk.com
Wiley	United States	Wiley.com
Wizpac Ltd	Germany	Txtr.com

(Source: Lightning Source)

7

THE LIGHTNING SOURCE INC. ('LSI')
PRINT-ON-DEMAND MODEL

I suppose true sexual equality will come when a general called Anthea is found having an unwise lunch with a young, unreliable model from Spain.
John Mortimer 1923–2009 English novelist, barrister, and dramatist: *The Spectator* 26 March 1994

This chapter covers:

- the power of the POD model
- Ingram, Lightning Source
- personal reflections on using Lightning Source's model
- setting up an account as a publisher with Lightning Source
- Lightning Source book specification issues: a comparison with book specifications available from digital short run printers
- LSI payment terms
- description of the Lightning Source model for smaller publishers and self-publishers

Updating or correcting content: the power of POD
It's strange but true that errors in your book manuscripts may escape your attention after numerous readings on a computer monitor, but once your book is printed they'll leap off the page – all too frequently if you haven't used a proficient proofreader and copy-editor. I recall my shock at spotting an error in *Buchanan's Dictionary of Quotations for right-minded people* which I had published without reviewing a full proof copy. George Bush Sr was described as a Democratic politician. I still have stock from the print run for the British and European markets. But the edition selling in North America, the imaginatively-titled *Buchanan's Dictionary of Quotations for right-minded Americans*, had been produced by POD. Only a few copies had been sold by the time I spotted the error, but as it was being printed by the POD model it was the work of a few minutes to send a revised PDF to LSI along with the associated fee of £25.20. I took the opportunity to dedicate the book to Ronald Reagan. The revised version was then made available to North American buyers.

This illustrates one of the advantages of the POD model. But it goes further. You might want to make minor revisions of a book sold through the POD model not only to make corrections, but also to keep it updated, or to make any revisions that occur to you. This can be especially valuable where you don't want to claim enough fresh material to justify a new edition of your book. Buyers will understandably be aggrieved if they've bought two editions of your book only to find little difference between them.

Americans have a gift for creating business models which transform industries. Ingram Book Company, an American company, is the largest book wholesale distributor in the world, offering immediate access to over two million titles. Lightning Source Inc (henceforth 'LSI'), one of Ingram's divisions, has developed a business model which is revolutionising the publishing sector, and it's accessible to self-publishers. I use it myself, and this book was originally launched only through the POD model worldwide. I paid LSI £50.40 to process the two constituent PDFs: the content and the cover. For £7.00 per title per year I have – and you can have – individual titles made visible and available to buyers around the world.

LSI are digital printers with two plants in the US, one in the UK, in 2010 they opened a plant in France in association with Hachette, and in August 2011 a plant in Australia became operational. The UK plant is in Milton Keynes, and they kindly granted me a factory tour and answered a number of questions I had about using them to print my titles. The average print run length at the facility in Milton Keynes, when I visited in 2008, was 1.6 copies.

LSI *only* print to order so their customers – such as yourself, possibly – need not have any physical stock of their titles. Or they can use LSI simply as a printer, and fulfil orders in other ways. If you visit their British website Lightningsource.co.uk you'll also be able to access their websites translated into French, German, Italian and Spanish but not yet (at the time of writing this in August 2011) Australian.

Upon receipt of an order – generally of a single copy of a book – LSI manufactures the exact number of books ordered (in paperback, hardback, and other formats) and mails them to the buyer, wholesaler or distributor.

If you want to set up an account and a title or titles with LSI you'll need to review and then agree their contract terms, supply them with full cover and content PDFs to their specifications, a JPG front cover (RGB format), provide them with your bank account details, pay them a sum to process cover and content PDFs (£25.20 per PDF in August 2011), decide which geographical markets you want them to supply (US/UK/Europe/Australia), decide the retail price and wholesaler discount in each market, and returns policy – I recommend you don't accept any returns – and, er, that's it.

The LSI POD model has been described to me by the business development director of a leading vanity publisher as 'the only true POD model in the world', although it seems to me that the Amazon CreateSpace POD model is arguably even 'leaner'. His company uses LSI almost exclusively to distribute its titles throughout the world. A number of companies claim to offer POD but you might like to ask them if their service includes order fulfilment, as LSI's does. If you're not looking for order fulfilment their offerings might suit you better than LSI's. CPI Antony Rowe have a POD offering along with Gardners, which might be worth exploring.

At the current time for self-publishers and even for first-time self-publishers the question is almost not why you would use LSI to print your titles, but why you wouldn't – especially if your titles have black text content with a colour (or black and white) cover. My own experience of LSI has been excellent, and I use them to distribute my suitable titles globally other than in the UK.

Currently (August 2011) the only drawback for me with the LSI model – and hopefully this will change in the fullness of time – is that LSI cannot produce books with colour plate sections on coated paper and the remainder of the content on 'standard' paper.

If you have a book with a colour plate section then the only option (other than ebooks) is to use a printer offering short print runs. CPI's ultra low print model will allow you to have as few as one copy produced, while MPG Biddles will insist on a minimum of 100 copies – though it may be worth asking for a shorter run as printers are always hungry for new customers.

The paper specification used by LSI – at their plants in both the US and UK, at least – is thinner and smoother than the 80gsm paper stock familiar to British book buyers. That's not a negative, but the obvious result will be a thinner book. However, buyers of your books won't know the thickness of it when they order it, unless they're geeky enough to look up the book dimensions on, for example, Amazon. Until late August 2011 *The Marriage Delusion* sold for $30.00 in the US, on Amazon and elsewhere, and I winced when I saw the LSI proof because it was markedly thinner than the edition printed by a British digital printer (14.5 millimetres versus 20 millimetres). But I haven't had any negative feedback from buyers over the thickness of my POD editions.

The cover PDF you send to LSI will need to be slightly different to that used for books printed by most British printers. Download the cover design template from LSI's website to ensure you get it right. It will be emailed to you as an attachment – several formats are available to choose from – and will be usable by your book cover designer. It will include the ISBN and associated bar code (which can be moved) and retail prices too if you want.

Other than the paper specification and colour plate section issues, factors which might incline you (or not) to LSI rather than conventional digital printers include ink density. The characters in books I've had produced by LSI have been less pronounced than in books produced by MPG Biddles. Neither better nor worse in terms of visual impact, just different. This means that with LSI books small print (I'd say 7 point or below for many people) might be a little harder to read. But fonts of 8 point or 9 point and above shouldn't give the majority of readers a problem.

LSI offers a narrower range of book specification options than conventional digital printers. When my hardback *The Marriage Delusion* was published in 2008, LSI offered hardback covers (on the book itself, under the dust jacket) in only two colour options, light blue or light grey, which hardly suited the book. The books printed by other printers had black hardback covers, better echoing the book's cover design.

LSI stress that they're not a publisher, so if you want services that writers would want from a publisher you'll have to go elsewhere. The site does, however, have details of a range of service providers.

I discovered LSI after I'd already had one or two titles printed in the conventional manner, so I could already present LPS as a publisher with a publisher's website (Lpspublishing.co.uk). On LSI's online application form you'll be asked for how many titles you (as a publisher, not as a writer) have already published. '0' isn't presented as an option.

If you haven't self-published any titles before, LSI might decline your application to open an account. So try this approach. Before you even contact LSI, have your forthcoming title set up by Nielsen and wait a week or two for its details to appear on the websites of Amazon, Waterstone's etc. Make sure you have a credible publisher name. If your name is John Smith, don't publish under 'John Smith Publishing'.

You don't have to use Nielsen's Publisher Enhanced Services for this exercise. When the book is visibly and widely available, *then* contact LSI to set up an account. In any communications describe yourself as a publisher, not an author. They'll presumably check that the publisher name you're using relates to a *bona fide* publisher. If asked, you might say that you plan to publish a number of titles over coming years, even if you don't. My hunch is that as long as you interact with them in a businesslike fashion and don't expect them to show the remotest interest in the content of your books there should be no problem. The online application form asks, 'Is this your first project?' Select the 'No' option.

LSI report sales on a monthly basis, by email, and show the calculations behind the 'Publisher's Compensation', which will be paid directly into your nominated bank (or building society) account. The account need not be a business account. The proceeds of sales outside the territory in which your currency is valid will be converted by LSI into your own currency.

You can view your sales online by title and see your forthcoming income at any time, for the current 'period' (four or five weeks) or as far back as the last three periods. I look at my LSI sales first thing every morning – before checking if I have any more reviews from Amazon buyers – and if I have either new sales or new Amazon reviews it always lifts my spirits. An encouraging start to the day. As a publisher you'll be given a nominated customer representative. Mine, in the Milton Keynes office, is excellent.

My only gripe about LSI is their payment terms. Early each month they will notify you of your sales in the preceding month, but the money will only be paid into your account three months later – so your income for sales in January will hit your account at the start of May. It's just the price you have to pay for accessing an incredible business model.

The remainder of this chapter is drawn from the LSI website Lightningsource.co.uk, mainly the sections outlining the benefits of their model for small publishers.

Freedom in print-on-demand starts here
As a publisher, you're about to discover the fastest, most economical way to get your books into the hands of an eager buyer. The Lightning Source model is the most comprehensive and highly individualized approach for printing and delivering books in the publishing world today.
   As a small publisher you benefit from:
   - fast fulfilment of all sales opportunities
   - reactivation of backlist sales
   - new revenue streams from backlists and alternative versions of titles
   - dramatic reduction of warehousing and returns

Print-to-Order
With this service the publisher sets the retail price, wholesale discount and return policy. We send the data out to our Distribution partners (including leading distributors such as Ingram, Baker & Taylor, Barnes & Noble, Amazon.com and others). They capture the demand from booksellers, libraries and consumers and we print to fill the order. We collect the wholesale price, deduct the print cost and pay the publisher the balance. The price for this service is $12.00 a year per title. Just one dollar a month. [Author's note: thanks for helping with the calculation there, chaps.]
   Barnes & Noble purchases through Ingram Book Group. Lightning Source titles are listed in the Print-to-Order program – an exclusive service that allows Ingram to display 100 copies on hand at all times. As part of this arrangement, and to avoid book buyers from having to backorder, we at Lightning Source guarantee books ordered by Ingram will be printed and returned to their shipping dock within 8–12 hours, generally in time to be included in the book buyer's regular order.
   Offset printing isn't a component of Print-to-Order. We also offer traditional printing services for titles that require large print orders.

Print to Publisher
With this programme we fill orders placed by the publisher and ship them in any quantity to any location. That can be one book to a reviewer or 5,000 to a warehouse. As part of that service we offer Offset printing on paperback quantities of over 2,000 or hardback quantities of over 750. Turnaround time on digital printing is days, turnaround time of offset is about 7–10 days depending on the book's specifics.

Enter our digital warehouse

Currently housing 500,000 titles with instant access to each one, our digital warehouse is a technological wonder. Instead of filling your warehouse and flooding the marketplace with books that may never sell, we print only what is needed to meet your current demand – whether that's a single book or 10,000. And you'll profit from every sale.

Once an order is placed, we have all the electronic data necessary to print and deliver the book to its intended destination. The distance between book-maker and book-reader has never been shorter. Instead of worrying about logistics and inventory management, you simply deposit checks for books that have been sold in the month. On a typical day, we add 500 titles to our digital warehouse, manufacture more than 50,000 books, and fulfil 27,000 orders.

How do I enter my titles into the Lightning Source System?

In a word, easily. Submit your titles and we handle everything else. Titles can be submitted as electronic files or as hard copy to be digitised. You pay only a minimal set-up charge but the benefits are enormous. Once entered into our system, your titles are ready to start generating profits on every sale and information about your titles enters the catalogues of the world's largest distribution channel of wholesalers, retailers and booksellers. We handle all aspects of order management including receipt of payment, printing, fulfilment, and paying you for your books that have been purchased each month. There has never been an easier way to profit from your catalogue.

Not only are we fast, we are good

When it comes to producing books, speed is not our only strength. We work fast but we also pay close attention to craftsmanship, conducting 10 quality control checks on each book before it is shipped. We keep your spec options wide open. Choose from all the most popular book types, bindings, and trim sizes. Our sharp graphics and crisp text make it virtually impossible to distinguish our on-demand books from offset copies. Our facilities are equipped with the most advanced technology in the world delivering great products in the most efficient and effective manner and we are committed to continuous improvement as new innovations prove viable.

Paperback Books

Trade paperback books, available with perfect binding, are our most popular offering. Current sizes:

5 x 8" (203 x 127mm)
5.06 x 7.8" (198 x 129mm)
5.25 x 8" (203 x 133mm)
5.5 x 8.5" (216 x 140mm)
5.83 x 8.27" (210 x 148 mm) A5
6 x 9" (229 x 152mm)
6.14 x 9.21" (234 x 156mm)
6.69 x 9.61" (244 x 170mm)
7 x 10" (254 x 178 mm)
7.44 x 9.69" (246 x 189mm)

7.5 x 9.25" (235 x 191mm)
8 x 10" (254 x 203mm)
8.25 x 11" (280 x 210mm)
8.268 x 11.693" (297 x 210mm) A4
8.5 x 11" (280 x 216mm)

Hardback Books
Hardcover book are available in case laminate, cloth or jacketed with such marks of craftsmanship as embossing available upon request. Current sizes:

5.5 x 8.5" (216 x 140mm) Casebound
6 x 9" (229 x 152mm) Casebound
6.14 x 9.21" (234 x 156mm) Casebound
7 x 10" (254 x 178mm) Casebound
8.5 x 11" (280 X 216mm) Casebound
5.5 x 8.5" (216 x 140mm) Dustjacket
6 x 9" (229 x 152mm) Dustjacket
6.14 x 9.21" (234 x 156mm) Dustjacket

[Author's note: 'casebound' means the book's cover itself is printed, so there is no dust jacket.]

Colour Books
Colour books are available in saddle-stitch and perfect bindings with a minimum of only 4 pages required for saddle stitch and 24 for perfect-bound books. Current sizes:

5.5 x 8.5" (216 x 140mm)
6 x 9" (229 x 152mm)
6.14 x 9.21" (234 x 156mm)
7 x 10" (254 x 178mm)
8 x 10" (254 x 203mm)
8.5 x 8.5" (216 x 216mm)
8.5 x 11" (280 x 216mm)

Choosing the right model for your needs
At Lightning Source, we offer a print and distribution model for every publisher, every title and every situation. Because these are complete vertical integration models, a single communication drives the production process all the way to order fulfilment. Provide us with the quantity and the destination and we'll handle all the necessary details.

Print to Order (Wholesale, Distribution)
With print to order, the traditional model is turned upside down by selling titles on a publisher's behalf and paying the publisher the wholesale price of the book, less print costs for each book sold through the largest network of distribution partners. Using your ISBNs as identifiers, we print as orders are received from wholesalers, retailers, or consumers, so you're never out of stock of a desired book.

Ingram Distribution Channel

Using the distribution strength of our parent company, Ingram Book Company, your book always appears in stock and available to all Ingram customers. With over 30,000 wholesalers, retailers and booksellers in over 100 countries your titles will gain the maximum exposure in the market today. With print to order, your book is printed and ready for shipment in 12 hours or less.

Other Distribution Channels

We maintain relationships with the most comprehensive portfolio of booksellers serving consumers today, as is evidenced by the list below. The practices of individual wholesalers and retailers determine whether your titles show as 'in stock.'

Lightning Source Distribution Partners

UNITED KINGDOM:
Adlibris.com
Amazon.co.uk
Bertrams
Blackwell
Book Depository
Coutts
Gardners
Mallory International
Paperback Shop
Eden Interactive Ltd.
Aphrohead
IBS–STL UK

UNITED STATES:
Ingram
Amazon.com
Baker & Taylor
Barnes & Noble
NACSCORP
Espresso Book Machine

Thank you for your interest in Lightning Source. If you are a publisher and want to become a customer please proceed to our New Account page.

Please note that Lightning Source does not provide design, file work, editorial, promotional or marketing services. These are solely the responsibility of the publisher. If you are not a publisher and require publisher services, like design, editorial and marketing services, please contact an author services company.

Let's finish with a couple of testimonials from the LSI website. The first is from the head honcho of one of the world's leading publishers, Simon & Schuster. I haven't checked their financial figures but I believe they may be a larger company than LPS publishing.

Our success with Lightning Source as a print-on-demand provider, together with their digital fulfilment and eBook enabling services, makes our partnership with them an important one for both Simon & Schuster and our authors. With the support they provide, we are making a wider array of titles available in a way that gives consumers the choice, selection and reading experience that are keys to growth in this arena.

Jack Romanos, President and Chief Operating Officer, Simon & Schuster

The first edition of my book *Friendshifts: The Power of Friendship and How It Shapes Our Lives* (Hannacroix Creek Books) completely sold out when I was asked to appear on Oprah as a friendship expert. Fortunately, the second revised edition was ready to go as a digital file at Lightning Source. When the show aired just two days later, Lightning Source came to the rescue and fulfilled the overwhelming demand for books that the Oprah appearance generated.

Dr. Jan Yager, Sociologist & Author

8

MAKING YOUR BOOKS VISIBLE AND AVAILABLE TO POTENTIAL BUYERS

Make visible what, without you, might perhaps never have been seen.
Robert Bresson 1901 or 1907–99 French film director

This chapter covers:

- ISBNs
- Nielsen Book's Publisher Seminar
- registering your titles
- submitting your book's details and cover image
- free listing service and Enhanced Service
- Nielsen PubWeb, an online editing tool
- receiving orders from Nielsen
- contact details for Nielsen Book's services and key departments
- BIC mandatory fields
- Nielsen Enhanced Service information requirements

As a self-publisher you need to understand and make the most of how the book retailing market works. And that means understanding how you can increase the likelihood of potential buyers – around the world – coming across your book, so as to maximise sales.

International Standard Book Numbers (ISBNs) are unique book identifiers, originally introduced in the late 1960s. Those issued since 2007 have all contained 13 digits. If you wish to have your books available for sale with retailers they must have ISBNs, because virtually all the ways in which potential buyers will come across your books, and then order them, rely on the book having an ISBN.

How you obtain your ISBNs depends on who the publisher is. Usually, if you use a vanity publisher's services, they will be the publisher and will provide you with ISBNs as required. If your books are in the English language and you are going to be the publisher – as opposed to another organisation publishing your work – you will need to source ISBNs from

Nielsen Book's ISBN Agency (if you're resident in the UK or Ireland), or from Bowker if you're resident in North America. As a British self-publisher all my experience to date has been with Nielsen Book, and the remainder of this chapter relates to the services available from them.

Nielsen Book charges newly registered publishers for batches of ten ISBNs, the minimum quantity. Subsequent batches of ten can be purchased as required. To find the latest costs and more information go to Isbn.nielsenbook.co.uk/controller.php?page=123.

If you're new to self-publishing, or you're not familiar with what Nielsen Book does, I recommend you attend their publisher seminar, usually held in June, in which their offerings – and how you could benefit from them – are explained in detail. The seminar is free – hell, they even throw in a nice buffet lunch, what more could you ask for? – and held at their offices in Woking, in Surrey. To book a place send them an email (contact details in Appendix 2). The topics generally covered in the publisher seminar are:

- overview of Nielsen Book's services
- how does good data assist book sales?
- what are the benefits for booksellers and libraries?
- how can you benefit from electronic trading?
- market overview and making the most of sales data
- question and answer session
- breakout sessions covering the key services in more detail: you have to book sessions in advance, but Nielsen Book promotes its events widely through its e-bulletins (you can sign up for these – see later in this chapter)

Assuming you wish to register as a publisher with Nielsen Book and also register your first title, you will need to go through the following process. I'm grateful to Nielsen Book for the remaining material in this chapter.

1. Purchase a publisher prefix and an ISBN allocation (ten numbers) from the ISBN Agency (part of Nielsen Book). Your first allocation of ten ISBNs will be provided once payment is received and you can then purchase subsequent batches as required. For the latest prices and further details go to Isbn.nielsenbook.co.uk.

2. Registering your first title will be actioned automatically by the ISBN Agency passing your Title Information Form to the Nielsen Book editorial team. However, details for subsequent titles requires that you carry out the first two of the following three actions, while if you plan to distribute your books yourself you also need to carry out the third action as well:

    (a) Submit your book details (the book's size, number of pages, weight etc.) through a choice of two options:

        (i) Nielsen PubWeb (Nielsenbookdata.co.uk); click on the 'PubWeb' button on the right-hand side.

        (ii) Nielsen Book Title Information Form; download from Nielsenbookdata.co.uk/controller.php?page=88, complete, and email to Newtitles.book@nielsen.com.

    (b) Supply a jacket/cover image. Nielsen Book displays a jacket/cover image free of charge. Email your image to Images.book@nielsen.com. Image specification requirements are on Nielsenbookdata.co.uk/controller.php?page=88.

    (c) Receive book orders by email notification: if you self-distribute it's essential that you supply an email address to Nielsen Book's TeleOrdering service. You can contact Nielsen Book's Technical Help Desk at Help.book@nielsen.com, or see later in this chapter for a direct link to register online.

3. There are two ways to list your titles on Nielsen Book's database:

    (a) Free listing service: Basic information about your title will be listed free of charge on the Nielsen Book database. It must, however, meet the Book Industry Communication (BIC) Standard. These are industry standards and are available to view at Bic.org.uk.

(b) BookData Enhanced Service (optional): This is a subscription service and provides far more information about your book to potential book buyers, such as short and long descriptions of the book, the table of contents, author biographies and reviews, and more. This should help drive higher sales volumes, but it is subject to a subscription charge. For more information and current prices email Publisher.services.book@nielsen.com.

4. Information about your title will now be held on the Nielsen Book database, which means that after a week or two it will become visible to Nielsen Book's 3,500-plus customers worldwide (Amazon, booksellers etc.), whether they're searching for books online or using the services of 'bricks and mortar' booksellers such as Waterstone's.

5. It's important that you keep Nielsen Book up-to-date with any changes relating to your titles, such as price, availability, and distribution information. You can do this in one of two ways:

    (a) At Nielsen PubWeb use the online editing tool available at Nielsenbookdata.com/pubweb/PubLogon. The timescale for details to go 'live' will be dependent on whether the data needs to be checked by the editorial team. If you need to know a rough time period, email: Pubhelp.book@nielsen.com.

    (b) Email the details to the Trade Data Department on tradedata.book@nielsen.com or go to their website for a form: Nielsenbookdata.co.uk/controller.php?page=88#Change_your_distributor_details. You should allow time for the data to be checked and output. If you need to know a rough time period email tradedata.book@nielsen.com.

In the UK orders for your books originating from buyers not ordering through your own channels will generally reach you via Nielsen BookNet TeleOrdering service and the best means of receiving these is via BookNet Online Order Collection Service (once you have registered). This will be true whether the order originated from a book shop or an individual ordering online. You'll be notified by emails from Nielsen Book, which will arrive around 5.30 a.m. For most suppliers this service is free, but to find out more email sales.booknet@nielsen.com.

6. If you need further help or assistance on any of Nielsen Book's services for publishers, contact their Publisher Help Desk (General Enquiries) on pubhelp.book@nielsen.com.

Important information and contact details for Nielsen Book's services and key departments

ISBN Agency for UK & Ireland:
Tel: +44 (0) 870 777 8712
Email: Isbn.agency@nielsen.com

Nielsen Book Editorial Services:
New titles: Newtitles.book@nielsen.com
Jacket/cover images: Images.book@nielsen.com
Trade Data: Tradedata.book@nielsen.com
Publisher Help Desk: Pubhelp.book@nielsen.com
Nielsen PubWeb: Nielsenbookdata.com/pubweb/PubLogon, Nielsenbookdata.co.uk

To view a simple chart with their services, go to:
Nielsenbookdata.co.uk/uploads/NewPublisherIntroGuide_Jul09(2).pdf

BookData Information Services:
Tel: +44 (0)1483 712 200
Email: Sales.bookdata@nielsen.com

Publisher Services:
BookData Enhanced Service: Publisher.services.book@nielsen.com
BookData Online: Nielsenbookdataonline.com

BookNet Transaction Services:
Tel: +44 (0)1483 712 200
Email: Sales.booknet@nielsen.com

Online Order Collection Service:
http://bookorders.nielsenbooknet.com/login.do, Nielsenbooknet.co.uk

Technical Help Desk: +44 (0)1483 712 260

BookScan Sales Analysis Services:
Tel: +44 (0)1483 712 222
From simple ad hoc reports to full subscription services
Email: Sales.bookscan@nielsen.com, Nielsenbookscan.co.uk

Publisher seminar and e-bulletins:
These are organised by the Nielsen Book marketing team. To find out more email Marketing.book@nielsen.com. You can also request that you are added to the circulation of their regular e-bulletin for publishers.

Please note: these URLs could change and you should refer to Nielsen Book if any of the links break.

The following are the BIC mandatory fields which should be supplied to Nielsen if you're *not* subscribing to their Enhanced Service:

EAN 13 Bar Code	Validated ISBN can be used to create an ISBN
Title	Full details should be supplied, not shortened or abbreviated
Product Format	Is it a book or audio book etc? If it's a book, what type of book? Hardback, paperback etc.
Subject Classification	BIC Subject Classification Code (at least to level 2, version 2) – you can download details from the BIC website: Bic.org.uk/7/Subject-Categories. Please provide as much information as possible.
Imprint / Publisher / Supplier identification	This must be sufficient to allow Nielsen Book to link each book record to all order sources (such as a distributor) for booksellers.
Publication Date	Either unconfirmed 'future' (not yet published) or confirmed 'actual' for books already published.
Availability Status Code	e.g. OP/RP/NP/TU/UR/NY/IP
Territorial Market Rights	The publishing rights that attach to a particular product, answering the question, 'where can this product be sold?' Rights for UK, Ireland, US, Canada, Australia, New Zealand and South Africa should be explicit wherever possible. A statement covering the whole world is preferred.

Further information is available if needed.

Prices   All known prices for each item – please indicate
                                    currency. UK price should also include VAT
                                    detail for non-book or mixed-media items.

Jacket / Cover Images   JPG format. A minimum 650 pixels high, 100dpi
                                    (dots per inch), with the ISBN as the filename e.g.
                                    978123456789.jpg. Upload small numbers of
                                    images via Nielsen PubWeb or email:
                                    Images.book@nielsen.com.

When you have registered as an Enhanced Service publisher with
Nielsen, you will be given access to their PubWeb service. For each new
title you'll have to complete fields in some or all of the following areas,
each of which has an associated 'Help' facility:

UK Price and Availability
ISBN number (13 digits):
UK Retail Price (£ inc VAT):
Tax Rate (zero / mixed / standard):
Publication Date:
Publication status: (Not yet published / In print / Out of print / Reissue /
  Abandoned)

Publisher Information
Imprint name: [Author's note: the name you wish the book to be presented as being
published by – this can be your actual publishing name, or an imprint if you want to
distinguish between the different genres you're going to publish]

Title Information
Title:
Sub-Title:
Volume / Part Title:
Volume / Part No:
Edition:
ISBN of previous edition:
Series Name:
No (within series):
Series ISSN:

Physical Details
Height (mm):
Width (mm):
Spine Width (mm):
Number of pages: [Author's note: all pages to be included including preliminaries,
appendixes, indexes etc. – not only those formally 'numbered' in the book.]

Weight (g): [Author's note: LSI have a tool for calculating weight; if you're not using them then your printer will be able to tell you the weight of your forthcoming book.]

Format: [Author's note: 103 options, reflecting the large number of item types Nielsen cover. But you'll probably be selecting one of the first two options, 'Paperback' or 'Hardback'.]
Additional Format Information:
Pack Contents:
Illustrations:
No of items:

Contributors
Up to 3 individuals may be specified for each of the following roles:

Author
Editor
Illustrator
Translator
Reviser
Corporate Author
Reader
Volume Editor
Volume Author

Subject Classification
This helps potential book buyers track down your book by its key subject matter(s). PubWeb gives access to the BIC Subject Category Selection Tool and the BIC Classification scheme guidelines. The Primary BIC subject code describes the most important subject area of the book. Use the Supplementary Code and Qualifiers where appropriate to add further subject detail.

Primary BIC Subject Code:
Supplementary BIC Subject Code:
Subject Qualifiers:

Audience (readership)
Audience Code: (27 options including General, Professional and vocational…)

Children's Book Marketing Code (CBMC)
CBMC values should be provided for all children's books (including books for Young Adults up to c. 16 years). Select one value from each field. All five fields must be filled to create a valid CBMC valid. CBMC codes are used in sales and marketing analysis of children's books.

Age Range: (0–5 / 5–7 / 7–9 / 9–11 / 12+ / unknown)
Broad subject: (6 options)
Type / Format (10 options)
Character: (Character / Non-Character, unknown)

Tie-in: (TV or film tie-in / Non tie-in / unknown)

Territorial rights
Please indicate the publishing rights you own for, and wish to apply to, this particular product, answering the question, 'where can this book be sold?'

Worldwide: (None / exclusive / non-exclusive / not for sale)

Please use EITHER worldwide OR list below: (None / exclusive / non-exclusive / not for sale)

United Kingdom
Ireland
USA
Canada
Australia
New Zealand
South Africa
Rest of World

Descriptive Information
Short Description (maximum 350 characters):
Long description:
Table of Contents:
Author Biography:
Reviews:
[Author's note: don't limit yourself with respect to reviews: include reviews from Amazon buyers, other individuals…]

Languages
Language of Publication (if not English):
Original Language:

Prizes
[Author's note: I asked Nielsen if they would insert 'None yet' in this field for all my titles. Sadly, they declined.]

9

DEALING WITH AMAZON AND OTHER ONLINE AND 'BRICKS AND MORTAR' BOOKSELLERS; DISTRIBUTION IN THE UK AND ELSEWHERE

When I took office, only high energy physicists had ever heard of what is called the Worldwide Web... Now even my cat has its own page.
Bill Clinton 1946– 42nd President of the United States (1993–2001): announcement of the Next Generation Internet initiative (1996)

This chapter covers:

- why Amazon is so important to self-publishers
- supplying information to Amazon
- Amazon's selling schemes: Advantage, Fulfilment by Amazon, others
- selling on Amazon's international websites
- Amazon and POD
- 'Look Inside'
- distribution in the UK and internationally
- the energetic Ros Wesson

Why Amazon is so important to self-publishers
For self-publishers the internet in general, and Amazon in particular, provides the opportunity to make their books and their books' content visible to a global audience at no cost.

I have one gripe with Amazon, and it's one that authors and publishers share: copies of books sold by Amazon resellers are sometimes described as 'New' even when the reseller in question cannot have genuinely new stock from the publisher. At best such copies should be described as 'Used – Like New' but the reality is that both sellers and buyers alike know what's going on. The problem is that the copies sold by resellers undermine the publisher's own sales. In my early days of self-publishing I emailed Amazon when instances came to my attention, but in the end I gave up the effort; it was taking up too much time. I consoled myself with the knowledge that Amazon provides a remarkable route to market for self-publishers and publishers alike.

Amazon is a company which self-publishers ignore at their peril. Many book buyers buy most and possibly almost all of their books from Amazon. So it's important to know how to get the best out of the Amazon model, because how they present your books could be crucial to the books' success. I shall be considering the Amazon model as operated through their British website Amazon.co.uk but their other websites appear to operate a very similar model.

From time to time my publishing website Lpspublishing.co.uk isn't operational, mainly when I'm not convinced of its merits and money happens to be tight. Then Amazon's websites become my 'shop window'. You can, indeed, even use them to present your books in a *dedicated* shop window. From information supplied by Lightning Source earlier this year I know that about 80% of the UK orders for my (POD) books originate with Amazon, while only 20% of the non-UK orders do. I don't know how representative this experience is of self-publishers in general, but it's clear you must make your presence on Amazon's websites as professional-looking as possible. Upload a biography on at least the American and British websites including a few words on each of your titles. It's a great way to connect with your potential readership. On a number of occasions I've had orders for titles resulting directly from people looking at my biography on Amazon.

Supplying information to Amazon

If you use Nielsen's Publisher Enhanced Service, comprehensive information about your book(s) will be passed by Nielsen directly to Amazon's British and other websites. Amazon 'refreshes' its book information every week or two, so that will be the delay to expect after Nielsen makes the information available.

If you don't use Nielsen's Enhanced Service but use their basic (free) service, only basic information will be passed to Amazon – not even the table of contents will be included, so your prospect of sales will be diminished. To make more information available to Amazon you'll need to register with them as a seller, ideally using your publishing name, and submit details such as the table of contents directly to them.

Amazon has a variety of selling schemes of differing levels of suitability for the self-publisher. You may find that some schemes are suitable for some titles, other schemes suitable for others. You may even find yourself using a number of the schemes at the same time for individual titles. Taking each scheme in turn:

Amazon Advantage

This scheme will seldom be suitable for self-publishers, in my view, at least not until individual titles start selling in reasonable quantities, at which time they should be produced by the offset litho printing model to bring the 'per copy' cost right down, and by that time they should be selling through traditional bookstores too.

Under the Advantage scheme Amazon stores the publisher's books in their warehouse. You have to pay for the bulk delivery to their warehouse, and you can't deliver them yourself. And if any of the books are subsequently returned to you, you'll pay for that too.

Amazon takes a standard discount rate of 60 per cent from the list price (which the publisher sets). With an apology to maths and math graduates, this means that if your book's list price is £10.00, you'll get £4.00, and you'll get it about 30 days after the end of the month in which the sale is made. If turnover through the scheme rises to over £50,000 annually the premium discount rate of 55 per cent applies.

Amazon's ordering software will automatically place orders for your titles by email, order quantities being of a size to give Amazon an estimated 7–14 days' stock at current demand levels.

Publishers pay an annual fee of £23.50 to join the scheme. Amazon claims that the great benefit of the scheme for publishers is that books are shown as being 'in stock', which improves their appeal to buyers and consequently drives sales. But my own titles produced by the POD model, which sell through Amazon.com and Amazon's other non-British websites, are almost always shown as being in stock, whatever Amazon's Mr Nard says. They're sometimes shown as, 'Only 1 copy in stock – order soon (more on the way)', presumably to stimulate wavering buyers.

If you're having your books produced by the short print run model you'll have to have written a compelling book justifying a high price to make any money out of the Amazon Advantage model. But even then you'll run into another problem. While you set the book's list price, Amazon will set the price *they* sell the book for, at their complete discretion. So not only will you be getting a poor margin, Amazon will be reducing your sales through other more profitable channels.

If you're selling titles which you can claim to be 'high-price, low-velocity' titles aimed at professional, technical and medical markets, you may be able to join Amazon's Advantage Professional scheme. The discount rate then falls to 40 per cent, and if turnover rises to over £25,000 annually, it will fall further to 35 per cent.

Fulfilment by Amazon

This is a useful scheme and I've used it on occasion for a number of titles although it would help to be a qualified accountant to understand the financial aspects of the scheme. Under the scheme – henceforth 'FBA' – Amazon stocks the books, but here's an odd thing. Unless the title is held in stock by Amazon already, or presumably available through POD, it won't show up as being 'in stock'. I've just looked on Amazon.co.uk at the entry for *Two Men in a Car*. The entry says 'Usually dispatched within 5 to 10 days'. It's only when I click on <u>2 New</u> that I'm taken to a page where it's clear the book is available not only from Amazon but also from 'lpsbooks2', the name LPS publishing trades under with Amazon, as a reseller.

It's also made clear that the title if bought from lpsbooks2 is 'Fulfilled by Amazon', which presumably helps drive sales. I'm personally more inclined to use resellers using the FBA scheme. There's one little thing I'd recommend you do to promote yourself as a reseller. Use the facility to add a short amount of text, which may persuade the potential book buyer to buy from you rather than another reseller. I always make a point of signing my books, and the buyer is not going to know that it will be signed regardless of where he buys it from. In the case of *Two Men in a Car* I've added the note:

The books are new and signed by myself, the author and publisher. Thanks for the order. I hope you enjoy the book. Mike Buchanan.

A very powerful promotional message, I think you'll agree. Customers who buy your FBA titles will enjoy 'Free Super Saver Delivery' and 'Amazon Prime' shipping discounts. FBA listings on Amazon.co.uk feature the same delivery messaging Amazon uses for its own listings. There are no additional set-up charges or subscription fees when you add FBA to your seller account. FBA fees vary depending on the type of item sold, its dimensions and weight, and the shipping method used. For a detailed explanation of FBA and its associated costs you should visit their website. Or have your accountant do so.

All FBA orders are shipped in Amazon branded boxes. The packing slip displays the Amazon brand and the name of the seller.

Other Amazon selling schemes
On Amazon's website we come to the prosaically titled section 'Sell Your Stuff', another Amazon scheme for sellers: one in which Amazon neither store your stock nor fulfil orders. The scheme comes in two forms: one for 'individual sellers' who expect to sell fewer than 35 items per month, one for 'Pro-Merchant subscribers'.

The first scheme is only applicable to products already available to order from Amazon – so you could apply for it as soon as their website is showing the title as available to order; it wouldn't have to be physically in stock at an Amazon facility. Amazon charges a £0.86 per item 'completion fee' and a 'closing fee' of 17.25 per cent of the sales price. There's also a 'variable closing fee' – £0.49 for books – which is deducted from the delivery charge Amazon takes from the buyer. So the sum you get paid for each sale is:

List price + buyer delivery charge – completion fee – closing fee – variable closing fee

The second scheme is identical other than a monthly fee of £28.75 being payable, but no completion charges are then payable. Sellers that want to sell items not yet available to order from Amazon need to choose this option to access the scheme. But it's equally open to sellers when the items are available to order from Amazon. That's clear, then.

Selling on Amazon's international websites
It could be that your book has sales potential in a number of international markets. Data supplied through Nielsen will feed through not only to Amazon's British and American websites, but also to their websites aimed at buyers in:

Canada	Amazon.ca
France	Amazon.fr
Germany	Amazon.de
Japan	Amazon.co.jp
China:	Amazon.cn

I believe the individual countries have the option of displaying or not displaying titles. *Profitable Buying Strategies* was published in a Simplified Chinese edition in January 2010. I was intrigued to see if it had received any buyer reviews on the Chinese website at the time of writing (July 2010) and sure enough it did, a single two-star review:

> 0 / 0 people think this review helpful :
> **Do not feel like** 2009-11-08 11:01:57
> quooler View all comments quooler
> Buy this book open to see , how could not stand it also may be foreigner way of thinking and we do not the same. In general , do not like this book .

Well, that's just marvellous. Thanks for that. According to Wikipedia the population of China in 2009 was 1,338,612,968. For a second or two, anyway. And the only review of my book which those 1,338,612,968 people can read online is this one. Hang on. I've just spotted the term 'could not stand'. So the buyer has mobility problems. What on earth has that to do with my book? Really. I've a good mind to boycott the Chinese takeaway restaurant near my house.

Amazon and POD

The combination of Lightning Source and Amazon provides an ideal way to supply your books into markets which you could not readily supply with stock for a variety of reasons. LPS titles available to order on Amazon.com are manufactured by Lightning Source, and I have yet to receive any adverse buyer reactions on any grounds. Amazon.com offer their own POD model and details may be found on Createspace.com.

'Look Inside'

This interesting feature of Amazon's websites allows potential buyers to look at selected elements of the book they're interested in, to help them better gauge the value of the book to them, thereby minimising the risk of an unsuitable purchase. The rationale of the feature is that if a potential reader uses it and decides not to buy the book, none of the key parties involved – the writer, the publisher, Amazon – have lost anything. But if it raises sales, then the key parties will benefit. You simply have to email content PDFs to the Amazon sites. No need to send cover files because they'll have got those through Nielsen.

I think I'm right in saying that until some point in the past year or two Amazon.com allowed the visitor to view more book content than would be visible on Amazon.co.uk. By clicking on the book cover image – which has 'Click to LOOK INSIDE!' at the top of the image, to show the feature is enabled – you will get through to the content made readily available to the potential buyer. Amazon alone decides what content they'll make visible in this way, but there is a pattern to it. Content that indicates the scope of a work – the contents page, the index, the back cover etc. – is *always* made available. Part or most of the first chapter is made available.

I'm currently disinclined to offer the 'Look Inside' feature on most of my books, especially the books which I think other writers may trawl for ideas for their own books. I might reconsider as and when Amazon starts to allow publishers to specify what content is made viewable through the feature.

If you use my model for creating distinctive content-rich books you won't want lazy oiks stealing your ideas. The least that lazy oiks can do is to buy my books before stealing my ideas, I feel. Aaron Shepard has managed to self-publish the three top-selling titles on self-publishing without employing the tool, and I'll do likewise. Thanks, Aaron. Pop in for a cold beer if you're ever passing by.

Amazon say they will remove the tool within 24 hours upon request, and I have found they actually do so. But – if memory serves me right, and it sometimes doesn't – I believe their official contract terms say otherwise. My advice is to get written confirmation from Amazon of how quickly it can be removed, before you start using it.

Distribution in the UK and internationally

Gardners are 'Britain's leading book DVD and Blu-ray wholesaler', according to their website. They're based near Eastbourne. Their 'Small Publisher Helpline' can be contacted on Sph@gardners.com.

Over the past couple of years I've despatched possibly ten times more books to Gardners than to the other major distributor/wholesaler in the UK, Bertrams. This is, I believe, because Gardners fulfil orders for Amazon and Waterstone's, the principal sources of orders for my books over that period.

Bertrams are 'the UK's leading book wholesaler, library and publisher distribution business', reports their website. They're based near Norwich whose citizens are said to greet one another by raising their hands, palms facing forward, then crying out loud, 'Give me six!' before slapping the other person's raised hand.

Their website is Bertrams.com. The only phone contact I could find on the site was for their business development manager, Ros Wesson, contactable on 0871 803 6603, also by email on Ros.wesson@bertrams.com. The Customer Services page contains her contact details only, and there are no contact details here or elsewhere on the site for customer services. The British are not world leaders when it comes to customer service, as Americans are apt to spot. Still, let's see what the website has to say:

> #### Customer Services
> The Customer Service team has strong industry wide connections with an in-depth knowledge of trade customers both in the UK and internationally. All Customer Services staff undertake a 6 week induction and in house training programme; the majority are members of the Institute of Call Centre Operatives and have completed a Customer Services NVQ. Our Customer Services department is open from 8.30am

until 5.30pm each weekday and flex up and down depending on clients' needs.

You have to wonder if, as members of the enchantingly-titled Institute of Call Centre Operatives, the Customer Services staff are confused to be sitting by desks every day on which sit phones that never ring; while poor Ms Wesson is handling five phone calls and ten emails per minute.

In the UK virtually all of your non-Amazon orders (and some from Amazon too) will be processed through Nielsen and delivered to either Gardners or Bertrams. I've had a few orders from independent bookshops and allowed them the same 20 per cent discount I allow Gardners and Bertrams. Orders from Amazon come with a guarantee of payment. I recommend you do not extend credit to other organisations or individuals, nor process orders with cheques until the cheque clears.

Until and unless your books sell in significant numbers you'll probably struggle to find overseas distributors, so POD is the obvious way to satisfy overseas orders. If you sell from your own website, have differential pricing to cover the additional postage costs. The PayPal tool for this is very sound. When you add new titles you'll be asked if you want to retrieve an existing button and modify it. You then simply send the button to your website designer to process – unless your IT skills are better than mine and you can do this yourself.

10

MARKETING YOUR BOOKS

pixel, n.: A mischievous, magical spirit associated with screen displays. The computer industry has frequently borrowed from mythology: Witness the sprites in computer graphics, the demons in artificial intelligence, and the trolls in the marketing department.
Jeff Meyer screenwriter and director of American situation comedies

This chapter covers:

- promoting your books
- the impact of BBC local radio interviews on book sales
- testimonials from 'leading lights'
- extraverts like promoting their books, introverts don't
- Paul Carrington, the ultimate book promoter
- Bedford: not the most literary of places
- Nielsen Publisher Enhanced Service
- promoting your *œuvre* in your new titles and on your dedicated website

Over 120,000 new book titles are published each year in the UK alone. The book-buying public isn't waiting with bated breath for your books. Or mine. Sorry. So you should think seriously about how you will promote your books.

Books on self-publishing often give the same advice about promoting your books; namely, that you should spend as much time in promoting them as you did writing them. This is another piece of advice I take delight in ignoring. I like writing, but I don't like promoting my books other than through the medium of writing. All things considered I should prefer to spend my time doing things I like rather than things I don't.

It's taken me some time to get to this position. When I published *The Marriage Delusion* I realised that the thesis put forward in the book was so different from most books on marriage and relationships that I had no choice but to promote the book, and I spent a good deal of time doing so.

I was interviewed by four BBC local radio stations. One was truly local – BBC Three Counties Radio – while the other three weren't; I was simply interviewed over the phone. I had only marketed to the first station; the BBC clearly maintains information databases of possible interviewees. I imagine I'm on a database of people with controversial views on marriage.

All four interviews went well. I was allowed to present the thesis of the book at length, and I was asked some searching and intelligent questions by both the radio presenters and their listeners. The interviews resulted in a modest uplift in sales of the book.

The other activity that helped increase sales, beyond word of mouth and buyer reviews on Amazon, was unplanned. The book contains a good deal of material on psychology, and how people are suited to – or not suited to – long-term intimate relationships with their partners. I thought it might therefore be of interest to leading psychologists, and I duly mailed complimentary copies to about 50 leading psychologists around the world, as well as leading writers of 'popular psychology' books.

One was the bestselling author and psychologist Oliver James. He emailed me a very positive critique, whereupon it struck me that I might seek a testimonial from him, which I could use for promotional purposes. He very kindly agreed to write one and I've used it ever since.

It then occurred to me that some of the other psychologists and writers also might be prepared to offer a testimonial, so I emailed them, citing Oliver James's testimonial and asking for one from them. Only one responded, Professor Alan Carr of Dublin University. It arrived in the form of an email one Sunday afternoon. I was surprised to receive a communication from a professor at the weekend – on reflection, I'd be surprised to receive one from a professor on a weekday too – and at first I assumed it was a hoax sent by one of his mischievous offspring, assuming he has any. But an exchange of emails satisfied me that it was a genuine testimonial.

My friend Paul Carrington has appeared in all my self-published books. He appears in *Guitar Gods in Beds.* as Thunderin' Paul Carrington, and he was my chauffeur in *Two Men in a Car.* He's the most extraverted person I've ever known. Now *he's* happy to promote my books, maybe because he's promoting himself at the same time. He even keeps copies of *Guitar*

Gods in Beds. and *Two Men in a Car* on the back shelf of his car and promotes them shamelessly whenever and wherever he can. He's been known to stop the car and try to sell copies to complete strangers walking by. My advice is to actively and personally promote your books if you enjoy doing so.

My adopted home town, the throbbing metropolis of Bedford, England, is not the most literary of places. The last bestseller to be written by a Bedford-based author was John Bunyan's *Pilgrim's Progress.* It was published in 1678 and it's never been out of print. It's been translated into more than 200 languages, and is said to be the most boring book in all of them.

When the local Waterstone's bookstore asked me to attend a book signing session I jumped at the offer. I wrote to the two local papers a week before the event, left copies of my latest book, and asked if they wanted to send a journalist and a photographer to record the event.

They didn't respond, and they didn't send anyone to cover the event. The papers clearly had more important stories to relate. Given that the event was in the spring, my story was probably kept off the front page by the customary lead story in Bedfordshire at that time of year, 'Sheep Has Lamb, Reports Local Farmer'.

I'm reminded of one of my father's anecdotes about local papers. He grew up in Stornoway, in the Western Isles of Scotland. Legend has it that some years before he was born, in 1912, *The Stornoway Gazette* ran the headline, 'Local man lost at sea'. The lengthy article was mainly about the man, but the final paragraph mentioned the vessel he'd been on when it sank, along with the estimated death toll. The ship was the *Titanic.*

Another of my father's stories relates to an advert he insists was placed in the local paper when he was a young man, by one of his neighbours, a crofter. The man had called the local paper and wanted to place an advertisement in the 'Lonely Hearts' section. It ran to 17 words, and he was told he could have an additional three words at no extra charge.

It started as:

> Crofter, 62, seeks woman for long term relationship, must own productive milk cow. Please send recent photograph.

And finished as:

> Crofter, 62, seeks woman for long term relationship, must own
> productive milk cow. Please send recent photograph of the cow.

The only promotion I normally do requires only writing on my part. I always ensure my books' full details are visible to book sellers and book buyers around the world through Nielsen's Publisher Enhanced Service. I include testimonials and reviews from every source including Amazon buyers. I make sure the title is worded such that it will be picked up by people searching on Amazon and elsewhere with keywords. And I generally cross-promote my books in each new book I write, often through including a few pages from them at the end. I find readers don't object to this practice so long as they find the material to be of interest, or it amuses them.

I sometimes finance a website Lpspublishing.co.uk but sales through it – processed by PayPal – are small and the expense simply isn't justifiable. The problem with author websites is driving traffic to them. On the plus side it gives me the highest margins I obtain for my books, it allows for differential pricing for different markets, and it has a facility for the book buyer to specify a dedication. It also enables me to fulfil orders for my books which are not available in some markets – for example, it enables me to make my books with colour plate sections (*Guitar Gods in Beds.* and *Two Men in a Car*) available to buyers around the world.

On Amazon I'm a reseller for most of my books (selling under the name 'lpsbooks2') and in the note section I write, 'The books are new and signed by the author. Please contact the seller through Amazon if you would like a dedication written by the author.'

When I need to order a new print run of a book I'll see how I can modify the Word file so as to promote all my books, including those published *after* the initial publication of the book I'm printing again. I'll ensure all my titles are shown on the 'By the same author' page and I state the year of the new print run on the preliminary page with the copyright details. I recently launched my first title in an ebook edition for major e-readers – *Two Men in a Car* – and I am in the process of having *The Joy of Self-Publishing* formatted by eBookIt.com. In the ebook edition of the latter ebook I'm including the plate section from *Two Men in a Car* both to show buyers how plate sections appear on e-readers, and to promote *Three Men in a Car* at the same time.

For both the POD and ebook editions of *The Joy of Self-Publishing* I've started the book with testimonials and reviews of a few of my titles. There's a risk of raising potential buyers' expectation levels excessively but it's a risk I'm prepared to take, because it encourages me to work even harder as a writer.

If you're prepared to spend time actively marketing your books, you could usefully read Alison Baverstock's *Marketing Your Book: An Author's Guide* or maybe – if you want to spend time promoting your books even more professionally – her *How to Market Books*. Her books are always worth reading and it was with some alarm that I spotted details of her forthcoming book on self-publishing, due to be published in October 2011, *The Naked Author – A Guide to Self-Publishing*. Please don't tell anyone looking for a book on self-publishing about that book, just direct them to this book instead. Thank you. Much appreciated.

11

WRITING OTHER PEOPLE'S AUTOBIOGRAPHIES

Develop interest in life as you see it; in people, things, literature, music – the world is so rich, simply throbbing with rich treasures, beautiful souls and interesting people. Forget yourself.
Henry Miller 1891–1980 American novelist and painter

This chapter covers:

- stumbling upon book topic ideas
- Bedfordshire's Dunstable Downs: England's equivalent of the Rocky Mountains
- indexes can stimulate sales
- colour plate sections can stimulate sales
- prats and popinjays

The first book I wrote was a business book in 2007, published internationally by Kogan Page the following year. After I submitted the final manuscript to Kogan Page I had a month remaining of the six-month sabbatical I'd taken for the project. I'd enjoyed writing the first book so it occurred to me that I might start on a second with a view to self-publishing it.

A number of book topics came to mind but I couldn't decide upon just one to progress. I stumbled across the idea which was to be the subject of my next book, a book which is still (about three years after publication) the fastest-selling local interest book in my local Waterstone's branch. It is of local interest because it relates the lives of local people, in their own words. But the model for writing it is, in effect, a model for writing other people's autobiographies, and it need not be restricted to the local interest market.

I'm a big fan of live guitar-based music and my adopted home town of Bedford has had a strong live guitar-based music scene since the early 1960s. My 50th birthday was on 8 December 2007 and I indulged myself by financing a concert at The Red Lion, a public house in the nearby village of Stevington. The performers were eight local (male) guitarists, and a glamorous lady performer on the tea chest bass. We called the concert 'Guitar Gods in Beds. (and a Goddess)'. For my non-British readers I should perhaps explain that 'Beds.' is the common abbreviation for the scenic county of Bedfordshire. North American readers might like to know that people living in the Rocky Mountains would feel very much at home in the county's Dunstable Downs.

I digress. Over the years, after watching countless gigs in Bedford and the surrounding areas, mainly in public houses – almost always for free – I'd come to know a number of the musicians and their spouses. I was chatting with Paul Carrington at a public house one typically balmy evening in November 2007. He was due to perform later that evening and was telling yet another story about his eccentric old father. I was laughing so much that I kept having to wipe tears from my eyes.

Later, while he was performing and I was indulging myself with my second and final half pint of Abbot Ale of the evening, a thought came to me. Paul and his fellow guitarists had given me a great deal of pleasure over the years; what might I do for them to show my appreciation? The answer was obvious. I would interview them and transcribe their life stories into a book, at the same time providing something of a history of the local music scene, which was not then available. And who better than the eight guitarists who were to perform at the 'Guitar Gods in Beds.' gig just a few weeks later?

And so it was that the *Guitar Gods in Beds. (Bedfordshire: a heavenly county)* project started. I learnt a lot from it, about writing biography and how to maximise sales of a book of strictly local interest. I interviewed the eight guitarists in their homes between November 2007 and August 2008, recording the interviews with a small digital voice recorder, an Olympus VN-1100. It wasn't expensive but it did have an option for transferring the material through a cable to my computer, so files could be emailed to a transcription service. I had neither the spare time nor the energy for volume transcribing on this scale, so I emailed the files to WNT Legal, contact details in Appendix 2.

I generally like and admire guitarists – one or two exceptions spring to mind, but let's move on – and I greatly enjoyed the discussions with these eight. I frequently had to switch the recorder off as either the guitarist or I – sometimes both – were helpless with laughter as he related some anecdote or other. One or two of them may have had one or two glasses of wine or beer before and during the interviews.

I've always been fond of the American habit of attaching an epithet to musicians' names – Ramblin' Jack Elliott and so on – but I wasn't sure I could be bothered to spend time thinking up epithets for all eight of the guitarists. Then it dawned on me that I was being apathetic about being epithetic so I made an effort and came up with the following names: Thunderin' Paul Carrington, Finger Pickin' Good Paul Bonas, Amazin' Max Milligan, Laughin' John Verity, Blindin' Dave King, Hollerin' Bob Foley, Mumblin' Cliff Hanson and Lightnin' Hands Pete Rose. Sizzlin' Sara Turner, the tea chest bass lady, declined to be interviewed.

In the autumn of 2008 the writing was completed. I had to do a little modification to the transcribed material so as to improve its flow, take my own spoken words out, and in effect created a series of mini autobiographies. As a matter of courtesy I sent the guitarists copies of their chapters, and some requested a few minor amendments, which took me minimal time to action. I was very happy with the final result. All of the guitarists had had interesting lives outside of the music scene as well as inside it, and the book had become a record of life over the past 60 years in the area. It was packed full of 'human interest' stories.

I then did something that I thought such a book deserved, and wrote a detailed index, which ended up stimulating sales, to my surprise. The index included all the individuals mentioned by the guitarists – along with much else – and almost ended up as an A to Z of the people of Bedford. A number of people who've bought a copy have told me that they did so after finding their own names, or the names of people they know, in the index.

The first edition of the book didn't contain photographs, but one day it occurred to me that sales might benefit from them. The printer was able to include a colour plate section (a fancy term for a section of photographs), and given the happy coincidence of a need for 16 photographs and there being eight guitarists, I decided to include two photographs of each guitarist, one taken when they were young, one taken more recently. I took four of the eight recent photographs.

One guitarist failed to provide a photograph of himself when younger – trying to organise musicians is like trying to herd cats, I find – so I decided to do a bit of cross-book promotion and included a photograph from my then half- finished *Two Men in a Car.* That book was eventually to become the travelogue of two long holidays in France with (Thunderin') Paul Carrington. The picture was of the two of us standing under a village sign in the Jura region of France, and the village rejoiced in the name of Pratz.

I wasn't sure that the English term 'prat' – a commonly-used and often affectionate term for a fool – would be known to North American readers, so I asked an acquaintance from Boston, Massachusetts, about the matter. He assured me that the equivalent word used by people in the United States would be 'popinjay'. Now I happen to be a big fan of the American sitcom *Frasier* and Niles Crane uses the term from time to time, so I know he's not pulling my leg.

The addition of the plate section added about £1.00 per copy to the cost of the ensuing 100 copy run at MPG Biddles, but it turned out to be a good investment. Sales of *Guitar Gods in Beds.* increased as soon as the new edition was available in the local Waterstone's store, and to this day it remains my only book which that store buys in minimum quantities of ten copies.

12

WRITING TRAVELOGUES

I shall be telling this with a sigh
Somewhere ages and ages hence:
two roads diverged in a wood, and I–
I took the one less traveled by,
And that has made all the difference.
Robert Frost 1874–1963 American poet who received four Pulitzer Prizes for Poetry during his lifetime: 'The Road Not Taken', *Mountain Interval* (1916)

This chapter contains:

- tax-deductible costs
- distinctiveness
- extracts from *Two Men in a Car* to illustrate various points
- The French Helpfulness Index

Travelogues remain in strong demand, so why not add your own offering in the genre? For British writers at least some of the costs can be tax-deductible, so if nothing else you'll effectively subsidise your travels if they are the subject of your book.

My accountant – who has always appeared to believe he's paid by Her Majesty's Revenue and Customs rather than by myself – tells me the HMRC would apply the 'reasonableness' test to claims of tax-deductible costs. I pointed out to him that the travelogues I planned to write would not be possible without, for example, expenditure on ferries and petrol to travel to the required destinations. So, I asked, could I charge the whole of such costs to the book project?

'It would depend on whether HMRC deemed that reasonable,' he replied.

'Okay,' I continued, 'let's say I spend eight hours a day writing. Can I charge, say, 50 per cent of the overall costs of the holiday to the project?'

'It depends,' he replied.

'On the reasonableness test?'

'Yes.'

I was rapidly losing the will to live and I shall mercifully spare you the remainder of the discussion.

I think most writers – even experienced ones – would be hard pressed to add anything commercially viable to the mountain of existing books about well-known countries, cities, and so on. The answer again is to be distinctive. You could write about interesting far-flung places, I suppose, but the problem with far-flung places is that few people are flung to them, so the book's potential market may be very limited.

Again, try to be distinctive. Draw on your opinions about things, and on your interactions with different people. My travelogue *Two Men in a Car* is both my highest-selling title and the one with the most positive reviews on Amazon.co.uk – 17 five-star reviews to date. One day someone will post a negative review and it will put me in a bad mood for a week because I don't handle criticism well, as my two ex-wives might possibly confirm.

The book's introduction starts as follows (here and in the remainder of this chapter I've put the extracts from the book in a box, to distinguish them from the other text):

INTRODUCTION

'What we need is rest', said Harris.
'Rest and a complete change', said George. 'The overstrain upon our brains has produced a general depression throughout the system. Change of scene, and absence of the necessity for thought, will restore the mental equilibrium.'
Jerome K Jerome *Three Men in a Boat* (1889)

I was reading the Victorian classic *Three Men in a Boat* in July 2007 when the above passage leapt from the page. My second wife and I had separated two weeks earlier and my spirits were very low. 'Rest and a complete change' were *exactly* what I needed, I realised. And why not go the whole hog, and adopt the continental habit of holidaying for the month of August?

The book's title was inspired by *Three Men in a Boat*, one of the finest comic travelogues ever written. I copied Jerome's approach to outlining the contents of chapters at the outset of the chapters – a common habit among Victorian writers, and one I'm fond of – leading to:

1

OUR FIRST WEEK WITH
ANNE AND MARK PHILLIPS

I refuse to grow up, on the grounds that I might not like it!
Paul Carrington (1950-)

The rocking chair – the heroic police officer – Mercedes S-class saloons – the problem with the ferry booking – Paul gets in touch with his 'inner child' – *When You Come to the End of Your Lollipop* – Anne and Mark – the witty dentist's receptionist – Cognac – 'a simple cup of English breakfast tea' – Super Mario – the problem with Hennessy's current cellarmaster – 'normal' cheese – the problem with French stamps – The French Helpfulness Index – window cleaning and shutter painting – the fetching waitress in Bordeaux – the helpful lady dentist – Louis, the flying dog – Paul spots something 'incredible' – the divine Château Mirambeau – a judgmental waiter in Jonzac – *Where do you go to, my lovely?* – Stanground boys and the art of bicycle borrowing – why the French are generally shorter than the English – funny sunflowers – Hiroshima – a tour of the Médoc wine region – *Madamoiselle Toptotty* and the 'magnificent warehouse' – 'Zey are *all* good vintages, monsieur' – Château Lynch-Bages and the awful lunch – French merde, German merde – *un trog, une trogette* – Quasimodo – an old lady crosses the road

SATURDAY 4 AUGUST
We couldn't fit the rocking chair into the car...

Two Men in a Car is distinctive in being a study of the contrast between two Englishmen, one firmly middle class (myself), the other firmly working class (Paul Carrington), and outlining opinions about France, the

French, and much else. The introduction contains the following biographical details:

	MIKE BUCHANAN	PAUL CARRINGTON
THE BUSINESSMAN AND THE CHAUFFEUR		
Background	Solidly middle class. Father worked in the Foreign Office. Public school, university, career with blue-chip organisations. Has run a management consultancy since 1999. Writer.	Solidly working class. Brought up on a houseboat in the village of Stanground, near Peterborough. Left school at 16, worked in brickworks, the Army, security. Self-employed chauffeur since 1983.
Age	50	57
Health and physical attributes, current marital status	5'9" tall, 235 lbs (107 kg). Highly unfit and averse to physical effort of any kind, hence his chauffeur, cleaner and gardener. This, combined with his fondness for good food and wine, has led to him being overweight for many years. Myopic, diabetic. Currently single, surprisingly.	6'1" tall, 210 lbs (94 kg). Interested in keeping himself fit even after suffering several lung collapses through emphysema. 5th Dan in the martial art Moo-duk-kwan-tang-soo-do. Six false teeth, and psoriasis on his head. Currently single, surprisingly.
Marital record and children	Two ex-wives (British). Two daughters, Sarah Mercedes (23) and Kerry Portia (22).	Three ex-wives (Yugoslavian, Italian, Ugandan). Three children, Louise (37), James (35) and Kristien (33).
Personality	An introvert until the wine kicks in. Tries to	An extrovert, and highly opinionated.

	respect opposing views to his, on complex issues. Invariably fails. Relishes variety and the finer things in life.	People call him arrogant, he prefers 'over confident'. A creature of habit, even with respect to his choice of biscuits.
Politics	Right-wing except on law and order issues.	Left-wing except on law and order issues, where he's to the right of the Taliban. Hanging is generally 'too good for 'em'.
Daily newspaper	*The Daily Telegraph.*	*The Express,* occasionally *The Sun.*
Favourite magazine	*The Economist.*	*Bike* (a motorcycling magazine).
Interest in sports	Interest limited to ladies' tennis – especially the Russian and East European players – and ladies' beach volleyball. The latter is rarely to be seen in Bedford.	Very interested in many sports.
Interest in fine food and wine	Substantial. Drinks *comme un trou* ('like a hole') as the French say. Helps makes life under the current Labour administration a little more bearable.	None. Has rarely been known to drink more than one glass of wine in a day.
Leisure pursuits	Live guitar-based music, reading, comedy, travelling in France. A good guitar owner.	Live guitar-based music, exercising, motorcycling. A good guitar player.
Attitude	Lifelong admirer of	Before the first holiday: 'I

towards France and the French	France, the French, their food, wine, language and… well, almost everything, to be honest.	love France, but I hate the French.' After the second: 'I love the southern half of France, which is scenic and warm, and the French people, but I'm not a fan of French food.'

A number of readers told me they bought the book partly because they were intrigued by the chapter titles. These are effectively the Table of Contents made visible through Nielsen's Publisher Extended Service. The chapter titles of the book are:

1. Our first week with Anne and Mark Phillips
2. Why my dinner cost 40 times more than Paul's
3. Hobnobbing with Ivana Trump in Monte Carlo
4. 'Would you like to have sex with my wife?'
5. We witness a miracle in Lourdes
6. In defence of *pâté de foie gras*
7. Paul worries about becoming a gay icon
8. Nuits-St-Georges is twinned with Hitchin!
9. 'It's always better if you have a big one!'

Paul and I enjoyed the first holiday (August 2007) so much that we went to France again in July 2008, and the book is the tale of both holidays. Whenever we meet we reminisce about the good times we had, and three years after the second holiday I still occasionally dip into the book. My spirits are invariably and quickly lifted as I relive those happy days – and isn't that enough of an incentive in itself to write a travelogue? I believe it is.

I close this chapter with The French Helpfulness Index.

TUESDAY 7 AUGUST 2007

An overcast day, we decided to go to Bordeaux after breakfast. During breakfast we realised that we needed a structured approach to defining our various terms of description for the French, and soon developed The French Helpfulness Index:

THE FRENCH HELPFULNESS INDEX (1)

Category	Points	Key pointers to identification
Un bon œuf (a good egg)	9 – 10	This person is friendly, helpful, maintains a well-repaired and clean house, a clean car and a well-tended garden. In response to a request for directions, this person will cheerfully point you in the right direction. We met a number of French people in this category, to our disappointment.
Un plonkeur / une plonkeuse	6 – 8	This person doesn't clean his windows, nor his car, nor repair his house, nor tend a garden. Many French people are in this category. Will respond to the enquiry *'Parlez-vous Anglais?'* with 'Oui, a leetel', and will actually make an effort if in a good mood. Best approached *after* lunch, i.e. 3.15 p.m.
Un tosseur / Une tosseuse	3 – 5	This person is unhelpful by nature, but more so once he/she discovers you are English, or you speak anything other than flawless French. Will respond to the enquiry *'Parlez-vous Anglais?'* with 'No, ah do nod spick a zingle wort of ze Onglish lonkwich, ah'm afret we shell eff to convorse in Fronch. Kandly prozeed wiss your onquerry.'
Un wankeur / une wankeuse	1 – 2	This person refuses to accept the very existence of the English language. Responds to your cheery 'good morning' – or 'good moaning', if you're willing to make an effort yourself – with a look of utter bewilderment. Responds to any enquiry with a fast torrent of French, in which no individual words could possibly be identified, even by a native French speaker.

(1) Scale of 1–10 points, 10 points representing extreme helpfulness.

13

CONCLUSION

Finally, in conclusion, let me say just this.
Peter Sellers 1925–80 English comedian and actor

EPILOGUE

I always wanted to write a book that ended with the word 'mayonnaise'.
Richard Brautigan 1935–84 American novelist, poet, and short-story writer

Well, here we are at the end of the book, or at least the end of the book before the appendices and indexes. I should like to record a few words of appreciation for a wonderful chain of British bookstores, Waterstone's. Paul, the manager of my local store in Bedford, has been unfailingly supportive since I showed him my first self-published book in 2008, *Guitar Gods in Beds*. He recently arranged a book signing session one Saturday lunchtime at which I – with the able support of Thunderin' Paul Carrington – met local readers of my books, and we sold a number of copies.

All Waterstone's stores appear to be staffed by knowledgeable, cheerful, hardworking and helpful people: qualities which are not always to be found in British store workers, a point which tends to be noticed by tourists of the American persuasion.

Any British writer clutching a copy of his new book – whether or not his first title – might like to copy my habit upon receiving the first copies. I spend a pleasant few hours in London with one or both of my daughters and during the course of the day we make our way to the largest bookstore in Europe, Waterstone's on Piccadilly.

I was taken aback a couple of years ago when I asked the salesperson if the store had a copy of *Guitar Gods in Beds*. After tapping the till keys he informed me that they didn't stock it but they soon would, as he'd just ordered a couple of copies. The same has happened in the case of my subsequent books. I was in London recently and took a little time out to check that the store was stocking all my titles, and sure enough it was. Honestly. I saw them with mayonnaise.

APPENDIX 1

QUOTATIONS ABOUT BOOKS AND RELATED MATTERS (MOSTLY)

(Sorted alphabetically by the surname of the speaker or the writer, or by the title of a play, show, television series or film.)

I love deadlines. I like the whooshing sound they make as they fly by.
Douglas Adams 1952–2001 English writer, dramatist, and musician

There is more beauty in the works of a great genius who is ignorant of all the rules of art, than in the works of a little genius, who not only knows but scrupulously observes them.
Joseph Addison 1672–1719 English poet, dramatist, and essayist: *The Spectator* 10 September 1714

After being turned down by numerous publishers, he had decided to write for posterity.
George Ade 1866–1944 American humorist and dramatist: *Fables in Slang* (1900)

The truth which makes men free is for the most part the truth which men prefer not to hear.
Herbert Agar 1897–1980 American poet and writer: *A Time for Greatness* (1942)

The English instinctively admire any man who has no talent and is modest about it.
James Agate 1877–1947 British diarist and theatre critic

A priest asked, 'What is Fate, Master?'
And he answered, 'It is that which gives a beast of burden its reason for existence. It is that which men in former times had to bear upon their backs. It is that which has caused nations to build byways from city to city upon which carts and coaches pass, and alongside which inns have come to be built to stave off hunger, thirst and weariness.'
'And that is Fate?' said the priest.
'Fate? I thought you said Freight,' said the Master.
'That's all right,' said the priest. 'I wanted to know what Freight was too.'
Kehlog Albran: *The Profit*

My one regret in life is that I am not someone else.
Eric Lax *Woody Allen and his Comedy* (1975)

All literature is a footnote to Faust. I have no idea what I mean by that.

I took a speed reading course and read *War and Peace* in 20 minutes. It involves Russia.

I don't want to achieve immortality through my work... I want to achieve it through not dying.

Money is better than poverty, if only for financial reasons.

How can I believe in God when just last week I got my tongue caught in the roller of an electric typewriter?
Woody Allen 1935– American film director, writer, and actor

We men have got love well weighed up; our stuff
Can get by without it.
Women don't seem to think that's good enough;
They write about it.
'A Bookshop Idyll' (1956)

If you can't annoy somebody with what you write, I think there's little point in writing.
Kingsley Amis 1922–95 English novelist and poet: in *Radio Times* 1 May 1971

Is there no beginning to your talents?
Clive Anderson 1952– English radio and television presenter, to Jeffrey Archer, English author, actor, playwright, convicted criminal, and former politician

This fictional account of the day-by-day life of an English gamekeeper is still of considerable interest to outdoor-minded readers, as it contains many passages on pheasant raising, the apprehending of poachers, ways to control vermin, and other chores and duties of the professional gamekeeper. Unfortunately one is obliged to wade through many pages of extraneous material in order to discover and savour these sidelights on the management of a Midlands shooting estate, and in this reviewer's opinion this book cannot take the place of JR Miller's *Practical Gamekeeping*.
Anonymous review of DH Lawrence's *Lady Chatterley's Lover*. Attributed to *Field and Stream*, c. 1928

Think different.
Apple Computers advertising slogan, 1997

People think that I can teach them style. What stuff it all is! Have something to say, and say it as clearly as you can. That is the only secret of style.
Matthew Arnold 1822–88 English poet and essayist: GWE Russell *Collections and Recollections* (1898)

You must keep sending work out; you must never let a manuscript do nothing but eat its head off in a drawer. You send that work out again and again, while you're working on another one. If you have talent, you will receive some measure of success – but only if you persist.
Isaac Asimov 1920–92 Russian-born biochemist and science fiction writer

Publishers are in business to make money, and if your books do well they don't care whether you are male, female, or an elephant.
Margaret Atwood 1939– Canadian novelist: Graeme Gibson *Eleven Canadian Novelists* (1973)

Some books are undeservedly forgotten; none are undeservedly remembered.

The Dyer's Hand (1963)

Geniuses are the luckiest of mortals because what they must do is the same as what they most want to do.

Dag Hammarskjöld *Markings* (1964)
WH Auden 1907–73 English poet

One of Edward's Mistresses was Jane Shore, who has had a play written about her, but it is a tragedy and therefore not worth reading.

The History of England (1791)

I declare after all there is no enjoyment like reading! How much sooner one tires of anything than of a book! When I have a house of my own, I shall be miserable if I have not an excellent library.

Pride and Prejudice (1811)

A large income is the best recipe for happiness I ever heard of. It certainly may secure all the myrtle and turkey part of it.

Let other pens dwell on guilt and misery. I quit such odious subjects as soon as I can.

Mansfield Park (1814)

I think I may boast myself to be, with all possible vanity, the most unlearned and uninformed female who ever dared to be an authoress.

letter, 11 December 1815
Jane Austen 1775–1817 English novelist

If I had been someone not very clever, I would have done an easier job like publishing. That's the easiest job I can think of.
AJ Ayer 1910–89 English philosopher (attr.)

I was obliged to be industrious. Whoever is equally industrious will succeed equally well.
JS Bach 1685–1750 German composer

If a man will begin with certainties, he shall end in doubts; but if he will be content to begin with doubts, he shall end in certainties.

The Advancement of Learning (1605)

Reading maketh a full man; conference a ready man; and writing an exact man.

Some books are to be tasted, others to be swallowed, and some few to be chewed and digested.

Books will speak plain when counsellors blanch.

Essays (1625)
Francis Bacon 1561–1626 English lawyer, courtier, philosopher, and essayist

The great pleasure in life is doing what people say you cannot do.
Prospective Review (1853)

Writers, like teeth, are divided into incisors and grinders.
Estimates of some Englishmen and Scotchmen (1858)

One of the greatest pains to human nature is the pain of a new idea.
Physics and Politics (1872)
Walter Bagehot 1826–77 English economist and essayist

The urge for destruction is also a creative urge!
Michael Bakunin 1814–76 Russian revolutionary and anarchist: *Jahrbruch für Wissenschaft und Kunst* (1842)

One of those big, fat paperbacks, intended to while away a monsoon or two, which, if thrown with a good overarm action, will bring a water buffalo to its knees.
reviewing a TV adaptation of MM Kaye's *The Far Pavilions*
Nancy Banks-Smith 1929– British television critic: *The Guardian* 4 January 1984

The writer must be universal in sympathy and an outcast by nature: only then can he see clearly.

Books say: she did this because. Life says: she did this. Books are where things are explained to you; life is where things aren't... Books make sense of life. The only problem is that the lives they make sense of are other people's lives, never your own.
Julian Barnes 1946– English novelist: *Flaubert's Parrot* (1984)

I do a lot of reading about serial killers, mostly *How To* books.
Roseanne Barr 1952– American actress, comedienne, writer, television producer, and director

[Author's note: where any individual has five or more lines of work attributed to them, you may safely assume the details are sourced from Wikipedia, not from a major dictionary of quotations. I'm convinced that the individuals, or their agents, specify their lines of work to Wikipedia. Should I ever have a Wikipedia entry, I shall ask to be described as a British writer, skydiver, winemaker, critic of radical feminism (gender Marxism) and of political correctness (cultural Marxism).]

It is all very well to be able to write books, but can you waggle your ears?
to HG Wells
JM Barrie 1860–1937 Scottish author and dramatist: JA Hammerton *Barrie: The Story of a Genius* (1929)

The world may be full of fourth-rate writers but it's also full of fourth-rate readers.
Stan Barstow 1928– English novelist: *Daily Mail* 15 August 1989

All that is beautiful and noble is the result of reason and calculation.
Charles Baudelaire 1821–67 French poet and critic: *The Painter of Modern Life* (1863)

Be daring, be different, be impractical, be anything that will assert integrity of purpose and imaginative vision against the play-it-safers, the creatures of the commonplace, the slaves of the ordinary.
Cecil Beaton 1904–80 English photographer: *Theatre Arts* May 1957

Where is human nature so weak as in the bookstore?
Henry Ward Beecher 1813–87 Congregationalist clergyman, social reformer, abolitionist, and speaker

When I am dead, I hope it may be said:
'His sins were scarlet, but his books were read.'
Hilaire Belloc 1870–1953 British poet, essayist, historian, novelist, and Liberal politician: 'On His Books' (1923)

It took me fifteen years to discover that I had no talent for writing, but I couldn't give up because by that time I was too famous.
Robert Benchley 1889–1945 American humorist: Nathaniel Benchley *Robert Benchley* (1955)

Writing is one-tenth perspiration and nine-tenths masturbation.

We were put to Dickens as children but it never quite took. That unremitting humanity soon had me cheesed off.
Alan Bennett 1934– English dramatist and actor: *The Old Country* (1978)

Why do writers write? Because it isn't there.
Thomas Berger 1924– American novelist

One is never obliged to write a book.
Henri Bergson 1859–1941 French philosopher

I have been commissioned to write my autobiography. Can anyone tell me where I was between 1960 and 1974 and what the hell I was doing?
Jeffrey Bernard 1932–97 British journalist reportedly fond of a lightly chilled dry sherry on a warm summer evening

A great writer reveals the truth even when he or she does not wish to.
Tom Bissell 1974– American journalist, critic, and fiction writer: *Truth in Oxiana* (2004)

No bird soars too high, if he soars with his own wings.
   The Marriage of Heaven and Hell (1790–3)

I must create a system, or be enslaved by another man's. I will not reason and compare: my business is to create.
William Blake 1757–1827 English poet and engraver: *Jerusalem* (1815)

Reading well is one of the great pleasures that solitude can afford you.
Harold Bloom 1930– American writer and literary critic: *O Magazine* April 2003

Of every four words I write, I strike out three.
Nicolas Boileau-Despréaux 1636–1711 French critic and poet: *Satire* (1665)

I have always imagined Paradise as a kind of library.
Jorge Luis Borges 1899–1986 Argentinean writer: *Seven Nights* (1984)

A losing trade, I assure you, sir: literature is a drug.
George Borrow 1803–81 English writer: *Lavengro* (1851)

Ideas are to literature what light is to painting.
Paul Bourget 1852–1935 French writer

You have to know how to accept rejection and reject acceptance.
Ray Bradbury 1920– American fantasy, horror, science fiction, and mystery writer

Striving for excellence motivates you; striving for perfection is demoralising.
Harriet Braiker

If we would guide by the light of reason, we must let our minds be bold.
Louis D Brandeis 1856–1941 American jurist: *Jay Burns Baking Co v Bryan* (1924) (dissenting)

I would rather read a novel about civil servants written by a rabbit.
on hearing that *Watership Down* was a novel about rabbits written by a civil servant
Craig Brown 1957– British artist, critic, satirist, and writer

Making a book is a craft, as is making a clock; it takes more than wit to become an author.
Jean de la Bruyère 1645–96 French essayist and moralist: *Les Caractères ou les Mœurs de Ce Siècle* (1688)

It's a great life if you don't weaken.
John Buchan 1875–1940 Scottish novelist, governor-general of Canada 1935–40: *Mr Standfast* (1919)

All that is necessary for the triumph of evil women is that good women do nothing.
on The Rt Hon Harriet Harman QC MP, a British radical feminist Labour party politician with very pretty eyes, and her like: *David and Goliatha: David Cameron – heir to Harman?* (2010)

It has become clear that the ultimate goal of leading radical feminists such as Harriet Harman never was equality of opportunity. That was simply a stage on the journey to what they really wanted, the ultimate validation of their dire philosophy: superiority of *outcome* for women. And if the happiness of the vast majority of British men and women has to be sacrificed to deliver that result, along with the economic viability of the country, well, that's a small price to pay.
The Glass Ceiling Delusion: the real reasons more women don't reach senior positions (2011)
Mike Buchanan 1957– British writer, skydiver, winemaker, critic of radical feminism and political correctness

Beneath the rule of men entirely great,
The pen is mightier than the sword.
Edward Bulwer-Lytton 1803–73 British novelist and politician: *Richelieu* (1839)

If Louisa May Alcott had really been sound, she'd have written a trilogy, and called the last one *Divorced Lesbian Sluts*.
Julie Burchill 1960– English journalist and writer: *Independent* 30 December 1995

So that's seven books I've written. Not bad for someone who's only read three.
George Burns 1896–1996 American comedian, actor, and writer: *All My Best Friends* (1989)

A loose, plain, rude writer... I call a spade a spade.
Robert Burton 1577–1640 English clergyman and scholar: *The Anatomy of Melancholy* (1621-51)

What literature can and should do is change the people who teach the people who don't read the books.
A S Byatt 1936– English novelist: interview in *Newsweek* 5 June 1995

A man must serve his time to every trade
Save censure – critics all are ready made.
    English Bards and Scotch Reviewers (1809)

I hate things all *fiction*... there should always be some foundation of fact for the most airy fabric and pure invention is but the talent of a liar.
    letter to John Murray, his publisher, 2 April 1817

The poem will please if it is lively – if it is stupid it will fail – but I will have none of your damned cutting and slashing.
    letter to John Murray, 6 April 1819

'Tis strange – but true. For truth is always strange;
Stranger than fiction.
    Don Juan (1819–24)
Lord Byron 1788–1824 English poet

You praise the firm restraint with which they write –
I'm with you there, of course:
They use the snaffle and the curb all right,
But where's the bloody horse?
Roy Campbell 1901–57 South African poet: 'On Some South African Novelists' (1930)

That's not writing, that's typing.
    on the work of Jack Kerouac (attr.)
Truman Capote 1924–84 American writer and novelist

What a sad want I am in of libraries, of books to gather facts from! Why is there not a Majesty's library in every county town? There is a Majesty's jail and gallows in every one.
    diary entry, 18 May 1832

A good book is the purest essence of a human soul.
    speech in support of the London Library, 24 June 1840

Blessed is he who has found his work. Let him ask no other blessing.
Thomas Carlyle 1795–1881 Scottish historian and political philosopher

'Where shall I begin, please your Majesty?' he asked. 'Begin at the beginning', the King said, gravely, 'and go on till you come to the end: then stop.'

'What is the use of a book', thought Alice, 'without pictures or conversations?'
Lewis Carroll (Charles Lutwidge Dodgson) 1832–98 English writer and logician: *Alice's Adventures in Wonderland* (1865)

I tell you there is such a thing as creative hate!
Willa Cather 1873–1947 American novelist: *The Song of the Lark* (1915)

Coleridge was a drug addict. Poe was an alcoholic. Marlowe was stabbed by a man whom he was treacherously trying to stab. Pope took money to keep a woman's name out of a satire; then wrote a piece so that she could still be recognised anyhow. Chatterton killed himself. Byron was accused of incest. Do you still want to be a writer – and if so, *why*?
Bennett Cerf 1898–1971 American humorist: *Shake Well Before Using* (1948)

When in doubt have a man come through the door with a gun in his hand.
(attributed)

If my books had been any worse, I should not have been invited to Hollywood, and if they had been any better, I should not have come.
letter to Charles W Morton, 12 December 1945

The more you reason, the less you create.
letter, 28 October 1947
Raymond Chandler 1888–1959 American detective fiction writer

The original writer is not he who refrains from imitating others, but he who can be imitated by none.
François-René Chateaubriand 1768–1848 French writer and diplomat: *Le Génie du Christianisme* (1802)

Authors with a mortgage never get writer's block.
Mavis Cheek 1948–: in *Bookseller* 19 September 2003

A writer must be as objective as a chemist: he must abandon the subjective line; he must know that dung-heaps play a very reasonable part in a landscape, and that evil passions are as inherent in life as good ones.
Anton Chekhov 1860–1904 Russian dramatist and short-story writer: letter to MS Kiselev, 14 January 1887

There is no such thing on earth as an uninteresting subject; the only thing that can exist is an uninterested person.
Heretics (1905)

The men who really believe in themselves are all in lunatic asylums.
Orthodoxy (1908)

Hardy went down to botanise in the swamp, while Meredith climbed towards the sun. Meredith became, at his best, a sort of daintily dressed Walt Whitman: Hardy became a sort of village atheist brooding and blaspheming over the village idiot.
The Victorian Age in Literature (1912)

He had long held one of the most fundamental of all literary convictions, that the world owed him a living.

A good novel tells us the truth about its hero; but a bad novel tells us the truth about its author.

There is a great deal of difference between an eager man who wants to read a book and the tired man who wants a book to read.
GK Chesterton 1874–1936 English essayist, novelist, and poet

Mr Gladstone read Homer for fun, which I thought served him right.
  My Early Life (1930)

I confess myself to be a great admirer of tradition. The longer you can look back, the farther you can look forward.
  speech, March 1944

This is the sort of English up with which I will not put.
  after an official had gone through one of his papers moving prepositions away from the ends of sentences
  Ernest Gowers *Plain Words* (1948): 'Troubles with Prepositions'

Broadly speaking, the short words are the best, and the old words best of all.

Success is the ability to go from one failure to another with no loss of enthusiasm.
Winston Churchill 1874–1965 British Conservative statesman, soldier, painter, writer

As repressed sadists are supposed to become policemen or butchers, so those with an irrational fear of life become publishers.
  Enemies of Promise (1938)

He could not blow his nose without moralising on the state of the handkerchief industry.
  of George Orwell: *Sunday Times* 29 September 1968

Better to write for yourself and have no public, than to write for the public and have no self.
Cyril Connolly 1903–74 English writer

My task which I am trying to achieve is by the power of the written word, to make you hear, to make you feel – it is, before all, to make you *see*. That – and no more, and it is everything.
  The Nigger of the Narcissus (1897) preface

For me, writing – *the only possible writing* – is just simply the conversion of nervous force into phrases.
  letter, October 1903
Joseph Conrad 1857–1924 Polish-born English novelist

Nothing in the world can take the place of persistence. Talent will not; nothing is more common than unsuccessful men with talent. Genius will not; unrewarded genius is almost a proverb. Education will not; the world is full of educated derelicts. Persistence and determination are omnipotent. The slogan 'press on' has solved and always will solve the problems of the human race.
Calvin Coolidge 1872–1933 American Republican statesman: attributed

In America only the successful writer is important, in France all writers are important, in England no writers are important, and in Australia you have to explain what a writer is.
Geoffrey Cottrell

'Till authors hear at length, one gen'ral cry,
Tickle and entertain us, or we die.
The loud demand from year to year the same,
Beggars invention and makes fancy lame.
William Cowper 1731–1800 English poet: 'Retirement' (1782)

Quality has to be caused, not controlled.
Philip Crosby 1926–2001 American businessman and author: *Reflections on Quality* (1995)

A truly great book should be read in youth, again in maturity and once more in old age, as a fine building should be seen by morning light, at noon and by moonlight.
Robertson Davies 1913–95 Canadian novelist

It has been my experience that one cannot, in any shape or form, depend on human relations for lasting reward. It is only work that truly satisfies.
Bette Davis 1908–89 American actress: *The Lonely Life* (1962)

It is not enough to have a good mind; the main thing is to use it well.

The reading of good books is like a conversation with the best men of past centuries – in fact like a prepared conversation, in which they reveal only the best of their thoughts.
René Descartes 1596–1650 French philosopher and mathematician: *Le Discours de la Méthode* (1637)

If I had to select one quality, one personal characteristic that I regard as being highly correlated with success, whatever the field, I would pick the trait of persistence. Determination. The will to endure to the end, to get knocked down seventy times and get up off the floor saying, 'Here comes number seventy-one!'
Richard M DeVos 1955– American businessman and politician

[Author's note: hopefully Mr DeVos won't give this advice to his two sons, should they take up boxing.]

There is no Frigate like a Book
To take us Lands away
Nor any Coursers like a Page
Of prancing Poetry.
Emily Dickinson 1830–86 American poet: 'A Book (2)' c. 1873

I write entirely to find out what I'm thinking, what I'm looking at, what I see and what it means. What I want and what I fear.
Joan Didion 1934– American writer

I don't really read books: there's not enough space in my life. When I have an empty space in my brain, it's cool, it's OK. I don't want to fill it with anything.
Celine Dion 1968– French-Canadian *chanteuse*: *Sunday Times Magazine*, October 1999

When I want to read a novel, I write one.
  W Monypenny and G Buckle: *Life of Benjamin Disraeli* (1920)

You know who the critics are? The men who have failed in literature and art.
  Lothair (1870)

An author who speaks about his own books is almost as bad as a mother who talks about her own children.
  at a banquet in 1873

The best way to become acquainted with a subject is to write a book about it.
Benjamin Disraeli 1804–81 British Tory statesman and novelist

It is with publishers as with wives: one always wants someone else's.
Norman Douglas 1868–1952 Scottish-born novelist and essayist: quoted in *The Frank Muir Book* (1968)

Quality in a product or service is not what the supplier puts in. It is what the customer gets out and is willing to pay for. A product is not quality because it is hard to make and costs a lot of money, as manufacturers typically believe. This is incompetence. Customers pay only for what is of use to them and gives them value. Nothing else constitutes quality.
Peter Drucker 1909–2005 American writer of Austrian-Hungarian extraction, management consultant, and self-described 'social ecologist'

Great wits are sure to madness near allied,
And thin partitions do their bounds divide.
John Dryden 1631–1700 English poet, critic, and dramatist: *Absalom and Achitopel* (1681)

In language, the ignorant have prescribed laws to the learned.
Richard Duppa 1770–1831 English artist and writer: *Maxims* (1830)

Men like women who write. Even though they don't say so. A writer is a foreign country.
Marguerite Duras 1914–96 French writer: *Practicalities* (1987)

Genius is one per cent inspiration, ninety-nine per cent perspiration.
Thomas Edison 1847–1931 American inventor: said c. 1903

Imagination is more important than knowledge.
Albert Einstein 1879–1955 German-born theoretical physicist: *Saturday Evening Post* 26 October 1929

Books are the quietest and most constant of friends; they are the most accessible and wisest of counsellors, and the most patient of teachers.
Charles W Eliot 1834–1926 American academic: *The Happy Life* (1896)

Is it so bad, then, to be misunderstood? Pythagoras was misunderstood, and Socrates, and Jesus, and Luther, and Copernicus, and Galileo, and Newton, and every pure and wise spirit that ever took flesh. To be great is to be misunderstood.
Essays (1841)

[Author's note: my uncle Henry is frequently misunderstood, but you wouldn't call him great. Stupid, possibly, but not great.]

The reward of a thing well done, is to have done it.
Essays: Second Series (1844)

Art is a jealous mistress.
The Conduct of Life (1860)

In the highest civilisation, the book is still the highest delight. He who has once known its satisfactions is provided with a resource against calamity.
Letters and Social Aims (1876)
Ralph Waldo Emerson 1803–82 American philosopher and poet

The central function of imaginative literature is to make you realise that other people act on moral convictions different from your own.
William Empson 1906–84 English poet and literary critic: *Milton's God* (1981)

If you can react the same way to winning and losing, that is a big accomplishment. That quality is important because it stays with you the rest of your life.
Chris Evert 1954– attractive American tennis player of the female persuasion

It would be equally correct to say that sheep are born carnivorous, and everywhere they nibble grass.
commenting on Rousseau's 'Man was born free, and everywhere he is in chains'
Émile Faguet 1847–1916 French writer and critic

The writer's only responsibility is to his art. He will be completely ruthless if he is a good one... if a writer has to rob his mother, he will not hesitate; the *Ode on a Grecian Urn* is worth any number of old ladies.
William Faulkner 1897–1962 American novelist: *Paris Review* spring 1956

The pen is mightier than the sword, and considerably easier to write with.
Marty Feldman 1934–82 English comedy writer, comedian, and actor

Writers should be read and not seen. Rarely are they a winsome sight.
Edna Ferber 1885–1968 American writer

What I cannot create, I cannot understand.
Richard Feynman 1918–88 American theoretical physicist (attributed)

If at first you don't succeed, try, try again. Then quit. No use being a damned fool about it.
WC Fields 1880–1946 American humorist (attributed)

The way British publishing works is that you go from not being published no matter how good you are, to being published no matter how bad you are.
Tibor Fischer 1959– British novelist

I've been drunk for about a week now, and I thought it might sober me up to sit in a library.
F Scott Fitzgerald 1896–1940 American novelist: *The Great Gatsby* (1925)

Books are made not like children but like pyramids… and they're just as useless! and they stay in the desert!… Jackals piss at their foot and the bourgeois climb up on them.
Gustave Flaubert 1821–80 French novelist: letter to Ernest Feydeau, November/December 1857

Normal is not something to aspire to, it's something to get away from.
Jodie Foster 1962– American actress, film producer, and director

Writing is easy. All you have to do is stare at a blank piece of paper until drops of blood form on your forehead.
Gene Fowler 1890–1960 American journalist, author, and dramatist

When a thing has been said and well said, have no scruple: take it and copy it.

Never lend books; no one ever returns them. The only books I have in my library are books other people have lent me.
Anatole France 1844–1924 French novelist and man of letters

Sometimes a cigar is just a cigar.
Sigmund Freud 1856–1939 Austrian psychiatrist

Seventeen publishers rejected the manuscript, at which time we knew we had something pretty hot.
Richard S 'Kinky' Friedman 1944– American singer, songwriter, novelist, humorist, politician, and columnist

No tears in the writer, no tears in the reader.
No surprise for the writer, no surprise for the reader.
  Collected Poems (1939) 'The Figure a Poem Makes'
Robert Frost 1874–1963 American poet

An original idea. That can't be too hard. The library must be full of them.
Stephen Fry 1957– English actor, writer, journalist, comedian, television presenter, and film director: *The Liar* (1991)

It is a far, far better thing to have a firm anchor in nonsense than to put out on the troubled seas of thought.
JK Galbraith 1908–2006 American economist: *The Affluent Society* (1958)

It is the quality of our work which will please God and not the quantity.

I believe in equality for everyone, except reporters and photographers.
Mahatma Gandhi 1869–1948 Indian political and spiritual leader

I'll not listen to reason… Reason always means what someone else has got to say.
Elizabeth Gaskell 1810–65 English novelist: *Cranford* (1853)

The great thing about a computer notebook is that no matter how much you stuff into it, it doesn't get bigger or heavier.
Bill Gates 1955– American business magnate, philanthropist, author, chairman of Microsoft: *Business @ The Speed of Thought* (1999)

We will discover the nature of our particular genius when we stop trying to conform to our own or to other peoples' models, learn to be ourselves, and allow our natural channel to open.
Shakti Gawain 1948– American authoress

What we need is hatred. From it our ideas are born.
Jean Genet 1910–86 French novelist, poet, and dramatist: *The Blacks* (1959)

Unprovided with original learning, unformed in the habits of thinking, unskilled in the arts of composition, I resolved to write a book.
Edward Gibbon 1737–94 English historian

The first thing a writer has to do is find another source of income.
Ellen Gilchrist 1935– American novelist, short-story writer, and poet

Mr Quarmby laughed in a peculiar way, which was the result of long years of mirth-subdual in the Reading-room.
George Gissing 1857–1903 English novelist: *New Grub Street* (1891)

There's no greater bliss in life than when the plumber eventually comes to unblock your drains. No writer can give that sort of pleasure.
Victoria Glendinning 1937– English biographer and novelist: *Observer* 3 January 1993

The deed is all, the glory nothing.
Johann Wolfgang von Goethe 1749–1832 German poet, novelist, and dramatist: *Faust* (1832)

Blanche Deveraux: I have writer's block. It's the worst feeling in the world.
Sophia Petrillo: Try ten days without a bowel movement sometime.
The Golden Girls

A man does not achieve the status of Galileo merely because he is persecuted: he must also be right.
Stephen Jay Gould 1941–2002 American palaeontologist: *Ever Since Darwin* (1977)

Imaginative readers rewrite books to suit their own taste, omitting and mentally altering what they read.
Robert Graves 1895–1985 English poet: *The Reader Over Your Shoulder* (1947)

Any fool may write a most valuable book by chance, if he will only tell us what he heard and saw with veracity.
Thomas Gray 1761–71 English poet: letter to Horace Walpole, 25 February 1768

There is a splinter of ice in the heart of a writer.
Graham Greene 1904–91 English novelist: *A Sort of Life* (1971)

The key part of your brand is a quality product. Creating exceptional content is the number one thing.
Rufus Griscom [Author's note: an American chap, I believe: *Building Buzz for Your Web Project, SXSW* (2006)]

Climb ev'ry mountain, ford ev'ry stream,
Follow ev'ry rainbow, till you find your dream!
Oscar Hammerstein II 1895–1960 American songwriter: *Climb Ev'ry Mountain* (1959 song)

Asking a working writer what he thinks about critics is like asking a lamp-post what it feels about dogs.
Christopher Hampton 1946– British playwright: *Sunday Times Magazine* 16 October 1977

It's red hot, mate. I hate to think of this sort of book getting into the wrong hands. As soon as I've finished this, I shall recommend they ban it.
Tony Hancock 1924–68 British actor and comedian: *Hancock's Half Hour*

If this sort of thing continues, no more novel-writing for me. A man must be a fool to deliberately stand up and be shot at.
of a hostile review of *Tess of the D'Urbervilles*, 1891
Thomas Hardy 1840–1928 English novelist and poet: Florence Hardy *The Early Life of Thomas Hardy* (1928)

Equality, blah, blah, blah, glass ceiling, blah, blah, blah, sexism, blah, blah, blah, discrimination, blah, blah, blah, ageism, blah, blah, blah . . .

[Author's note: the above is a précis of Harriet Harman's speeches, interviews, and writings, 1982–]

What must men do... They will have to... They will have to... Then they will feel able to... They must begin to... They must dramatically increase... They must... Men must... They must... They must... they must...
Extracts from three successive paragraphs in Harriet Harman's *The Century Gap (20th Century Man, 21st Century Woman* (1993), in a section titled 'Men Contributing More'. Available from Amazon resellers for £0.01 (plus postage and packaging).

[Author's note: on behalf of men everywhere, may I respond feebly with, 'But *why* must we, Mistress Harriet? What will happen to us if we don't?']

Harriet Harman 1950– attractive British radical feminist Labour party politician (1982–)

America is now given over to a damned mob of scribbling women.
Nathaniel Hawthorne 1804–64 American novelist

My mother drew a distinction between achievement and success. She said that, 'achievement is the knowledge that you have studied and worked hard and done the best that is in you. Success is being praised by others, and that's nice, too, but not as important or satisfying. Always aim for achievement and forget about success.'
Helen Hayes 1900–93 American actress

No author is a man of genius to his publisher.
(attributed)

Wherever books will be burned, men also, in the end, will be burned.
Almansor (1823)
Heinrich Heine 1797–1856 German poet

All modern American literature comes from one book by Mark Twain called *Huckleberry Finn*.
Green Hills of Africa (1935)

The most essential gift for a writer is a built-in, shock-proof shit detector. This is the writer's radar, and all great writers have had it.
Paris Review spring 1958
Ernest Hemingway 1899–1961 American novelist

The defendant, Mr Haddock, is, among other things, an author, which fact should alone dispose you in the plaintiff's favour.
AP Herbert 1890–1971 English writer and humorist: *Misleading Cases* (1935)

Woe be to him that reads but one book.
George Herbert 1593–1633 English poet and clergyman

Do give books – religious or otherwise – for Christmas. They're never fattening, seldom sinful, and permanently personal.
Lenore Hershey

Between us and excellence, the gods have placed the sweat of our brows.
Hesiod Greek poet, 7th century BC: *Works and Days*

I always had my nose in a book. My parents couldn't afford Kleenex.
Joe Hickman

We must know.
We will know.
David Hilbert 1862–1943 German mathematician: epitaph on his tombstone

Why buy a book when you can join a lending library?
Benny Hill 1924–92 English comedian, actor, and singer

Everyone has a book in them and that, in most cases, is where it should stay.
Christopher Hitchens 1949– English-American author and journalist

The praise of ancient authors proceeds not from the reverence of the dead, but from the competition, and mutual envy of the living.
Thomas Hobbes 1588–1679 English philosopher: *Leviathan* (1651)

When people are free to do as they please, they usually imitate each other. Originality is deliberate and forced, and partakes of the nature of a protest.
  Passionate State of Mind (1955)

They who lack talent expect things to happen without effort. They ascribe failure to a lack of inspiration or ability, or to misfortune, rather than to insufficient application. At the core of every true talent there is an awareness of the difficulties inherent in any achievement, and the confidence that by persistence and patience something worthwhile will be realized. Thus talent is a species of vigor.
Eric Hoffer 1902–83 American social writer and philosopher

When I think of talking, it is of course with a woman. For talking at its best being an inspiration, it wants a corresponding divine quality of receptiveness, and where will you find this but in a woman?
Oliver Wendell Holmes 1809–94 American physician, professor, lecturer, and author

Life-transforming ideas have always come to me through books.
bell hooks (Gloria Jean Watkins) 1952– American author, feminist, and social activist: *O Magazine* December 2003

He has gained every point who has mixed profit with pleasure, by delighting the reader at the same time as instructing him.
Horace (Quintus Horatius Flaccus) 65–8 BC Roman poet: *Ars Poetica*

Three minutes' thought would suffice to find this out; but thought is irksome and three minutes is a long time.
AE Housman 1859–1936 English poet: *D Iunii Iurenalis Saturae* (1905) preface

How many a man has thrown up his hands at a time when a little more effort, a little more patience would have achieved success?
Elbert Hubbard 1856–1915 American writer, publisher, artist, and philosopher

Popularity? It is glory's small change.
  Ruy Blas (1838)

An invasion of armies can be resisted, but not an idea whose time has come.
  Histoire d'un Crime (written 1851–2, published 1877)

Imagination is intelligence with an erection.
Victor Hugo 1802–85 French poet, novelist, and dramatist

Beauty is no quality in things themselves; it exists merely in the mind which contemplates them.
David Hume 1711–76 Scottish philosopher, historian, and writer

The prigs who attack Jeffrey Archer should bear in mind that we all, to some extent, reinvent ourselves. Jeffrey has just gone to a bit more trouble.
Barry Humphries 1934– Australian entertainer: *Observer* 19 December 1999 'They said what…?'

The proper study of mankind is books.
  Crome Yellow (1921)

Those who believe that they are exclusively in the right are generally those who achieve something.
Proper Studies (1927)
Aldous Huxley 1894–1963 English novelist

If a little knowledge is dangerous, where is the man who has so much as to be out of danger?
'On Elementary Instruction in Physiology' (1877)

Logical consequences are the scarecrows of fools and the beacons of wise men.
Science and Culture and Other Essays (1881)

The necessity of making things plain to uninstructed people was one of the very best means of clearing up the obscure corners in one's own mind.
Man's Place in Nature (1894) preface
TH Huxley 1825–95 English biologist

One almost begins to feel that the reason some women worked feverishly to get into men's clubs is to have a respite from the womanised world feminists have created.
Carol Iannone American conservative writer and literary critic: *Good Order* (1994) ed. Brad Miner 'The Feminist Perversion'

What is originality? Undetected plagiarism.
William Ralph Inge 1860–1954 English writer, Dean of St Paul's 1911–34: *Labels and Libels* (1929)

Margaret Thatcher sounds like *The Book of Revelations* read out over a railway station public address system by a headmistress of a certain age wearing calico knickers.
Clive James 1939– Australian critic, novelist, TV presenter, poet, and essayist

Summer afternoon. The two most beautiful words in the English language.
Henry James 1843–1916 Anglo-American writer

I believe that political correctness can be a form of linguistic fascism, and it sends shivers down the spine of my generation who went to war against fascism.
PD James 1920– English writer of detective stories: *Paris Review* (1995)

The moral flabbiness born of the exclusive worship of the bitch-goddess *success.*
William James 1842–1910 American philosopher: letter to HG Wells 11 September 1906

All any author wants from a review is six thousand words of closely reasoned adulation.
Sir Antony Jay 1930– English writer: speech at a booksellers' luncheon, Birmingham (1967)

I find that the harder I work, the more luck I seem to have.
Thomas Jefferson 1743–1826 American Democratic-Republican Party co-founder and statesman, political philosopher

I like work: it fascinates me. I can sit and look at it for hours. I love to keep it by me: the idea of getting rid of it almost breaks my heart.
Jerome K Jerome 1859–1927 English writer: *Three Men in a Boat* (1889)

Be a yardstick of quality. Some people aren't used to an environment where excellence is expected.
Steve Jobs 1955– American business magnate and inventor, co-founder, and chief executive officer of Apple

A man may write at any time, if he will set himself doggedly to it.

A man ought to read just as inclination takes him; for what he reads as a task will do him little good.

Why, Sir, if you were to read Richardson for the story, your impatience would be so much fretted that you would hang yourself.

Every man has a lurking wish to appear considerable in his native place.

He was dull in a new way, and that made many people think him *great*.
Of Thomas Gray

I never think I have hit hard, unless it rebounds.

The greatest part of a writer's time is spent in reading, in order to write: a man will turn over half a library to make one book.

No man but a blockhead ever wrote, except for money.

Why, that is because, dearest, you're a dunce.
to Miss Monckton, later Lady Corke, who said that Laurence Sterne's writings affected her
James Boswell *Life of Samuel Johnson* (1791)

What is written without effort is in general read without pleasure.
William Seward: *Biographia* (1791)

The only end of writing is to enable the readers better to endure life, or better to enjoy it.
A Free Enquiry (1757)

He whom nature has made weak, and idleness keeps ignorant, may yet support his vanity by the name of critic.
The Idler 9 June 1759
Samuel Johnson 1709–84 English poet, critic, and lexicographer

The worst thing about new books is that they keep us from reading the old ones.
Joseph Joubert 1754–1824 French moralist and essayist

One man is as good as another until he has written a book.
Benjamin Jowett 1817–93 English classicist

Writing in English is the most ingenious torture ever devised for sins committed in previous lives. The English reading public explains the reason why.
James Joyce 1882–1941 Irish novelist: letter, 5 September 1918

Many suffer from the incurable disease of writing, and it becomes chronic in their sick minds.
Juvenal 60–130 Roman satirist: *Satires*

A book should serve as an axe for the frozen sea within us.
Franz Kafka 1883–1924 Czech novelist

Writing is like the world's oldest profession. First you do it for your own enjoyment. Then you do it for a few friends. Eventually, you figure, what the hell, I might as well get paid for it.
Irma Kalish

Dare to know! Have the courage to use your own reason! This is the motto of the Enlightenment.
Immanuel Kant 1724–1804 German philosopher: *What Is Enlightenment?* (1784)

For the sake of a few fine imaginative or domestic passages, are we to be bullied into a certain philosophy engendered in the whims of an egotist?
    on the overbearing influence of Wordsworth upon his contemporaries
    letter to JH Reynolds, 3 February 1818

If poetry comes not as naturally as the leaves to a tree it had better not come at all.
    letter to John Taylor, 27 February 1818

That which is creative must create itself.
    letter to Hessey, 8 October 1818

Fine writing is next to fine doing the top thing in the world.
    letter to JH Reynolds 24 August 1819
John Keats 1795–1821 English poet

Few men are willing to brave the disapproval of their fellows, the censure of their colleagues, the wrath of their society. Moral courage is a rarer commodity than bravery in battle or great intelligence. Yet it is the one essential, vital quality for those who seek to change a world which yields most painfully to change.
Robert F Kennedy 1925–68 American politician

If you don't have the time to read, you don't have the time or the tools to write.

If you want to be a writer, you must do two things above all others: read a lot and write a lot... I usually get through 70 or 80 books a year, mostly fiction. I don't read in order to study the craft; I read because I like to read.
Stephen King 1947– American writer: *On Writing* (2000)

I keep six honest serving-men
(They taught me all I knew);
Their names are Why and What and When
And How and Where and Who.
Rudyard Kipling 1865–1936 English writer and poet: *Just So Stories* (1902)

A writer's ambition should be... to trade a hundred contemporary readers for ten readers in ten years' time and for one reader in a hundred years.
Arthur Koestler 1905–83 Hungarian-born writer: *New York Times Book Review* 1 April 1951

When my sonnet was rejected, I exclaimed, 'Damn the age; I will write for Antiquity!'

Books think for me.
Last Essays of Elia (1833)
Charles Lamb 1775–1834 English writer

Mr Cobb took me into his library and showed me his books, of which he had a complete set.
Ring Lardner 1885–1933 American writer: RE Drennan *Wit's End* (1973)

Deprivation is for me what daffodils were for Wordsworth.
Required Writing (1983)

I am afraid the compulsion to write poems left me about seven years ago, since when I have written almost nothing. Naturally this is a disappointment, but I would sooner write no poems than bad poems.
Letter, 11 August 1984

When I get sent manuscripts from aspiring poets, I do one of two things: if there is no stamped self-addressed envelope, I throw it into the bin. If there is, I write and tell them to fuck off.
Philip Larkin 1922–85 English poet

Keep right on to the end of the road,
Keep right on to the end.
Tho' the way be long, let your heart be strong,
Keep right on round the bend.
Harry Lauder 1870–1950 Scottish music-hall entertainer: 'The End of the Road' (1924 song)

When I read Shakespeare I am struck with wonder
That such trivial people should muse and thunder
In such lovely language.
'When I read Shakespeare' (1929)

If you try to nail anything down in the novel, either it kills the novel, or the novel gets up and walks away with the nail.
Phoenix (1936)
DH Lawrence 1885–1930 English novelist and poet

The best fame is a writer's fame: it's enough to get a table at a good restaurant, but not enough that you get interrupted when you eat.
Observer 30 May 1993

Your life story would not make a good book. Don't even try.
Fran Lebowitz 1950– American writer

Hilary Clinton said in her book it was a challenge to forgive Bill, but she figured if Nelson Mandela could forgive, she could give it a try. Isn't that amazing? I didn't know Clinton hit on Mandela's wife.
Jay Leno 1950– American comedian and television host

There's only one real sin, and that is to persuade oneself that the second-best is anything but the second-best.
Doris Lessing 1919– British novelist and short-story writer

Don't use words too big for the subject. Don't say 'infinitely' when you mean 'very'; otherwise you'll have no word left when you want to talk about something really infinite.

Even in literature and art, no man who bothers about originality will ever be original: whereas if you simply try to tell the truth (without caring twopence how often it has been told before) you will, nine times out of ten, become original without ever having noticed it.
CS Lewis 1898–1963 English literary scholar

Some things in life are bad,
They can really make you mad.
Other things just make you swear and curse.
When you're chewing on life's gristle,
Don't grumble, give a whistle,
And this'll help things turn out for the best,
And always look on the bright side of life.

Life's a piece of shit,
When you look at it.
Life's a laugh and death's a joke, it's true.
You'll see it's all a show,
Keep 'em laughing as you go.
Just remember that the last laugh is on you,
And always look on the bright side of life.
Life of Brian 1979 'Always Look on the Bright Side of Life' (song)

People who like this sort of thing will find this the sort of thing they like.
  judgement of a book
  GWE Russell *Collections and Recollections* (1898)

So you're the little woman who wrote the book that made this great war!
  on meeting Harriet Beecher Stowe, author of *Uncle Tom's Cabin*
Abraham Lincoln 1809–65 American Republican statesman

The quality of a person's life is in direct proportion to their commitment to excellence, regardless of their chosen field of endeavour.
Vincent T Lombardi (1930–70) American football coach

All books are either dreams or swords,
You can cut, or you can drug, with words.
Amy Lowell 1874–1925 American poet: 'Sword Blades and Poppy Seed' (1914)

Nothing can be created out of nothing.
Lucretius 94–55 BC Roman poet: *De Rerum Natura*

If all the earth were paper white
And all the sea were ink
'Twere not enough for me to write
As my poor heart doth think
John Lyly 1554–1606 English poet and dramatist

Yer pashin' doon ma leg!

I didnae come doon the Clyde on a wotter biscuit!
Ellen MacPartlane (1970–) beautiful and witty Scottish lady who worked for the author when he worked as a business consultant for Grant's Whisky, near Glasgow, in 1995 [Author's note: I had said something which she had taken to be a joke, and she responded with the first of the above lines. Spotting my puzzlement, she claimed at first that it was a Gaelic expression, then burst out laughing and explained it was a common Glaswegian saying, roughly translated into polite English as, 'You have to be joking!' Whenever she felt someone was treating her with less seriousness than she deemed appropriate she would respond with the second line.]

Writing books is the closest men ever come to child-bearing.
Norman Mailer 1923–2007 American novelist and essayist

This book is dedicated to my brilliant and beautiful wife without whom I would be nothing. She always comforts and consoles, never complains or interferes, asks nothing and endures all. She also writes my dedications.
Albert Malvino

Resolve to edge in a little reading every day, if it is but a single sentence. If you gain fifteen minutes a day, it will make itself felt at the end of the year.
Horace Mann 1796–1859

A writer is a person for whom writing is more difficult than it is for other people.
Thomas Mann 1875–1955 American educationalist

I'm a writer first and a woman after.
Katherine Mansfield 1888–1923 New Zealand-born short-story writer: letter to John Middleton Murray, July 1917

The world must be all fucked up when men travel first class and literature goes as freight.
Gabriel García Márquez 1928– Colombian novelist: *One Hundred Years of Solitude* (1967)

If you want to get rich from writing, write the sort of thing that's read by persons who move their lips when reading.
Don Marquis 1878–1937 American poet and journalist (attributed)

I like a woman with a head on her shoulders. I hate necks.
Steve Martin 1945– American actor, comedian, writer, playwright, producer, musician, and composer

From the moment I picked up your book until I laid it down, I was convulsed with laughter. Some day I intend reading it.

I find television very educating. Every time somebody turns on the set, I go into the other room and read a book.

Outside of a dog, a book is man's best friend. Inside of a dog it's too dark to read.
Groucho Marx 1890–1977 American film comedian

When I read a book I seem to read it with my eyes only, but now and then I come across a passage, perhaps only a phrase, which has a meaning for me, and it becomes part of me.
Of Human Bondage (1915)

An author spends months writing a book, and maybe puts his heart's blood into it, and then it lies about unread till the reader has nothing else in the world to do.
The Razor's Edge (1943)
W Somerset Maugham 1874–1965 English novelist

The mind of man is capable of anything.
Guy de Maupassant 1850–93 French novelist and short-story writer: 'The Tress of Hair' (1884)

Writers should be read, but neither seen nor heard.
Daphne du Maurier 1907–1989 English author and playwright

The reader's fancy makes the fate of books.
Terentianus Maurus Roman writer of the late 2nd century AD

Fame is an accident; merit a thing absolute.
Herman Melville 1819–01 American poet and novelist: *Mardi* (1849)

Gutenberg made everyone a reader. Xerox made everyone a publisher.
Marshall McLuhan 1911–80 Canadian communications scholar: *Guardian Weekly* 12 June 1977

Why did you bring that book that I didn't want to be read to out of up for?
HL Mencken 1880–1956 American journalist and literary critic

The adjuration to be 'normal' seems shockingly repellent to me; I see neither hope nor comfort in sinking to that low level. I think it is ignorance that makes people think of abnormality only with horror and allows them to remain undismayed at the proximity of 'normal' to average and mediocre. For surely anyone who achieves anything is, essentially, abnormal.
Dr Karl Menninger 1893–1990 American psychiatrist

If all mankind minus one were of one opinion, and only one person were of the contrary opinion, mankind would be no more justified in silencing that one person, than he, if he had the power, would be justified in silencing mankind.
On Liberty (1859)

Ask yourself whether you are happy, and you cease to be so.
Autobiography (1873)
John Stuart Mill 1806–73 English philosopher and economist

Eeyore was saying to himself, 'This writing business. Pencils and what-not. Over-rated, if you ask me. Silly stuff. Nothing in it.'
AA Milne 1882–1956 English writer for children: *Winnie-the-Pooh* (1926)

A good book is the precious life-blood of a master spirit, embalmed and treasured up on purpose to a life beyond life.

As good almost kill a man as kill a good book: who kills a man kills a reasonable creature, God's image; but he who destroys a good book, kills reason itself, kills the image of God, as it were in the eye.
Areopagitica (1644)

The mind is its own place, and in itself
Can make a heaven of hell, a hell of heaven.
Paradise Lost (1667)
John Milton 1608–74 English poet

If you steal from one author, it's plagiarism; if you steal from many, it's research.
Wilson Mizner 1876–1933 American dramatist: Alva Johnston *The Legendary Mizners* (1953)

I always write a good first line, but I have trouble in writing the others.
Les Précieuses Ridicules (1659)

Reading and marriage don't go well together.
Molière (Jean-Baptiste Poquelin) 1622–73 French comic dramatist: *Les Femmes Savantes* (1672)

When I am attacked by gloomy thoughts, nothing helps me so much as running to my books. They quickly absorb me and banish the clouds from my mind.

There is more business in interpreting interpretations than in interpreting things, and more books on books than on any other subject: all we do is gloss each other. All is a-swarm with commentaries: of authors there is a dearth.
Michel de Montaigne 1533–92 French moralist and essayist: *Essais* (1580)

'You want to be a writer?' my father said. 'My dear boy, have some consideration for your poor wife. You'll be sitting around the house all day, wearing a dressing-gown, brewing tea, and stumped for words.'
John Mortimer 1923–2009 English novelist, barrister, and dramatist: *Clinging to the Wreckage* (1982)

Erratum. In my article on the Price of Milk, 'Horses' should have read 'Cows' throughout.
JB Morton 1893–1979 English humorous writer: *The Best of Beachcomber* (1963)

Oxymoron is a literary device whereby two contradictory concepts are juxtaposed: as for example in 'the witty Jane Austen'.
Patrick Murray

[Author's note: the last quotation is an example of one from an individual with no biographical details provided in the source I used. Wikipedia has four people with this name who lived after the publication of Jane Austen's works. I shall leave it for you to guess the most likely candidate:

(1) The Irish Roman Catholic theologian (1811–82).
(2) The Canadian lumber merchant and politician (1880–). Note that in the absence of a year of death, according to the ever-reliable Wikipedia the man is still alive, and currently 131 years old. I'll be happy to send him a complimentary copy of this book if he writes to me and encloses a copy of his birth certificate along with a written statement from his father to confirm it's a genuine copy.
(3) The English actor (1956–) who played the role of Mickey Pearce in the situation comedy *Only Fools and Horses*.
(4) The reggae singer and toaster Pato Banton (b. Patrick Murray) (1960–); a rare example of a person having a line of employment which has unfortunately been made obsolete by a cheap kitchen appliance.]

He mobilised the English language and sent it into battle to steady his fellow countrymen and hearten those Europeans upon whom the long dark night of tyranny had descended.
  of Winston Churchill, broadcast 30 November 1954
Edward R Murrow 1908–65 American broadcast journalist: *In Search of Light* (1967)

First you're an unknown, then you write one book and you move up to obscurity.
Martin Myers

Curiously enough, one cannot *read* a book: one can only reread it. A good reader, a major reader, an active and creative reader is a rereader.
Vladimir Nabokov 1899–1977 Russian novelist: *Lectures on Literature* (1980)

Let us pause to consider the English,
Who when they pause to consider themselves they get all reticently thrilled and tinglish,
Because every Englishman is convinced of one thing, viz.:
That to be an Englishman is to belong to the most exclusive club there is.
Ogden Nash 1902–71 American poet: 'England Expects'

The Ten Commandments contain 297 words, the Bill of Rights 463 words, and Lincoln's Gettysburg Address 266 words. A recent federal directive regulating the price of cabbage contains 26,911 words.
Johann von Neumann 1903–57 Austro-Hungarian-born American mathematician and scientist: *New York Times*

Just the knowledge that a good book is awaiting one at the end of a long day makes that day happier.
Kathleen Norris 1880–1966 American novelist: *Hands Full of Living* (1931)

Yesterday American and British troops handed out food to hundreds of Iraqis. Not surprisingly, the Iraqis handed the British food back.
Conan O'Brien 1963– American television host, comedian, comedy writer

The vote, I think, means nothing to women. We should be armed.
Edna O'Brien 1932– Irish novelist and short story writer

Some savage faculty of observation told him that most respectable and estimable people usually had a lot of books in their houses.
The Best of Myles (1968)

Waiting for the German verb is surely the ultimate thrill.
The Hair of the Dogma (1977)
Flann O'Brien 1911–66 Irish novelist and journalist

Everywhere I go I am asked if university stifles writers. My opinion is that it doesn't stifle enough of them.
Flannery O'Connor 1925–64 American novelist, short-story writer, and essayist: *Wise Blood* (1952)

If men were shouted down for being sexist when they used the word 'postman', then asking if there was any chance of a quick shag seemed like a bit of a non-starter.
John O'Farrell 1962– British author, broadcaster, and comedy scriptwriter

Always read stuff that will make you look good if you die in the middle of it.
PJ O'Rourke 1947– American political satirist, journalist, and author

Roast beef and Yorkshire, or roast pork and apple sauce, followed by suet pudding and driven home, as it were, by a cup of mahogany-brown tea, have put you in just the right mood... In these blissful circumstances, what is it that you want to read about? Naturally, about a murder.
Decline of the English Murder and Other Essays (1965) title essay, written 1946

Don't you see that the whole aim of Newspeak is to narrow the range of thought? In the end we shall make thought crime literally impossible, because there will be no words in which to express it.
Nineteen Eighty-Four (1949)

Political language – and with variations this is true of all political parties, from Conservatives to Anarchists – is designed to make lies sound truthful and murder respectable, and to give an appearance of solidity to pure wind.

If liberty means anything at all, it means the right to tell people what they do not want to hear.

Good prose is like a window pane.
George Orwell 1903–50 English novelist, journalist, literary critic, poet

Being politically correct means always having to say you're sorry.
Charles Osgood 1933– American radio and television commentator

The writer's way is rough and lonely, and who would choose it while there are vacancies in more gracious professions, such as, say, cleaning out ferryboats?

It is our national joy to mistake for the first-rate, the fecund rate.
review of Sinclair Lewis *Dodsworth* in *New Yorker* 16 March 1929

I hate women. They get on my nerves.
quoted in *Women's Wicked Wit* ed. Michelle Lovric (2000)

This is not a novel to be tossed aside lightly. It should be thrown with great force.
RE Drennan *Wit's End* (1973)
Dorothy Parker 1893–1967 American critic and humorist

Get the advice of everybody whose advice is worth having – they are very few – and then do what you think best yourself.
Charles Stewart Parnell 1846–91 Irish nationalist leader: Conor Cruise O'Brien *Parnell* (1957)

The last thing one knows in constructing a work is what to put first.

When we see a natural style, we are quite surprised and delighted, for we expected to see an author and we find a man.
Blaise Pascal 1623–62 French mathematician, physicist, and moralist: *Pensées* (1670)

Thus, in a real sense, I am constantly writing autobiography, but I have to turn it into fiction in order to give it credibility.
Katherine Paterson 1932– British author of books for children: *The Spying Heart* (1989)

He who does not bellow the truth when he knows the truth makes himself the accomplice of liars and forgers.
Charles Péguy 1873–1914 French poet and essayist: *Basic Verities* (1943)

A man came to my door and said, 'I'd like to read your meter.' I said, 'Whatever happened to the classics?'

My favourite writers are Joyce, Tolstoy, Proust and Flaubert, but right now I'm reading *The Little Engine That Could*.

Grandmother's brain was dead, but her heart was still beating. It was the first time we ever had a Democrat in the family.

Women: you can't live with them, and you can't get them to dress up in a skimpy Nazi uniform and beat you with a warm squash.

I discovered my wife in bed with another man, and I was crushed. So I said, 'Get off me, you two!'
Emo Philips 1956– American comedian

For the mind does not require filling like a bottle, but rather, like wood, it only required kindling to create in it an impulse to think independently and an ardent desire for the truth.
Plutarch 46–120 Greek philosopher and biographer: *Moralia*

Those who dream by day are cognizant of many things which escape those who dream only by night.
Edgar Allan Poe 1809–49 American writer, poet, editor, and literary critic: *Eleanora* (1842)

Sometimes I'm charmed by the fact that there are women with whom you can discuss the theory of light all evening, and at the end they will ask you what is your birth sign.
Roman Polanski 1933– French-born and resident Polish film director, producer, writer, and actor

But those who cannot write, and those who can,
All rhyme, and scrawl, and scribble, to a man.
Alexander Pope 1688–1744 English poet: *Imitations of Horace* (1737)

Properly, we should read for power. Man reading should be man intensely alive. The book should be a ball of light in one's hand.
Ezra Pound 1885–1972 American poet

The Librarian was, of course, very much in favour of reading in general, but readers in particular got on his nerves . . . He liked people who loved and respected books, and the best way to do that, in the Librarian's opinion, was to leave them on the shelves where Nature intended them to be.
  Men at Arms (1993)

Most modern fantasy just rearranges the furniture in Tolkien's attic.
  Stan Nicholls (ed) *Wordsmiths of Wonder* (1993)

I'm up to my neck in the real world, every day. Just you try doing your tax return with a head full of goblins.
  Sunday Times 27 February 2000

Multiple exclamation marks are a sure sign of a diseased mind.
Sir Terence Pratchett 1948– English science fiction writer

I've never heard such a load of *merde de taureau* in all my life!
Bill Price quality director of Revlon UK in the 1990s, when the author worked there, disagreeing on a point made by his French colleague Véronique Robert during a large meeting of senior executives, 1992

'Thou shalt not' might reach the head, but it takes 'Once upon a time' to reach the heart.
Philip Pullman 1946– English writer: *Independent* 18 July 1996

I wish thee as much pleasure in the reading, as I had in the writing.
Francis Quarles 1591–1644 English poet: *Emblems* (1635) 'To the Reader'

There's a certain kind of conversation you have from time to time at parties in New York about a new book. The word 'banal' sometimes rears its by-now banal head; you say 'underedited', I say 'derivative'. The conversation goes around and around various literary criticisms, and by the time it moves on one thing is clear: No one read the book; we just read the reviews.
Anna Quindlen 1953– American author, journalist, and columnist

I was having a cup of tea with Mum in the living room, when Ken the Man [Author's note: Myfanwy's nickname for her beloved father] hollered from upstairs, 'Myfanwy, I'm in the bedroom. Would you please come upstairs and help me with my dongle?' I exploded with laughter and a jet of tea flew halfway across the living room, creating brown patches on Mum's new cream carpet. She didn't look too happy.
Myfanwy Rees 1970– eminent Welsh businesswoman

I am sitting in the smallest room of my house. I have your review before me. In a moment it will be behind me.
Max Reger 1873–1916 German composer, in a letter to the music critic Rudolph Louis, 1906

You can't think rationally on an empty stomach, and a whole lot of people can't do it on a full stomach either.
Lord Reith 1899–1971 British administrator and politician: D Parker *Radio: The Great Years* (1977)

Writing is the only profession where no one considers you ridiculous if you earn no money.
Jules Renard 1864–1910 French novelist and dramatist

To say Agatha Christie's characters are cardboard cut-outs is an insult to cardboard.
Ruth Rendell 1930– English crime writer

For years a secret shame destroyed my peace –
I'd not read Eliot, Auden or MacNiece.
But then I had a thought that brought me hope –
Nor had Chaucer, Shakespeare, Milton, Pope.
Justin Richardson 1900–75 British poet: 'Take Heart, Illiterates' (1966)

I would like to say that my wife, Elaine, possessed all the patience of a loving wife, but in fact she just said to me, 'Oh, will you just shut up about it, and finish it.'
Jon Ronson 1967– Welsh journalist, documentary filmmaker, radio presenter, and author: *Them* (2001) preface

No one can make you feel inferior without your consent.
Eleanor Roosevelt 1884–1962 American humanitarian and diplomat: *Catholic Digest* August 1960

The only reason for being a professional writer is that you can't help it.
Leo Rosten 1908–97 American writer and social scientist

I hate books; they only teach us to talk about things we know nothing about.
Jean-Jacques Rousseau 1712–78 French philosopher and novelist: *Émile* (1762)

One of the things a writer is for is to say the unsayable, speak the unspeakable and ask difficult questions.

Independent on Sunday 10 September 1995

A book is a version of the world. If you do not like it, ignore it; or offer your own version in return.

O Magazine April 2003
Salman Rushdie 1947– Indian-born British novelist

We call ourselves a rich nation, and we are filthy and foolish enough to thumb each other's books out of circulating libraries!

Sesame and Lilies (1865)

Quality is never an accident; it is always the result of intelligent effort.

All books are divisible into two classes, the books of the hour, and the books of all time.

How long most people would look at the best book before they would give the price of a large turbot for it.

Say all you have to say in the fewest possible words, or your reader will be sure to skip them; and in the plainest possible words or he will certainly misunderstand them.

John Ruskin 1819–1900 English art and social critic

What is wanted is not the will to believe, but the will to find out, which is its exact opposite.

Free Thought and Official Propaganda (1922)

The opinions that are held with passion are always those for which no good ground exists; indeed the passion is the measure of the holder's lack of rational conviction.

Sceptical Essays (1928)

One should as a rule respect public opinion in so far as is necessary to avoid starvation and to keep out of prison, but anything that goes beyond this is voluntary submission to an unnecessary tyranny.

One of the symptoms of approaching nervous breakdown is the belief that one's work is terribly important, and that to take a holiday would bring all kinds of disaster.

To be without some of the things you want is an indispensable part of happiness.

The Conquest of Happiness (1930)
Bertrand Russell 1872–1970 British philosopher and mathematician

If you really want to hear about it, the first thing you'll probably want to know is where I was born and what my lousy childhood was like, and how my parents were occupied and all before they had me, and all that David Copperfield kind of crap.

opening words

What really knocks me out is a book that, when you're all done reading it, you wish the author that wrote it was a terrific friend of yours and you could call him up on the phone whenever you felt like it.
JD Salinger 1919– American novelist and short-story writer: *Catcher in the Rye* (1951)

Writing is the hardest way to earn a living, with the possible exception of wrestling alligators.
William Saroyan 1908–81

I genuinely try as hard as I can to buy British. In consequence, my house is full of slightly second-rate crap. Imagine if there were no Japanese, and the British had invented the Walkman. It would be a big teak box covered in leatherette, with the headphones out of a Lancaster bomber.
Alexei Sayle 1952– English stand-up comedian, actor, and author

The skill of writing is to create a context in which other people can think.
Edwin Schlossberg 1945– American designer, author, and artist

Writing gives you the illusion of control, and then you realise it's just an illusion, that people are going to bring their own stuff into it.
David Sedaris 1956–: interview in *Louisville Courier-Journal* 5 June 2005

It is quality rather than quantity which matters.
Seneca the Younger 5 BC – 65 AD Roman Stoic philosopher, statesman, dramatist, and humorist: *Epistles*

When I step into this library, I cannot understand why I ever step out of it.
Marie de Sévigné 1626–96 French aristocrat

All my wife has ever taken from the Mediterranean – from that whole vast intuitive culture – are four bottles of Chianti to make into lamps.
Peter Shaffer 1926– English dramatist: *Equus* (1973)

Brevity is the soul of wit.

Polonius: What do you read, my lord?
Hamlet: Words, words, words.
William Shakespeare 1564–1616 English dramatist: *Hamlet* (1601)

A man of great common sense and good taste, meaning thereby a man without originality or moral courage.
  notes to *Caesar and Cleopatra* (1901)

The reasonable man adapts himself to the world: the unreasonable one persists in trying to adapt the world to himself. Therefore all progress depends on the unreasonable man.

Of all human struggles there is none so treacherous and remorseless as the struggle between the artist man and the mother woman.

But a lifetime of happiness! No man alive could bear it: it would be hell on earth.
Man and Superman (1903)

All great truths begin as blasphemies.
Annajanska (1919)

One man that has a mind and knows it can always beat ten men who haven't and don't.
The Apple Cart (1930)

No man who is concerned in doing a very difficult thing, and doing it well, ever loses his self-respect.

The man who writes about himself and his own time is the only man who writes about all people and all time.
George Bernard Shaw 1856–1950 Irish dramatist

Learn to write well, or not to write at all.
John Sheffield, 1st Duke of Buckingham and Normanby 1648–1721 poet and Tory politician: 'An Essay upon Satire' (1689)

You write with ease, to show your breeding,
But easy writing's vile hard reading.
Richard Brinsley Sheridan 1751–1816 Irish dramatist and Whig politician: 'Clio's Protest' (1771)

If writing did not exist, what terrible depressions we should suffer from.
Sei Shōnagon 966–1013 Japanese diarist and writer: *The Pillow Book of Sei Shōnagon*

My advice to aspiring writers: marry money.
Max Shulman 1919–88 American writer and humorist

Pay no attention to what the critics say. No statue has ever been put up to a critic.
Jean Sibelius 1865–1957 Finnish composer: quoted in Bengt de Törne *Sibelius: A Close Up* (1937)

Writing is not a profession but a vocation of unhappiness.
Georges Simenon 1903–89 Belgian novelist: *Paris Review* summer 1955

Homer Simpson: Kids, you tried your best, and you failed miserably. The lesson is, never try.

Marge Simpson: Homer, are you coming with us to the book fair?
Homer Simpson: If it doesn't have Siamese twins in a jar, it's not a fair.
The Simpsons

I enjoyed talking to her, but thought *nothing* of her writing. I considered her 'a beautiful little knitter'.
of Virginia Woolf

My personal hobbies are reading, listening to music, and silence.

Eccentricity is not, as dull people would have us believe, a form of madness. It is often a kind of innocent pride, and the man of genius and the aristocrat are frequently regarded as eccentrics because genius and aristocrat are entirely unafraid of and uninfluenced by the opinions and vagaries of the crowd.
Edith Sitwell 1887–1964 English poet and critic

Consistency is the quality of a stagnant mind.
John Sloan 1871–1951 American socialist painter

People say that life is the thing, but I prefer reading.

No furniture so charming as books.

A best-seller is the gilded tomb of a mediocre talent.
   Afterthoughts (1931)

What I like in a good author is not what he says, but what he whispers.
   All Trivia (1933)
Logan Pearsall Smith 1865–1946 American-born man of letters

I never read a book before reviewing it; it prejudices a man so.
Sydney Smith 1771–1845 English clergyman and essayist: H Pearson *The Smith of Smiths* (1934)

I think for my part one half of the nation is mad – and the other not very sound.
   The Great Adventures of Sir Lancelot Greaves (1762)

A man may be very entertaining and instructive upon paper (said he), and exceedingly dull in common discourse. I have observed, that those who shine most in private company, are but secondary stars in the constellation of genius – A small stock of ideas is more easily managed, and sooner displayed, than a great quantity crowded together.
Tobias Smollett 1721–71 Scottish novelist: *The Expedition of Humphry Clinker* (1771)

Our current obsession with creativity is the result of our continued striving for immortality in an era when most people no longer believe in an afterlife.
Arianna Stassinopoulos 1950– Greek-born American writer: *The Female Woman* (1973)

Reading is to the mind what exercise is to the body.
Richard Steele 1672–1729 Irish-born essayist and dramatist: *The Tatler* 18 March 1710

Everybody gets so much information all day long that they lose their common sense.
Gertrude Stein 1874–1946 American writer: *Reflections on the Atomic Bomb* (1946)

All the world's greats have been little boys who wanted the moon.
   Cup of Gold (1953)

Unless the bastards have the courage to give you unqualified praise, I say ignore them.

Nobody wants advice – only corroboration.
John Steinbeck 1902–68 American novelist

For those who have tasted the profound activity of writing, reading is no more than a secondary pleasure.
Stendhal (Henri Beyle) 1783–1842 French novelist: *De l'Amour* (1822)

Knowledge is good. It does not have to look good or sound good or even do good. It is good just by being knowledge. And the only thing that makes it knowledge is that it is true. You can't have too much of it and there is no little too little to be worth having.
Tom Stoppard 1937– British dramatist: *The Invention of Love* (1997)

Write something to suit yourself and many people will like it; write something to suit everybody and scarcely anyone will care for it.
Jesse Stuart 1907–84 American short-story writer, poet, and novelist

When a true genius appears in the world, you may know him by this sign, that the dunces are all in confederacy against him.
Jonathan Swift 1667–1745 Anglo-Irish poet and satirist: *Thoughts on Various Subjects* (1711)

Biting my truant pen, beating myself for spite,
'Fool,' said my Muse to me; 'look in thy heart and write.'
Philip Sydney 1554–86 poet, courtier, and soldier

Poetry is not the most important thing in life… I'd much rather lie in a hot bath reading Agatha Christie and sucking sweets.
  Joan Wyndham *Love is Blue* (1986)
Dylan Thomas 1914–53 Welsh poet

Our life is frittered away by detail… Simplify, simplify.

How many a man has dated a new era in his life from the reading of a book.
Henry David Thoreau 1817–62 American writer: *Walden* 'Reading' (1854)

Disinterested intellectual curiosity is the life-blood of real civilisation.

Education has produced a vast population able to read but unable to distinguish what is worth reading, an easy prey to sensations and cheap appeals.
GM Trevelyan 1876–1962 English historian: *English Social History* (1942)

In modern America, anyone who attempts to write satirically about the events of the day finds it difficult to concoct a situation so bizarre that it may not actually come to pass while the article is still on the presses.

I'm in favour of liberalised immigration because of the effect it would have on restaurants. I'd let just about everybody in, except the English.
Calvin Trillin 1935– American journalist, humorist, food writer, poet, memoirist, and novelist

Never think that you're not good enough yourself. A man should never think that. My belief is that in life people will take you very much at your own reckoning.
  The Small House at Allington (1864)

Take away from English authors their copyrights, and you would very soon take away from England her authors.

Three hours a day will produce as much as a man ought to write.

Of all the needs a book has, the chief need is that it be readable.
  Autobiography (1883)
Anthony Trollope 1815–82 English novelist

One editor said to me, 'You could be the next Dorothy Parker.' I thought, 'What? Keep slashing my wrists and drinking shoe polish?'
Lynne Truss 1955– English writer and journalist

A good book is the best of friends, the same today and forever.
Martin Tupper 1810–89 English writer: *Proverbial Philosophy* (1838)

I share no one's ideas. I have my own.
Ivan Turgenev 1818–83 Russian novelist: *Fathers and Sons* (1862)

I know of no genius but the genius of hard work.
JMW Turner 1775–1851 English painter: John Ruskin *Notes by Mr Ruskin on His Collection of Drawings by the Late JMW Turner* (1878)

Persons attempting to find a motive in this narrative will be prosecuted; persons attempting to find a moral in it will be banished; persons attempting to find a plot in it will be shot.
  'Notice to Readers' at the start of *Adventures of Huckleberry Finn*

Pilgrim's Progress: a book about a man that left his family. It doesn't say why.
  Adventures of Huckleberry Finn (1884)

All you need in this life is ignorance and confidence; then success is sure.
  letter to Mrs Foote 2 December 1887

As to the Adjective: when in doubt, strike it out.
  Pudd'nhead Wilson (1894)

Jane Austen's books, too, are absent from this library. Just that one omission alone would make a fairly good library out of a library that hadn't a book in it.

To me Edgar Allen Poe's prose is unreadable – like Jane Austen's. No, there is a difference. I could read his prose on a salary, but not Jane's.

Also, to be fair, there is another word of praise due to this ship's library: it contains no copy of Oliver Goldsmith's *The Vicar of Wakefield*… a book which is one long waste-pipe discharge of goody-goody puerilities and dreary moralities…
  Following the Equator (1897)

I like a thin book because it will steady a table; a leather volume because it will strop a razor; and a heavy book because it can be thrown at a cat.

The man who doesn't read good books has no advantage over the man who can't read them.

It seems a great pity they allowed Jane Austen to die a natural death.
Mark Twain 1835–1910 American writer and humorist

There are only two kinds of PG Wodehouse readers: those who adore him, and those who have never read him.
Richard Usborne 1910–2006 British journalist and author

I cannot help it that my pictures do not sell. Nevertheless the time will come when people will see that they are worth more than the price of the paint.
Vincent Van Gogh 1853–90 Dutch painter: letter to his brother Theo, 20 October 1888

Whenever a friend succeeds, a little something in me dies.
Gore Vidal 1925– American novelist and critic: *Sunday Times Magazine* 16 September 1973

The multitude of books is making us ignorant.
Voltaire 1694–1778 French writer and philosopher

To see him fumbling with our rich and delicate language is to experience all the horror of seeing a Sèvres vase in the hands of a chimpanzee.
of Stephen Spender

Anyone could write a novel given six weeks, pen, paper, and no telephone or wife.
Henry ('Chips') Channon diary 16 December 1934
Evelyn Waugh 1903–66 English novelist: *The Tablet* 5 May 1951

Publish and be damned.
replying to a blackmail threat prior to the publication of Harriet Wilson's *Memoirs* (1825)
Duke of Wellington 1769–1852 British soldier and statesman, attributed: Elizabeth Longford *Wellington: The Years of the Sword* (1969)

Go away. I'm all right.
last words
HG Wells 1866–1946 English author

Writing is so difficult that I often feel that writers, having had their hell on earth, will escape all punishment hereafter.
Mary Jessamyn West 1902–84 American short-story writer and novelist

A classic is classic not because it conforms to certain structured rules, or fits certain definitions (of which its author had quite probably never heard). It is classic because of a certain eternal and irrepressible freshness.
Edith Wharton 1862–1937 American novelist

The best thing for being sad… is to learn something.
TH White 1906–64 English novelist: *The Sword in the Stone* (1938)

Ideas won't keep. Something must be done about them.
Alfred North Whitehead 1861–1947 English philosopher and mathematician: *Dialogues* (1954)

One should not be too severe on English novels; they are the only relaxation of the intellectually unemployed.
Owen Dudley Edwards (ed.) *The Fireworks of Oscar Wilde* (1989)

We have really everything in common with America nowadays except, of course, language.
The Canterville Ghost (1887)

Education is an admirable thing, but it is well to remember from time to time that nothing that is worth knowing can be taught.
All art is immoral.

It is through Art, and through Art only, that we can realise our perfection; through Art, and through Art only, that we can shield ourselves from the sordid perils of actual existence.

Meredith! Who can define him? His style is chaos illuminated by flashes of lightning.
Intentions (1891)

The moment that an artist takes notice of what other people want, and tries to supply the demand, he ceases to be an artist, and becomes a dull or an amusing craftsman, an honest or dishonest tradesman.
'The Soul of Man Under Socialism' (1891)

There is no such thing as a moral or an immoral book. Books are well written, or badly written.
The Picture of Dorian Gray (1891) preface

We are all in the gutter, but some of us are looking at the stars.
Lady Windermere's Fan (1892)

I always pass on good advice. It is the only thing to do with it. It is never of any use to oneself.
An Ideal Husband (1895)

The good ended happily, and the bad unhappily. That is what fiction means.

I never travel without my diary. One should always have something sensational to read in the train.
The Importance of Being Earnest (1895)

I have nothing to declare but my genius.
at the New York Custom House: Frank Harris *Oscar Wilde* (1918)

I suppose publishers are untrustworthy. They certainly always look it.
letter, February 1898

A thing is not necessarily true because a man dies for it.
The Portrait of Mr WH (1901)

I was working on the proof of one of my poems all the morning, and took out a comma. In the afternoon I put it back again.

One must have a heart of stone to read the death of Little Nell without laughing.
Oscar Wilde 1854–1900 Anglo-Irish dramatist and poet

Unable obtain bidet. Suggest handstand in shower.
    cabled response to his wife's cabled complaint from Paris just after the Second World War, that her accommodation did not have a bidet, and could he arrange to have one sent to her?
Billy Wilder 1906–2002 American film director and writer

The nice thing about quotes is that they give us a nodding acquaintance with the originator which is often socially impressive.
Kenneth Williams 1926–88 English actor: *Acid Drops* (1980)

I myself have always deprecated... in crisis after crisis, appeals to the Dunkirk spirit as an answer to our problems.
    in the House of Commons 16 July 1961

I believe that the spirit of Dunkirk will carry us through... to success.
    speech to the Labour Party Conference 12 December 1964
Harold Wilson, Baron Wilson of Rievaulx 1916–95 British Labour Party politician, prime minister of the United Kingdom 1964–70, 1974–6

Never read a book through merely because you have begun it.
John Witherspoon 1723–94 Scottish-born American clergyman, the only active clergyman to sign the United States Declaration of Independence

To my daughter Leonora without whose never-failing sympathy and encouragement this book would have been finished in half the time.
PG Wodehouse 1881–1975 English writer, an American citizen from 1955: dedication in *The Heart of a Goof* (1926)

The General... repeated nearly the whole of Gray's Elegy... adding, as he concluded, that he would prefer being the author of that poem to the glory of beating the French tomorrow.
James Wolfe 1727–59 British general, captor of Quebec: J Playfair *Biographical Account of J. Robinson* in *Transactions of the Royal Society of Edinburgh* (1815)

Jackie: *(very slowly)*   Take Tube A and apply to Bracket D.
Victoria: Reading it slower does not make it any easier to do.
Victoria Wood 1953– British writer and comedienne: *Mens Sana in Thingummy Doodah* (1990)

The scratchings of pimples on the body of the bootboy at Claridges.
    of James Joyce's *Ulysees*
    letter to Lytton Strachey, 24 April 1922

A woman must have money and a room of her own if she is to write fiction.

Literature is strewn with the wreckage of men who have minded beyond reason the opinions of others.
    A Room of One's Own (1929)

As an experience, madness is terrific... and in its lava I still find most of the things I write about.
    letter to Ethel Smyth, 22 June 1930

She stinks like a civet cat that had taken to street walking.
    on Katherine Mansfield

Her mind is a very thin soil, laid an inch or two upon very barren rock.
    on Katherine Mansfield
Virginia Woolf 1882–1941 English novelist

She is so odd a blend of Little Nell and Lady Macbeth. It is not so much the familiar phenomenon of a hand of steel in a velvet glove as a lacy sleeve with a bottle of vitriol concealed in its folds.
    of Dorothy Parker
Alexander Woollcott 1887–1943 American writer: *While Rome Burns* (1934)

Never forget what I believe was observed to you by Coleridge, that every great and original writer, in proportion as he is great and original, must himself create the taste by which he is to be relished.
William Wordsworth 1770–1850 English poet: letter to Lady Beaumont 21 May 1807

I'm writing a book. I've got the page numbers done.
Steven Wright 1955– American comedian, actor, and writer

You who scribble, yet hate all who write...
And with faint praises one another damn.
    of drama critics
William Wycherley 1640–1716 English dramatist: *The Plain Dealer* (1677) prologue

A line will take us hours maybe;
Yet if it does not seen a moment's thought,
Our stitching and unstitching has been naught.
WB Yeats 1865–1939 Irish poet: *In the Seven Woods* (1904) 'Adam's Curse'

Rock journalism is people who can't write interviewing people who can't talk for people who can't read.
    Linda Botts *Loose Talk* (1980)

Without deviation from the norm, progress is not possible.
    New York 20 June 1994 (attr.)

I think it is good that books still exist, but they do make me sleepy.
Frank Zappa 1940–93 American rock musician and songwriter

Quit now, you'll never make it. If you disregard this advice, you'll be halfway there.
David Zucker 1947– American film director, producer, and screenwriter

APPENDIX 2

KEY ORGANISATIONS AND FREELANCE SERVICE PROVIDERS

Cartoons and caricatures
Martin Honeysett

Web: Martinhoneysett.com
Email: Honeysettmartin@yahoo.co.uk

Stan Hurr

Web: Stanhurr.co.uk
Email: Stanhurr@gmail.com

Copy-editing/proofreading
Charlie Wilson (Perfectly Write):

Web: Perfectlywrite.co.uk
Email: Info@perfectlywrite.co.uk

The Society for Editors and Proofreaders (Sfep.org.uk) has a directory of 440 members. A keyword search will lead you to individuals with the skills you're looking for.

Erico House
93–99 Upper Richmond Road
Putney
London SW15 2TG

Tel: 0208 785 5617
Fax: 0208 785 5618
Email: Administration@sfep.org.uk

Cover design
After an error with the cover design of my first self-published book I have mainly used one cover design firm, the one run by John Chandler. I highly recommend him and his team of designers. The office is in the centre of King's Lynn. The team's technical competence and creativity are excellent, I believe, and they're always a pleasure to work with. Their website Chandlerbookdesign.co.uk is worth visiting. They can be contacted through info@chandlerdesign.co.uk, or telephone 01553 660175.

I used a new graphic designer, Tony Whelan, for *The Glass Ceiling Delusion* cover design (using a Lightning Source template and InDesign software) and I'm happy to recommend him. I plan to use his services again for the cover design of my forthcoming book *Feminism*. He charges £30.00 per hour.

Tel: 01234 307936
Email: Tonywhelan@ntlworld.com

Data distribution to booksellers and book buyers on online booksellers
British self-publishers should visit Nielsen Publisher Services: Nielsenbook.co.uk.

North American self-publishers should visit Bowker on Bowker.com.

Distributors/wholesalers
The principal distributors/wholesalers in the UK:

Gardners:
Tel: 01323 521777
Web: Gardners.com
Small Publisher Helpline: sph@gardners.com

Bertrams:
Tel: 0871 803 6603
Web: Bertrams.com
Email: Ros.wesson@bertrams.com

Ebooks: formatting files for ebook e-readers

eBookIt!: eBookIt.com
Wordzworth: Wordzworth.com

eBookIt! offer book distribution to ebook retailers, while Wordzworth don't, at least not at the time of writing (August 2011).

Formatting and typesetting
I'm referring here to issues like having consistency of font styles and sizes, paragraph indenting, page numbering, and the countless other tasks which are required to arrive at a professional-looking manuscript. If you're not prepared to go through the effort required to develop your word processing skills to this level – and you have my full sympathies if you're not, believe me – I recommend a proficient typist be employed, unless you're lucky enough to have a friend or family member who will do it for a song. Is 'typist' one of the banned words of our time, like 'secretary'? I believe so. Find a pretty young lady typist (if you're a man) or a handsome young gentleman typist (if you're a lady) to tidy up your efforts.

I can strongly recommend the lady I've used on a couple of projects, Sharon Smith, my glamorous personal assistant. She's the fastest typist and secretary I've ever known. She used to work in the Foreign Office, and still does some work every day for Lord Someone-or-Other, a crossbencher in the House of Lords.

Sharon's based in Bedford, her website is Swanva.co.uk, and she can be contacted on 01234 930994 or sharon@swanva.co.uk. She currently (August 2011) charges a modest £30.00 per hour but charges by the minute. She's a pleasure to work with.

John Chandler (contact details under 'cover design') and Wordzworth (contact details under 'ebooks') provide typesetting services.

The Independent Publishers' Guild

A useful organisation for the British self-publisher. From the website Ipg.uk.com:

> The IPG supports around 480 members who have a combined turnover of £500m a year and who make enormous contributions to creative excellence and innovation in the UK. We supply our members with vital information, practical advice and great ideas to help them grow and prosper. We represent their interests in the wider publishing industry. And we provide a friendly community in which independent publishers can share knowledge and experiences.

An introduction to the IPG from Executive Director Bridget Shine

Publishing is a great business for companies to be in, but also a challenging one. Independent publishers' creativity, enthusiasm and contribution to the vibrant UK publishing industry should be celebrated and encouraged, and that's exactly what the IPG sets out to do. The IPG helps publishers to do better business and become part of a real community – somewhere to find advice, ideas and information. We give independent companies the support they need to get the most out of publishing and keep their businesses growing.

The need for the IPG has never been greater. Independent publishers face ever stiffer competition from larger rivals, and must be imaginative and agile to succeed. The IPG helps them by supplying a forum to exchange ideas and resources. Smaller companies also need a loud collective voice and the strength to make an impact in the wider publishing industry. Again, we provide this.

The IPG is in better shape than at any time in its 48 year history. Membership is at an all-time high of around 480 companies, sharing combined turnover of £500m a year. We represent publishers of all shapes and sizes, from one-person operations to medium sized companies to international heavyweights. Our different special interest groups under the IPG umbrella reflect the diversity of the membership, and give companies the chance to get advice and information that are specific to their own sector.

One of the most impressive things about the independent publishing community is its willingness to share its expertise, and new joiners get access to a mine of knowledge and experience, from both their fellow members and the IPG's own Board of Directors.

PO Box 12,
Llain
Whitland SA34 0WU

Tel: 01437 563335
Fax: 01437 562071
Email: info@ipg.uk.com
Web: Ipg.uk.com

Indexing

The *Writers' and Artists' Yearbook* (2012) has an article on the topic of indexing, and gives contact details of the Society of Indexers. Authors or publishers wishing to commission an indexer should consult *Indexers Available* on their website Indexers.org.uk.

Internet discussion forums

I include this topic here because it doesn't fit naturally anywhere else in the book. In the early summer of 2011 another self-publisher informed me of a couple of Yahoo discussion forums he'd found useful. Having now belonged to the forums for a couple of months myself, I can heartily recommend them. The majority of the forum members are of the American persuasion, a minority British or Canadian, with other nationalities occasionally making an appearance. Frequent contributors include Aaron Shepard and members of the forum can usually be assured of receiving enthusiastic, wide-ranging and knowledgeable attention to their queries. The first group is for self-publishers in general, the second for self-publishers with an interest in POD:

http://finance.groups.yahoo.com/group/self-publishing
http://finance.groups.yahoo.com/group/pod_publishers

Order fulfilment and warehousing

For a number of months I was unable to fulfil orders for my books due to heavy business commitments so I had to find a company to store my books, process my orders, and despatch the books. After a frustrating search I finally found a suitable order fulfilment company locally, in Wilstead. The company is myWarehouse, their website Orderfulfilment.co.uk. I found them flexible and economical, their contract terms were reasonable, and I recommend them. Telephone 0845 475 7354.

Photograph libraries

I've bought images from iStockphoto (iStockphoto.com) and Getty Images (Gettyimages.co.uk) and found both companies professional if frustratingly inflexible on pricing. There are a number of other online photo libraries and it may pay to shop around. I started to use Bigstockphoto.com with the cover image for *The Glass Ceiling Delusion* (the image cost £6.99) and I plan to use them again for the image on the cover of *Feminism*.

Photographer

Roger Day (Rogerdayphotography.com).

Printers (POD, digital short print run, offset lithography)
Until the POD edition of this book all my books – both hardbacks and paperbacks –
sold in the UK were printed in the UK by MPG Biddles at their facility in King's
Lynn. I can't praise them highly enough. Their Nigel Mitchell must be the most
patient man on the planet, answering countless queries promptly, courteously, and
accurately. The company's informative website is Mpg-biddles.co.uk, telephone 01553
764728 or email Nigel at nmitchell@mpg-biddles.co.uk. MPG Biddles also manufacture
books printed by offset lithography, at their Bodmin plant.

Another printer that I expect to use one day is CPI Antony Rowe. Details of their
offering is at http://uk.cpibooks.com/short-run-and-pod. They're a division of CPI Books,
Europe's largest book manufacturer. I contacted their sales manager, Geoff Fisher,
because he's presented as their 'expert on self-publishing'. He was most helpful and
answered a lot of questions with impressive speed. He also explained that with their
technology they were able to print even single copies of books under the ultra low
print run model, and they can include colour plate sections on coated papers.
Telephone 01732 363897, mobile 07767 675262, email address gfisher@cpibooks.co.uk.
   CPI Books have divisions dealing with longer print runs than the Antony Rowe
division, and they offer offset lithography too.

The first edition of this book was made available through Lightning Source's LSI
model. Their American plant is in Tennessee, the British plant in Milton Keynes.
British self-publishers should contact:

Web: Lightningsource.co.uk
Email: Enquiries@lightningsource.co.uk
Tel: 0845 121 4567

North American self-publishers should contact:

Web: Lightningsource.com
Email: Inquiry@lightningsource.com
Tel: (615) 213-5815

Proofreading – see 'Copy-editing/proofreading'

The Society of Authors

The Society of Authors
84 Drayton Gardens
London SW10 9SB

Tel: 020 7373 6642
Fax: 020 7373 5768
Web: Societyofauthors.org
Email: info@societyofauthors.org

From the website:

> The Society of Authors has been serving the interests of professional writers in Great Britain for more than a century. Today it has more than 8,500 members writing in all areas of the profession.
>
> Whatever your specialisation, from novelists to doctors, textbook writers to ghost writers, broadcasters to academics, illustrators to translators, you are eligible to join as soon as you have been offered a contract.
>
> The staff are ready to help members with any query, however trivial or obscure, relating to the business of writing. Our services include the confidential, individual vetting of contracts, and help with professional disputes.
>
> In addition, the Society holds meetings and seminars, publishes a quarterly journal, *The Author*, and maintains a database of members' specialisations.
>
> It administers a wide range of prizes, as well as the Authors' Foundation, which is one of the very few bodies making grants to help with work in progress for established writers.
>
> A year's membership costs £90 (£64 for those aged under 35). The annual subscription includes the cost of specialist contract appraisals, and is tax deductible under Schedule D.

Full Membership is open to:
- writers, illustrators and translators who have had a full-length work published (not at the author's expense), broadcast, or performed commercially
- those who have had at least a dozen occasional items (e.g. articles or short stories) published or broadcast
- those who are the owners/administrators of a deceased author's estate
- those who have self-published and sold over 200 copies of a single title in a 12 month period

If you have not had any work published but fall into one of the following categories, Associate Membership may be offered as an alternative to Full Membership (where appropriate):
- those who have received an offer to publish or broadcast a full-length work (without subsidy by the author)
- those who have received an agreement from an agent but have had no work published
- those who have been published on a print-on-demand basis
- those who self publish
- those who have been offered a contract which asks for a contribution towards the costs of publication
- those who own one or more of the following: a pen, a pencil, a crayon, a manual typewriter or a computer

I may have made one of those up.

Transcription
I can recommend the company I used to transcribe my recordings for *Guitar Gods in Beds.*, the London-based WNT Legal.

Web: Wntlegal.co.uk
Email: info@wntlegal.co.uk
Tel: 0208 741 6622

Typesetting
See 'Formatting and typesetting'.

APPENDIX 3

INVOICE FORMAT

LPS publishing
8 Putnoe Heights
Bedford MK41 8EB

Email:	mikebuchanan@hotmail.co.uk
Tel:	bedford 7
Mob:	xxxxx xxxxxx

Gardners Books
1 Whittle Drive
Willingdon Drove
Eastbourne
East Sussex BN23 6QH

15 August 2011

SAN 0117567

Invoice LPSG109

Ordered and despatched: 15 August 2011

Your order D74048507
Two Men in a Car
ISBN 9780955878411
8 copies, RRP £12.00, 20% discount   £76.80

Your order D74868205
The Fraud of the Rings
ISBN 9780955878473
1 copy, RRP £12.00, 20% discount   £9.60

                                        TOTAL: £86.40

Terms: cheque made out to 'LPS publishing' by 1 October 2011

APPENDIX 4

CONTENTS OF
WRITERS' & ARTISTS' YEARBOOK (2012)

Foreword – William Boyd

Newspapers and magazines
Getting started
Writing features for newspapers and magazines
  – Merope Mills
Writing for newspapers – Richard Keeble
Writing for magazines – Richard Keeble

Listings
National newspapers UK and Ireland
Regional newspapers UK and Ireland
Magazines UK and Ireland
Newspapers and magazines overseas
Syndicates, news and press agencies

Books
Getting started
Dos and don'ts of approaching a publisher
  – Michael Legat
Writing a synopsis – Rebecca Swift
Understanding the publishing process
  – Bill Swainson
Spotting a bestseller – Alexandra Pringle
One hundred years of fiction bestsellers
  – Alex Hamilton
Notes from a successful fiction author
  – Joanna Trollope
Notes from a successful short story author
  – Chimamanda Ngozie Adichie
Writing stories – Alex Hamilton
Notes from a successful comic author
  – Kathy Lette
Notes from a successful fantasy author
  – Terry Pratchett
Notes from a successful crime author
  – Mark Billingham
Notes from a successful contemporary women's
  novelist – Adele Parks
Notes from a successful romantic novelist
  – Jane Green
Notes from a successful historical novelist
  – Bernard Cornwell
Notes from a successful biographer
  – Claire Tomalin
Notes from a successful travel author
  – William Dalrymple
The growth of travel guidebooks – Alex Hamilton
Notes from a successful non-fiction author
  – Simon Winchester

Notes from a successful 'Mind, Body & Spirit'
  author – William Bloom
Ghostwriting – Andrew Crofts
Books published from blogs – Scott Pack
Notes from a literary editor – Claire Armistead
Notes from a successful crossover author
  – Neil Gaiman
Notes from a successful children's author
  – JK Rowling
Writing and the children's book market
  – Chris Kloet
Is there a book in you? – Alison Baverstock
The state of commissioning – Nicholas Clee
Publishing agreements – Michael Legat
Notes from a successful self-publisher
  – GP Taylor
Doing it (self-publishing) on your own
  – Peter Finch
Self-publishing in ebook –Nicholas Clee
FAQs about ISBNs
Marketing, publicising and selling books
  – Katie Bond
Helping to market your book – Alison Baverstock
How to publicise your book – Isabel Losada
A year in view of the publishing industry
  – Tom Tivnan
Print on Demand – David Taylor
Who owns whom in publishing
Public Lending Right
Vanity publishing – Johnathon Clifford

Listings
Book publishers UK and Ireland
Book publishers overseas
Audio publishers
Book packagers
Book clubs

Poetry
Notes from a passionate poet
  – Benjamin Zephaniah
Getting poetry published – Michael Schmidt
Approaching a poetry publisher – Roddy Lumsden

Listings
Poetry organisations – Paul McGrane

Television, film and radio
Notes from a successful television screenwriter
  – Andrew Davies

APPENDIX 5

NOTES FROM A SUCCESSFUL BOOK COVER DESIGNER (JOHN CHANDLER)

Most of my company's work is designing bespoke book covers and formatting and typesetting their contents, and we work for both self-publishers and mainstream publishers. More and more of our work comes from self-publishers rather than publishers for a number of reasons, but mainly:

- the steady increase in the number of self-publishers because they can now make their books visible and available worldwide at low cost, thanks to the internet and companies such as Lightning Source and Amazon;
- writers increasingly want the full creative control that only self-publishing can offer; and
- publishers are reducing the number of authors they publish, concentrating on the small number who most reliably deliver them solid profits.

Our main services are cover design, and content formatting and typesetting from manuscripts submitted in Microsoft Word. We also do website design for our clients. We're happy to do as little or as much as the client wants, for example only today we had a request to add text to a pre-existing book cover illustration, and we were happy to do so.

We also design promotional materials for authors: postcards, flyers, posters and so on, with the designs usually echoing the book's cover design. If the client wants it, we can commission printers and illustrators for the book and promotional materials. Bestselling author Charlotte Bingham asked us to select the illustrator for her latest book *Mums on the Run*, for example. We also did the book's content formatting and typesetting.

We pride ourselves in delivering a bespoke service very different to that offered by vanity publishers to their clients. We are more expensive but the resulting designs are so superior that our clients are very happy to pay for the service. They often say the added value we provide dwarfs the cost of our services.

The vanity publishers can offer low prices – £100.00, say – for a cover design because they're largely working with design templates which make the whole job easier and faster. We offer a 'small budget' service relying on design templates, but it draws poorly on the designers' experience and expertise. But we do recognise that some authors are short of money.

The predictable result of using design templates is – almost without exception – uninspiring book cover designs. People judge books by their covers, even though the old adage says they shouldn't. It's basic human nature, I think. Book buyers in book stores – real or virtual – are surely more likely to open and review books with bespoke cover designs rather than template-based designs, aren't they?

We try to be flexible and go along with our clients' wishes wherever possible. Clients differ enormously with regard to the inputs and services they want from us, so each project is quoted for separately. We never incur costs without obtaining the client's approval in advance. The average quotation for the bespoke service is about five hundred pounds, which also covers the formatting and typesetting of the book content. We format and typeset with the InDesign software package, which is the professional tool for the job. I know Mike Buchanan does this himself in Microsoft Word, and the result looks professional, but it must take him *forever*. [Author's note: it does.] Word wasn't designed to format or typeset such large documents as books. We offer formatting and typesetting as a standalone service if a client wants it.

A few of our clients like to be very hands-on with respect to the cover design process, they visit our studio in King's Lynn and sit down with the designer until the job is done. We charge £75.00 per hour for this service, and only charge by the minute, there's no minimum fee. Mike is a good example of such a client. He emails us in advance any constituent materials such as design templates – increasingly from Lightning Source, as we're finding with other clients too – along with text as Word documents and photographs as JPGs. He makes comments and works with the designer, and it's a pretty intense process. Mike really enjoys himself. I'm not so sure the designer does though (laughs).

Mike is one of only a handful of writers who are highly involved in the cover design process and use our designers' time economically. He spends a lot of time selecting images, and for a writer he has a reasonable visual sense, although he'd be the first to tell you he doesn't have the skills required to bring a cover design to fruition. His book covers are always rather different to what he'd anticipated before coming into the studio, we always add one or two twists he likes. All the cover designs we've done for Mike, including the one John Rose did this morning for *The Joy of Self-Publishing*, have been completed in an hour or less, so he's paid £75.00 or less for each one. Most writers, we find, are happier to brief us with their thoughts on the cover design, either on the telephone or face-to-face here in the studio. They leave it to us to arrive at the final design, or something very close to it for their comment and adjustment. Some become agitated if they're here in the studio, and a lot of time can be wasted if they keep changing their minds. And they generally do. It can be costly for them too, bearing in mind the clock is ticking at £75.00 per hour: they often find they spend more by adopting this way of working than if they'd simply adopted our bespoke service, which includes formatting and typesetting.

We don't offer copy-editing or proofreading services ourselves, but we can provide our clients with contact details of freelance professionals. We have longstanding relationships with other freelancers too. One of our clients, an eighty-year-old man self-publishing his first book, went down to London with me to meet with the illustrator, and he agreed a substantial sum of money for her services. He's going to have a wonderful book at the end of all this and it will sell well, he's sure of that, because of huge interest in the project from a number of major bookstore chains on both sides of the Atlantic.

Writers such as Mike Buchanan are insistent that their books don't *appear* self-published, so they come to us. Over 90% of our business is repeat business, and we're very busy.

John Chandler was one of the founding directors – along with his wife Frances – of Chandler Book Design, a bespoke book cover design and content formatting and typesetting specialist. More details of the company on Chandlerbookdesign.co.uk.

APPENDIX 6

NOTES FROM A SUCCESSFUL EBOOK FORMATTING SERVICE PROVIDER (DOUG MORRIS)

The process of getting a book to print has always been heavily dependent on the use of technology. There has been a fairly continuous improvement in the technology for the author and the typesetter as well as parallel developments for on-demand printing and distribution.

But what about the reader? Whilst various technologies have been heralded as superseding the printed book, the vast majority of book sales remain of the paperback and hardback variety. Well, maybe that is set to change. For books to be read in any volume electronically, the device has to be small and light, the resolution must be nothing short of superb, and the device itself must be an ergonomic masterpiece. Oh, and the individual title must look enticing as well.

Until now, this has proved a tough combination and most ebook readers and individual ebooks have fallen short. However, more recently devices like the Kindle and Apple iPad have finally bridged the gap to making truly readable, portable electronic books a reality. There are now (July 2010) two principal ebook formats – page layout and reflowable text. The page layout format effectively copies the printed book, the obvious standard being the PDF.

If your book is properly typeset then converting to PDF format is quick – select a sans-serif font that's easy to read on screen, set up bookmarks, references and linking for navigation, and convert using a PDF creation tool like Adobe Acrobat [Author's note: or recent versions of Microsoft Word]. Almost everyone has a copy of Adobe Acrobat Reader and you can easily distribute a PDF in the knowledge that it will look identical on every device as well as every PC and Mac.

But what of the advent of smaller hand-held devices? At Wordzworth we've been inundated with enquiries about formatting for the iPad ever since its launch in early 2010. The smaller the device, the less well PDF format tends to work. The print becomes very small and you spend a considerable amount of time zooming in and out on pages to make them comfortable to read.

The main alternative to the page layout format is reflowable text. This means that the text will reshape to fit the device. Reflowable text will be legible even on the smallest hand-held device as the reader can simply adjust the typeface, size and colours to their liking. However, giving the reader total flexibility has its drawbacks – the author no longer has total control over what his or her words will look like. Indeed, the appearance of an ebook can vary considerably from one device to another and from one reader to another.

The standard format for reflowable text is ePub. There are then a number of variants including the Amazon Kindle format which are basically adaptations of this same format. Under the covers an ePub is actually a zip folder containing multiple HTML files, all the pictures associated with the book, usually a style sheet, a manifest which defines all the electronic components in the book, and a table of contents. An ebook device then acts like a mini-browser which accesses all these files to display HTML on what looks like individual book pages.

However, creating a good-looking ePub from Word, InDesign or PDF files is not straightforward. Whilst there are plenty of converters available and even a number of low cost services, most will produce a book which may be technically valid, but will render extremely badly on most devices.

The art of book layout and typesetting has developed over hundreds of years and people in the industry have a very good understanding of what makes a book 'look good'. The same is not yet true for ebooks, particularly the reflowable text variety. ePub does not lend itself to complex text flows or columns and it's all too easy to end up with so much cramped text, strange styling and stretched pictures that the book is just painful to read.

Producing an ePub ebook which is a pleasure to read involves considerable manual effort beyond a simple conversion. It requires a mixture of technical skill combined with book layout knowledge which is proving hard to find for many authors. In particular, books with lots of illustrations, tables, quotations and different styles will need considerably more attention to ensure a totally consistent layout throughout.

So is it worth all the effort? Well, the iPad has proved a very popular piece of technology since its launch, and at the time of writing is in very short supply in the UK. It is quite superbly engineered: it is small and light, it has excellent resolution, and it is an ergonomic triumph. The iBooks reader comes with a free *Winnie-the-Pooh* ePub ebook which looks simply stunning. The mix of properly indented book text and glorious full colour illustrations combined with page turning at the flick of a finger produces, probably for the first time, an electronic reading experience to really rival the printed book. So maybe the tide is beginning to turn and ebook sales as a percentage of overall book sales will rise inexorably.

If this is true, then to truly reach out to their markets authors will need to consider producing books in printed, PDF and ePub formats, and there is likely to be a growth in book formatting services which offer the ability to take a completed manuscript and easily create all three.

Doug Morris is one of the founding directors of Wordzworth, an online document formatting business which provides typesetting, cover design and ebook conversion services to authors and publishers around the globe. More details of Wordzworth's services can be found at Wordzworth.com.

APPENDIX 7

NOTES FROM A SUCCESSFUL
FICTION AUTHOR (JOANNA TROLLOPE)

[Author's note: I am grateful to the publishers of *Writer's and Artists' Yearbook (2012)* for their kind permission to reproduce this and the next two appendices from their publication.]

I once said to a journalist – rather crossly – that it had only taken me 20 years to be an overnight success. This was in 1993, with my first number one (the paperback of *The Rector's Wife*) and the accompanying media assumption that I had come from nowhere to somewhere at meteoric speed.

People do, of course. Rare, rare people do, but most of us are trudging for years across the creative plateau, honing our skills and cajoling our sinking hearts and *hoping*. I wrote my first published book when my younger daughter was three. When *The Rector's Wife* appeared, she was nearly 23, and there'd been ten books in the interim. Hardly *Bridget Jones*. Scarcely *White Teeth*.

But, on reflection, the long haul suited me. I learned about structure and dialogue and pace and characterisation at my own pace. I might have started with a readership so small it was almost invisible to the naked eye, but it grew, and it grew steadily in a manner that made it feel reliable, as is the case with long-term friendships. It also meant that when success came, it was absolutely lovely, no question about that, but there was no question of it turning my middle-aged head.

When I wrote my first published book – a historical novel called *Eliza Stanhope* set around the battle of Waterloo – the publishing climate was very different to how it is now. Many of the great publishing individuals were still alive, agents were a scarcer breed and writing was not seen as a way to become instantly, absurdly rich (and, in my view, never should be). I sent my manuscript – poorly typed on thin paper – off to Hamish Hamilton in a brown paper parcel. It was politely returned. I sent it – heart definitely in sink – to Hutchinson. They wrote back – a letter I still have – and invited me, like a job interview, to 'come and discuss my future'.

Even if the rest is history, it is not easy or simple history. There weren't any great dramas, to be sure, no cupboards filled with rejection slips, no pulped copies (that came later), but what there was instead was a simply enormous amount of perseverance. I don't want to sound too austere, but I find I rather believe in perseverance when it comes to writing. As VS Pritchett once said, most people write better if they *practise*.

And I have to say that I am still practising. I think it very unlikely that I will ever feel I have got it right, and I would be uneasy if that feeling went away. After all, only a few geniuses – Sophocles, Shakespeare – could claim to be prophets or inventors. Most writers are translators or interpreters of the human condition, but no more. A hefty dose of humility in writing seems to me both seemly and healthy.

Readers, after all, are no fools. Readers may not have a writer's gift of the arrangements of events and people and language, but they know about life and humanity all right. They may even know much more about both than the writer. So not only must they never be forgotten, but they must never be underestimated or patronised either.

Which is one of the reasons, in my case, why I research my novels. For the reader's sake, as well as my own, I have to be as accurate as possible about, say, being the child of a broken home, or the widow of a suicide, or a mistress or an adopted man in his thirties. So, once I've decided upon the theme of a novel (and those can have brewed in my brain for years or be triggered by a chance remark overheard on a bus) I go and talk to people who are in the situation that I am exploring. And I have to say that in all the years of working this way, no one has ever turned me down, and everyone has exceeded my expectations.

This habit has had an unlooked-for advantage. During all the years I've been writing, the business of promotion has grown and grown, and fiction is notoriously difficult to talk about in any medium. But the research gives me – and journalists – subject matter which is, to my relief, honourably relevant but, at the same time, miles away from the inexplicable private, frequently uncomfortable place where writing actually goes on. 'Tell me,' people say, not actually understanding what they are asking, 'Tell me how you write.' Pass.

Joanna Trollope is the author of 14 contemporary novels, as well as a number of historical novels published under the name of Caroline Harvey, and a study of women in the British Empire called *Britannia's Daughters*. She lives in London.

APPENDIX 8

NOTES FROM A SUCCESSFUL NON-FICTION AUTHOR (SIMON WINCHESTER)

The research is all done, the reading is complete. Files have been pored over, archives have been plundered. Those Who Know have been consulted. That Which Was Unknown has been explained and one fondly prays, made clear. I am, in consequence, or so I hope, now fully steeped in facts and awash with understanding. The book I have been planning for so very long is at last all in the forefront of my mind – structure, content, tone, pace and rhythm are all there. What now remains is simply – would that it were *simply* – to write it: 100,000 words, says the contract, due in just 100 days.

I live on a farm in the Berkshire Hills of western Massachusetts, and I have a small and ancient wooden barn, 100 yards or so from the main house. I have furnished it with books and a long desk on which are a variety of computers and two typewriters, one manual, the other electric. The farm is where I live. The barn is where I work. Each morning, well before the sun is up, I leave the comforts of the farm and enter this spartan, bookish little universe, and shut the allurements of domesticity behind me for the day. For a hundred days, in fact: for a hundred days of a solitary, writerly routine that, for me at least, is the only way I know to get a book properly and fully written.

Inside the barn I tend to follow an unvarying routine. First, as the dawn breaks, I spend two hours looking back over what I wrote the day before: I examine it with what I hope is a sharp and critical eye, checking it for infelicities of language, improprieties of grammar, expanding the inexact, refining the imprecise, making as certain as I can the minutiae of fact and detail. Only when I feel satisfied (never smug) that what I have on the screen represents as good a first draft as I can offer do I press the *print* button on the keyboard: a few pages of A4 slither into the out-tray. Once that task is done I leave the barn and walk through the early sunlight back to the house for breakfast. I read the papers, drink enough coffee to kick-start both mind and body, and at nine exactly I head back again, this time to write for real.

I have a word counter at the top left of my computer screen. Purists may object, but my newspaper days have left me with deadline commitment, and this is the way that I like to work. Whenever I begin a book I set the counter with the start date, the number of words I have to write, the contract date and a very simple calculation – the number of words needed each day to meet the deadline. One hundred days, 100,000 words: 1,000 words each day is the initial goal. But things change: the writing life is imperfect, however noble the intentions. Some days are good and maybe I'll write 1,500 words, while others are much less satisfactory and, for a variety of reasons, I may write virtually nothing. So the following day's necessary word total will rise and fall depending on the achievement of the day before. It is that figure my system obliges me to set the night before that I'll see on my screen when I arrive in the cold dark before dawn: 1,245 words needed today, with 68 more days before the deadline? So be it.

I sit down, arrange my thoughts and hammer away without stopping for the next six hours – each day from nine in the morning until three in the afternoon. This is the solitary pleasure of writing – total concentration, pure lexical heaven. I write on, oblivious to everything about me. Except that I do know when I have done my six hours – because by the time the mid-afternoon is upon me, the sun will have shifted to the window in front of my desk, and in the wintertime I have to suffer an uncomfortable hour or so of the sunset's glare. This gives me a perfect excuse to end this second stage of the day and to go off to do something completely different: a run along my country road, usually, followed by tea. By then it is six or so, the sun has fully set and the glare has been replaced by twilight glow. Then I return, for the day's third and final phase: planning for the next day.

I go back to my desk and arrange the papers, books and thoughts that I think I need for the next day's writing. Then I close down the computers – having been sure, of course, to have made the necessary calculations and set the counter to tell me how many words are due on the morrow – and walk back to the house. For a while I try to forget about the book (though I never can). I have dinner, go to a movie, have friends around – and am in bed, invariably, by midnight.

The next day it begins all over again. As before, I spend the first two hours of the morning looking back over what I have written in those six sunlit hours of the day before. As soon as I have tinkered and tweaked, I press *print*. I stack the A4 sheets neatly on the pile from the preceding day. Millimetre by millimetre, day by day, the pile grows taller and thicker, looking ever more substantial. In the first week it has the look and feel of a newspaper essay; after ten days or so, a magazine article; by a month, it's an outline, a chapter, a monograph, a dissertation – until finally, on one heaven-sent morning, I pick up the pile of paper and it has heft, weight and substance. And then it all changes.

The dream has been made solid. The former featherweight piece of ephemera has been transformed by time into a work-in-progress, a book-in-the-making. After a precisely calculated number of sunrises and sunsets, after yet more walks between barn and farmhouse, after setting and resetting the counter a score of times, and after hours spent reviewing and re-doing and printing and piling and collating and collecting – there, suddenly, is a finished product.

The pile of printed paper and digital confection of finished text will now be placed in the hands of the publishers, who by mysterious dint of designing, printing, binding and jacketing, will in due course turn it into a full-fledged book. *My* new book. After 100 days it is ready to be offered to the world. As for its fate – well, there lies ahead of it what will seem a lifetime of hoping – hoping that it will be lucky, do well and be loved by all. The wish and the prayer of any new parent, who has taken time and care to bring a newborn into the world. But that, of course, is another story. This is just the writing. What follows next is the reading, and that is much less exact of a science.

Simon Winchester OBE worked as a foreign correspondent for the *Guardian* and the *Sunday Times* for 30 years before turning to full-time writing. He is the author of some 20 books, including *The Surgeon of Crowthorne*, *The Map that Changed the World*, *Krakatoa*, *A Crack in the Edge of the World* and *The Man Who Loved China*. His most recent book, *Atlantic: The Biography of an Ocean*, is due to be published by HarperPress in September 2010. He divides his time between his small farm in the Berkshire Hills of western Massachusetts and New York.

APPENDIX 9

NOTES FROM A SUCCESSFUL
SELF-PUBLISHER (GP TAYLOR)

Lying in bed and hearing that horrendous thud on the doormat is the unpublished author's worst nightmare. It is the thud of a returned manuscript – the tell-tale sound of rejection. Nevertheless, you get out of bed and grimly hold on to *faux* hope that this time the letter will read differently and that you've been accepted and will be published. But no, nothing is further from the truth. Instead, you're faced with a note, hastily typed by a spotty faced 16 year-old who says she enjoyed your manuscript but it doesn't 'fit in' with the list and the niche in the market for romantic-fantasy-gothic literature isn't as big as it once was.

The trouble is, there are just too many people writing these days. Since a certain young lady put pen to paper, fiction (especially children's fiction) has become a *perceived* means of gathering fame and fortune. Even the prestigious Faber and Faber have now closed its doors to the unsolicited manuscript. So why bother? Only a few titles get produced each year from new authors but I don't believe all is lost. The author has now, thanks to the advent of the internet and email, a publishing house at their fingertips.

Once self-publishing was known as the 'vanity press' – for those failed authors who didn't feel their pride would allow them to die without first seeing a book in print. For a monumental fee, you would receive five copies of your book along with the promise that your book would appear in their magazine for the entire world to see and that copies would be sent to reviewers so that they could herald your arrival to a greater world. Sadly, editors and reviewers knew the names of all the vanity press imprints and, once spotted, would be heaped at the back of the office and sent to the local charity shop once a year.

It was when I found out this information that I decided to avoid the usual route to publication and go it *alone*. In a nutshell, Mount Publishing Limited was born – established via Companies House and a credit card. I became the director, editor and tea boy of the newest and most prestigious name in publishing! However, I knew nothing and it showed. A PDF what? Typeset? Margins? All these were very new concepts, but thankfully there is help out there.

The first problem I faced was the printing. Very quickly I realised that the prices varied immensely. One company wanted to charge me £6 per paperback, which would have meant pricing my book at £12 – who would buy it at that price? This is the area where you have to be very careful. If you are self-publishing you have to keep the costs of your book down and there are many hidden overheads to look out for (don't forget postage!).

So, once again, reach out for help that's available. My blessing came in the shape of Mr David Sowter, who I found courtesy of the Society of Authors. David was the UK rep for WS Bookwell of Finland and quickly became the fount of all knowledge and good advice at the end of a phone. He knew what I wanted and where I should go, and was a guiding hand through the issues of file preparation and submission.

Within two weeks of sending off the manuscript to the printer I was greeted with 2,000 copies of my first book *Shadowmancer*. They filled my house – they were under the bed, in the toilet, I couldn't even enter my small office. All these books with nowhere to go. Now I faced my biggest problem so far: how to sell them.

Thankfully for us self-publishers, there is a ready supply of independent bookshops all too willing to help the new author on a 'sale or return' basis. [Author's note: many of these shops have closed since 2002, sadly.] The Whitby Bookshop quickly set me off on the right foot. A book signing and press call were all arranged for a rainy October morning, and as my wife tramped through the wet streets with a pram full of books, she turned to me and said, 'I bet JK Rowling didn't have to do this'. Too true – but the excitement and hope I was feeling at that point more than made up for it.

Very quickly I came across another hurdle – the national bookshop chains (known to self-publishers as the Mafia). No one would deal with me, no one would talk to me. 'Graham who?' was all they asked. 'Self-publisher? No thank you.' The kindly manager of my local Waterstone's suggested I contact a book distributor but when I did they turned me down flat. I then went to Bertram books, another wholesaler which supplies Waterstone's, and thankfully they opted to give me a chance. Bingo! I was now selling my book to the shops.

Luck was well and truly on my side. Somewhere around this time, the story of *Shadowmancer* was spreading by word of mouth. From nowhere, people from all over the country were ringing my home wanting copies of the book. I couldn't believe it! Suddenly, hundreds of people wanted to read *Shadowmancer* and my house started to empty of books. I knew I was doing well when copies were selling on Ebay for large sums of money – I was outbidding JK Rowling!

Within a matter of weeks of the start of my self-publishing venture, I was signed to Faber and Faber. It was good timing because every day was a constant stream of wrapping and posting books, an operation so large that my local Post Office could no longer accommodate me and I was forced to find alternative arrangements. Self-publishing is definitely not for the faint hearted!

From then on, the path to notoriety has been a fast one. *Shadowmancer* spent many weeks at the number one spot on the bestseller lists in both the USA and UK. The film rights were quickly bought by Universal Pictures and a multi-book deal was in the bag. I had sold out and gone the way of the establishment!

Would I recommend others to self-publish? Definitely. In fact, I receive several emails each day asking me what to do and how to do it. Ultimately, my advice is simple – research the area and check prices, get quotes and be as wary as a fox. Be prepared for disappointment as self-publishing is certainly not a get-rich-quick scheme. It cost me all I had in time, money and resources – and more! Finally, it is always best to set up a limited company just in case all goes wrong, oh and *never* remortgage your house – sell your vintage motorbike instead.

GP Taylor self-published his debut novel *Shadowmancer* in 2002. He was soon signed to Faber and Faber and GP Putnam & Son in the USA, and the book became an international bestseller, translated into 42 languages. His subsequent books *Wormwood, Tersias the Oracle* and *The Shadowmancer Returns: The Curse of Salamander Street* have also been bestsellers. His most recent books are *Mariah Mundi and the Midas Box* (2007) and *Mariah Mundi and the Ghost Diamonds* (2008). He used to be an Anglican vicar but now writes full-time.

QUOTATIONS:
INDEX OF WRITERS AND SPEAKERS

INDEX OF CITED PUBLICATIONS

INDEX

Lightning Source UK Ltd.
Milton Keynes UK
UKOW031424090112

185014UK00006B/40/P